The Limits of
Racial Domination

R. Douglas Cope

The Limits of Racial Domination

Plebeian Society in Colonial Mexico City, 1660–1720

The University of Wisconsin Press

The University of Wisconsin Press
1930 Monroe Street
Madison, Wisconsin 53711

3 Henrietta Street
London WC2E 8LU, England

Library of Congress Cataloging-in-Publication Data
Cope, R. Douglas.
    The limits of racial domination : plebeian society in colonial
Mexico City, 1660–1720 / R. Douglas Cope.
        234 p.   cm.
    Includes bibliographical references and index.
        ISBN 0-299-14040-7   ISBN 0-299-14044-X (pbk.)
    . 1. Mexico City (Mexico)—History. 2. Mexico—History—Span-
ish colony, 1540–1810. 3. Indians of Mexico—Mexico—Mexico City
—History. 4. Poor—Mexico—Mexico City—History. 5. Mexico
City (Mexico)—Race relations. 6. Mexico City (Mexico)—Social
conditions. I. Title.
    F1386.3.C66   1994
972'.53—dc20   93-23344

For My Parents

Contents

Figures   ix

Tables   xi

Acknowledgments   xiii

Introduction   3

1   Race and Class in Colonial Mexico City, 1521–1660   9

2   Life among the Urban Poor: Material Culture and
    Plebeian Society   27

3   The Significance and Ambiguities of "Race"   49

4   Plebeian Race Relations   68

5   Patrons and Plebeians: Labor as a System of Social Control   86

6   The Fragility of "Success": Upwardly Mobile Castas in
    Mexico City   106

7   The Riot of 1692   125

    Conclusion   161

    Appendix: List of Casta and Indian Wills   169

    Notes   171

    Selected Bibliography   201

    Index   211

Figures

3.1   Relationship between Juan Romero and Rosa María   58
3.2   Surname inheritance in the family of Pedro de Mora Esquivel   60
3.3   Surname inheritance in the family of Juan Jacinto   61
4.1   Casta burials, by year, in Sagrario Metropolitano Parish, 1672–1700   72

Tables

2.1 Ecclesiastical rentals in the Mexico City *traza*, 1660–1730   31

3.1 Most common male surnames in late-seventeenth-century Mexico City, Sagrario Metropolitano Parish   62

3.2 Most common female surnames in late-seventeenth-century Mexico City, Sagrario Metropolitano Parish   63

3.3 Most common surnames of casta men by race, Sagrario Metropolitano Parish, 1670–1672   64

3.4 Most common surnames of casta women by race, Sagrario Metropolitano Parish, 1670–1672   64

3.5 Most common surnames of *peninsulares* in Mexico City, 1689   65

3.6 Most common "casta" surnames among Spaniards in late-seventeenth-century Mexico City   66

3.7 "Casta" surnames among Spanish women marrying in Sagrario Metropolitano Parish, 1680–1682   67

4.1 Racial identification in casta burial records, 1672–1700   70

4.2 Racial identification in casta marriage records, 1675–1704   71

4.3 Casta burials in Sagrario Metropolitano Parish, 1672–1700   73

4.4 Casta marriages in Sagrario Metropolitano Parish, 1670–1704   74

4.5 Casta burials in Sagrario Metropolitano Parish during normal and "critical" years, 1672–1700   75

4.6 Racial variability among castas and Indians in Sagrario Metropolitano Parish   77

4.7 Marriage patterns in Sagrario Metropolitano Parish, 1694–1696   79

4.8 Conditional kappas and expected values by racial group, Sagrario Metropolitano Parish, 1694–1696   80

4.9 Casta marriage patterns in Sagrario Metropolitano Parish, 1670–1704   81

4.10 Casta marriage patterns in Sagrario Metropolitano Parish, 1686–1690   82

5.1 Racial composition of occupational groups in the Mexico City *traza*, 1753   88

5.2 Occupations of Indian men from San José Parish residing in the *traza*, 1692   90

5.3 The social control spectrum   95

5.4   Indian bakers in Antonio de la Peña's *panadería*, 1697   100
6.1   Possessions of Juan de Oliva y Olvera   110
6.2   Possessions of Teresa de Losada   111
6.3   Possessions of Josefa de la Cruz   112
6.4   Salvador de Cañas's credit network   115
6.5   Family size among casta testators   123
7.1   Sentences for riot participants   155
7.2   Sentences for riot participants, by race   157
7.3   Occupations of convicted defendants   158
7.4   Occupations of convicted Indian defendants   159

Acknowledgments

This book would not have been possible without the help of many friends, teachers, and colleagues. Colin Palmer introduced me to the study of colonial Mexico and to the issues around which my work revolves. My dissertation advisers, Steve J. Stern and Thomas E. Skidmore, provided indispensable criticism and encouragement at every stage of the research and writing process. Their scholarly ability is matched only by their remarkable sensitivity and patience. During my years at the University of Wisconsin–Madison, my fellow graduate students—Jackie Austin, Todd Diacon, Teresa Veccia, Joel Wolfe, and especially Anita Genger—gave me good advice, friendship, and vital moral support.

Financial support for my research came from a Fulbright-Hays Government Grant for Study Abroad and a National Endowment for the Humanities Summer Stipend. While in Mexico, I benefited from discussions with Enrique Florescano, Josefina Zoraída Vázquez, Moisés González Navarro, and Patricia Seed. I am also greatly indebted to the directors and staffs of the Archivo General de la Nación, the Archivo Histórico de la Ciudad de México, the Archivo Histórico del Instituto Nacional de Antropología e Historia, the Archivo de Notarías del Distrito Federal, the Archivo del Tribunal Superior de Justicia del Distrito Federal, and the Archivo de las Indias in Seville for their courteous and efficient aid.

In the manuscript's transformation from dissertation to book, I received much valuable criticism from Frederick P. Bowser and an anonymous reviewer for the University of Wisconsin Press. Charlene Mastrostefano, Karla Cinquanta, and Cherrie Guerzon supplied the typing and computer skills I so woefully lack. I also owe thanks to Sheila Berg, for her careful copy editing, and to Raphael Kadushin, my editor at the University of Wisconsin Press, for guiding my manuscript to publication.

Any faults that remain, despite the best efforts of these contributors, are strictly my own.

The Limits of
Racial Domination

Introduction

The fall of Tenochtitlán opened a vast new stage, continental in size, for Spanish imperialism. Appearing on this stage was a varied cast of characters, most of whom, a few decades earlier, had been unknown or of limited relevance to Europeans. The land's inhabitants, in all their millions, posed the first and most central problem of definition and classification.[1] Who (or what) were these "Indians"? They built cities, sent men into battle, traded enthusiastically, and maintained a properly hierarchical social order—all traits that in Spanish eyes bespoke a civilized society. Yet Spaniards also found many indigenous practices—notably, the bloodstained religious rituals—nauseating, savage, and diabolic. However they might marvel at the Aztecs' feats of engineering, the large and well-ordered marketplaces, or the "enchanted vision"[2] of Tenochtitlán itself, the Spaniards could only believe that their conquest represented the triumph of a superior, God-fearing civilization over paganism. The many peoples of Mexico, equally lacking in Christianity and European mores, were consigned to a single, subordinate category.

This distinction between Spaniard and Indian, conqueror and conquered, formed the basis of the colonial regime. The two societies remained largely separate. The Indians were governed at a distance, through native lords who retained local authority; these *caciques,* in return, funneled Indian tribute and labor services to the conquistadores residing in newly founded Hispanic cities. Mendicant friars and royal officials would soon erect an entire system of government on this ethnic dichotomy. By midcentury the crown officially recognized two sectors of society—the *república de los españoles* and the *república de los indios*—and (in theory) provided each one with the institutional arrangements most suited to its needs. Royal paternalism, however, could only disguise, not alter, the essentially exploitative relationship between the two "republics."[3]

Other groups played smaller but still significant roles in the new social order, particularly in urban areas. African slaves had accompanied the Spaniards from the beginning. Before the century's end, tens of thousands more would be imported. As foremen, managers, and skilled laborers, Africans provided invaluable aid to the process of Hispanic colonization; as slaves and thus potential insurrectionaries, they provoked the fear and con-

3

tempt of their masters. But for the Spanish, Africans were the devil they knew. Still more troublesome was the inevitable yet unexpected emergence of the _castas, products of miscegenation_, new kinds of people for whom names had to be invented: mestizos, _castizos, zambos_, and many others.

The Spaniards, of course, had always been a minority in Mexico, their scattered cities bulwarks against the indigenous countryside. But by the early seventeenth century, the rapid growth of the castas had created large non-Hispanic populations in Spanish urban centers and mining camps and even in the Spaniards' chief redoubt, Mexico City. How could the heirs of the conquistadores sustain their rule over this multiracial melange without the benefit of a standing army? Perhaps ideology could take the place of force. Patrick Carroll, discussing Veracruz, points out that "as victors, Spaniards thought themselves superior to the peoples they dominated. The trick lay in convincing Africans and Indians of this tautological line of reasoning. If accomplished, the . . . subordinate groups would become their own oppressors and sustain [the] Iberians' hegemony."[4] He argues that the Spaniards largely achieved these goals. Indeed, such "divide-and-conquer" models of Hispanic rule have long enjoyed wide acceptance among colonial historians. The Spanish, it is said, successfully propagated their ideology of racial hierarchy—a ranked series of categories, known as the _sistema de castas_, that placed the Spaniards themselves (naturally) on top, castas in the middle, and Indians and Africans at the bottom. Lower-ranking groups, acknowledging their position in the hierarchy, shaped their behavior accordingly. Ambitious castas, for example, scorned their inferiors and sought to marry "up" (into lighter-skinned groups). Racial ideology thus functioned as a system of social control, since it created status differences between groups (such as blacks and mulattoes) who might otherwise have united against their oppressors. For confirmation of these assertions, one need only look at the actual socioeconomic structure of urban society. The Spanish monopolized political power and dominated the elite occupations, thereby enjoying a grossly disproportionate share of Mexico's wealth. In contrast, Indians, Africans, and mixed-bloods languished in low-paying, low-prestige positions.

Elite disdain, prejudice, and discrimination confronted non-Spaniards at every turn. So much is undeniable. One may doubt, however, that Carroll's "trick" proved so easy to execute. We should not assume that subordinate groups are passive recipients of elite ideology. Mesoamerican Indians, for instance, demonstrated a remarkable ability to resist cultural impositions. Summarizing fifteen years of work on Nahuatl documents, James Lockhart concludes that "indigenous structures and patterns sur-

vived the conquest on a much more massive scale and for a longer period
of time than had seemed the case when we had to judge by the reports
of Spaniards alone. The indigenous world retained much social and cultural autonomy, maintaining its center of balance to a surprising extent,
concerned above all with its own affairs."[5]

Nor did such cultural survivals merely reflect salutary neglect of the
Indian communities by the Spaniards: consider the massive Christianization effort of the sixteenth century. Spanish missionaries baptized millions
of Indians in the belief that this would soon lead to complete acceptance of
Christian doctrine, only to discover later that the Indian conversions had
been "insincere" and that the natives had "relapsed" into paganism. For
their part, the Indians had most probably participated in Catholic rituals
to appease the new and powerful God and his representatives but without
accepting—or even understanding—Christianity's claims to exclusivity.[6]
Indeed, the Indians' response to Catholicism, which ranged from acceptance to rejection to anomie but was most characterized by creative
adaptation, the selective incorporation and reworking of those elements
of Christianity that made sense to them, has much to tell us about the
difficulties of imposing the rulers' ideology on the ruled.[7]

We would do better, then, to view culture as a contested terrain, in
which people from all walks of life (and not just the dominant group)
"engage in a continuous process of manipulating and constructing social
reality."[8] In a multiracial society such as colonial Mexico, ethnic identity
itself became a prime point of contention and confusion. Elite attempts
at racial or ethnic[9] categorizations met with resistance as non-Spaniards
pursued their own, often contradictory, ends: social mobility, group solidarity, self-definition. Once again, the indigenous population provides
a good example. To Spaniards, the term "Indian" seemed straightforward; not so for those who received this designation. Mexico's indigenous
peoples understood that when dealing with Spaniards and Spanish officialdom, they were "Indians." In community documents, however, they
continued to employ distinctive, highly localized ethnic referents as late
as the eighteenth century.[10]

The existence of such "double boundaries"[11] points to a broader principle: ethnic status is not fixed permanently at birth, by official fiat, but
constitutes a *social* identity that may be reaffirmed, modified, manipulated, or perhaps even rejected—all in a wide variety of contexts. In short,
"the use of ethnic identity is free, . . . flexible," and strategic.[12]

Now, it could be argued that one should not conflate the experience
of village-dwelling Indians with that of urban blacks and castas. Indigenous peoples could draw on the totality of their pre-Columbian heritage

in confronting a foreign ideology. A black slave might (or might not) have memories of an earlier life in Africa; an urban mestizo might have tenuous links with indigenous society. But they, unlike the Indians, lived in an essentially Hispanic milieu, speaking Castilian, working in a European-style economy for Spanish employers, and—in Mexico City—facing the full panoply of judicial and religious authority. Moreover, the Indians had a physical foundation for the preservation of cultural autonomy—the land-owning community, whose "essentially conservative native elites mediated the intrusion of alien goods and strategies."[13] The multiracial plebeians had no hereditary leaders, and their mechanisms for solidarity, such as *compadrazgo* and *cofradías*, were themselves Spanish in origin.

Does it in fact make sense to speak of casta "solidarity"? Since the sixteenth century, the castas have seemed anomalous and marginal and have been largely defined by antithesis. In Eric Wolf's classic account, *Sons of the Shaking Earth*, the castas ("mestizos") appear as middlemen who, in mediating between different cultures and social sectors, failed to forge a secure identity of their own. Lacking the advantages of either the dominant Spaniards or the telluric Indians, castas lived in a kind of twilight world; they operated on the fringes of legality, surviving by wits and guile, lusting after legitimacy and power, yet plagued with self-doubt.[14] Here Wolf's analysis joins the divide-and-conquer school: the rootless castas became avid social climbers, eager to discard their shameful racial status.

Wolf is open to criticism for too readily accepting the official Hispanic view of the castas, in lieu of empirical studies, and thus seeing the entire group as pathological. More recent research, for instance, suggests that the mestizo vagabond, that notorious bogeyman of so many official reports, was largely a myth.[15] However, as we shall see, the castas' bad reputation also sprang precisely from their reluctance to acquiesce in their stipulated inferiority. Indeed, Wolf points out that the castas possessed a "subterranean strength," that they busily molded "informal network[s]" that would propel them to power after independence.[16] Wolf hints at, but does not quite formulate, the concept of an unofficial, oppositional culture, which he would describe as "mestizo" but which might be more accurately characterized as "plebeian."

Race, after all, was not the only dividing line in colonial Mexico. Nor was it the only principle of social organization. Mexican society was riven with fissures, not the least of which was the immense gap between the rich and the poor. A high degree of social uniformity between the two can hardly be taken for granted. We must not be too eager to fit plebeian behavior into systems of meaning devised by the elite. A mulatto marries a mestiza. Who can say what combination of affection, sexual desire, family consider-

[handwritten margin note: mixed race / as confused / rejected, / social / climbers / ...]

ations, and economic calculation went into this decision? We cannot know, from that act itself, whether one partner exulted in an opportunity or the other agonized over marrying "down." Yet marriage registers have been the single most important source for studies of colonial racial structures. The problem requires a more comprehensive, well-rounded approach. We simply need to know more about the urban poor, particularly about the castas. What material and social constraints shaped their world? What sort of lives did they lead at work and at home? What role did race play among plebeians? How did their beliefs compare with those of the elite? And what kinds of relations existed between these two components of society?

The following pages will explore the social organization of Mexico City during the late seventeenth and early eighteenth centuries. Mexico City was chosen for two reasons. First, New Spain's capital housed the colony's most racially diverse population, making it ideal for the study of the relationship between ethnicity and class. Second, Mexico City offers an unusually rich collection of sources: Inquisition and criminal cases, notarial records, a wide range of civil and ecclesiastical documents, and (after about 1660) parish registers covering both Spanish and casta baptisms, marriages, and burials. These materials will provide a far richer portrait of the castas than has been available previously. As for the book's time frame, the years 1660–1720 mark the period of greatest maturity and stability for the sistema de castas: its formative years lay behind, while its decline and dissolution were yet to come. If the sistema ever had a meaningful social function, it must have been during this period.

The book is organized as follows. Chapter 1 charts the development of a racially diverse population in Mexico City and describes the legal and ideological formulas created by the Spanish elite in reaction to this development. Chapter 2 argues for the existence of a "plebeian society" in seventeenth-century Mexico City, linked to the elite yet distinct from it in both material circumstances and cultural beliefs. The next two chapters further investigate plebeian values, focusing on the plebeians' resistance to elite racial ideology. Chapter 3 suggests that castas had a significantly different perception of race, and of lineage in general, than did upper-class Spaniards; chapter 4 then attempts to define the significance of ethnicity in lower-class society. Chapter 5 examines the most common elite/plebeian nexus: labor. The employer-employee link, which frequently broadened into a patron-client relationship, should be seen as the primary method of social control in colonial Mexico City. Labor relations and patronage provided a far more effective divide-and-conquer strategy than did racial ideology. Chapter 6 looks at "successful" castas and shows that upward mobility depended on an ever-tighter integration into the elite-dominated

patronage system. Chapter 7 analyzes the riot of 1692 and explains how
plebeians momentarily broke through their restraints to mobilize for political action and why the elite was able to reassert its authority so quickly
and decisively. The conclusion offers some remarks on the nature of the
social order in colonial Mexico City.

1

Race and Class in
Colonial Mexico City, 1521–1660

Like so many other great cities, past and present, colonial Mexico City was a study in contrasts. Stunning wealth and wretched poverty, elegance and squalor, and sophistication and ignorance all existed side by side. The capital's dark underside was inextricably woven into the fabric of daily life. The poor were not tucked away into hidden slums; they were visible—indeed, unavoidable—in the most fashionable quarters of the city. Government buildings and elite mansions did not house the rich alone: their lower levels were given over to slaves and servants. Interspersed among the checkerboard of main avenues were narrow alleyways, described as the "den[s] of thieves" who terrorized their neighborhoods day and night.[1] Mulatto street vendors plied their wares among the master silversmiths in the Calle de San Francisco, the address of highly elite families. But the fullest expression of the city's social complexity appeared at its very heart, the *plaza mayor*. Built on the ruins of the Aztec ceremonial center and surrounded by the cathedral, the viceregal palace, and the municipal buildings, the plaza demonstrated the unalterable triumph of Spaniard over Indian, the imposition of Hispanic order on a recalcitrant population. Yet the plaza's daily activities seemed to mock or even subvert these pretensions by affirming Mexico City's unquenchable ethnic diversity. In short, the elite faced a rising tide of mixed-bloods, blacks, Indians, and poor Spaniards that (in their view) threatened to submerge the city into chaos.

A complex, contradictory society had come into being with remarkable speed once Cortés had made his decision to rebuild ruined Tenochtitlán. The new city amid the waters of Lake Texcoco retained much of the majesty and allure of its famed predecessor[2] and achieved even greater economic and political primacy. As Ross Hassig points out, "The relative size of cities changed greatly. All the towns in the Valley of Mexico declined in relation to Mexico City. . . . Their prior importance as independent centers was undermined. They were no longer important in their own right, but only in relation to the capital."[3] Mexico City—political capital, economic center, cultural trendsetter—acted as a magnet for

9

travelers and immigrants, who, in turn, reinforced its status. The "flow of immigration" into New Spain had "reached flood proportions" as early as 1523.[4] Because of their background (most were town dwellers), the urban bias in Spanish culture, and a natural desire to congregate in already Hispanicized areas, these immigrants usually settled in cities—above all, in the capital.[5] By 1574, perhaps eighteen thousand Spaniards, about 30 percent of the colony's entire Hispanic population, lived in Mexico City.[6] The city's inhabitants were a remarkably varied group, running the gamut from viceroy to vagabond. The colonial elite resided there, and where the wealthy lived, so also dwelled their servants and retainers, including their African slaves. The concentration of riches also provided economic opportunities for traders and craftsmen. Artisanry flourished: within a dozen years of the conquest, artisans (including weavers, tailors, carpenters, and candle makers) comprised nearly half of Mexico City's Spanish population.[7] In 1542, the city's first artisan guild (the silk weavers' *gremio*) was officially established. By 1600, some two hundred guilds had been organized in New Spain, most operating in the capital.[8] Commerce also engaged both the poor and the wealthy. The city's markets trafficked in Indian as well as European goods; and its merchants included not only members of transatlantic trading houses but petty dealers such as Andrés Garcia, who bought and sold cacao, "Campeche wood, and cotton blankets and wax."[9] Many of the city's necessities—including the indispensable food of the poor, maize—continued to be delivered by canoe, via the still extensive system of canals.[10]

The city's indigenous infrastructure had its human counterpart as well. A Spanish island in an indigenous sea—the Valley of Mexico had been the most densely populated region in Mesoamerica—the capital tried to solve its Indian "problem" through segregation. The conquistadores had marked out an area of some thirteen square blocks in the center of the city. This sector, known as the *traza*, was reserved for Spanish occupancy. In fact, from the Spaniards' point of view, the traza was the city. The region surrounding the traza, earmarked for Indian residence, formed the indigenous community of San Juan Tenochtitlán. Like many Indian villages in the countryside, San Juan had a largely traditional political organization, one that included internal subdivisions (barrios), a full range of Indian officials, and even a claim to tribute from subject pueblos.[11] But the separation of Spaniard and Indian was more than a political convenience. It reflected the conquistadores' fear and mistrust of the Indians (the traza's houses and churches had a fortresslike solidity, in case of native uprising); their disdain for the social and cultural practices of their conquered foes; and, above all, their desire to exploit the resources of Indian society to support a sumptuous and noble life-style, worthy of Spanish hidalgos. The socioeconomic meaning of the Spanish-Indian dichotomy had been visible in Mexico City from the beginning, in the contrast between the Spaniards' "monumental public and private buildings" and "the Indians' shacks [*casuchas*] . . . which barely rise above the ground."[12]

By the seventeenth century, social and cultural diversity had become a hallmark of the capital, acknowledged (though sometimes uneasily) by residents and visitors alike. Colonial Mexico's greatest poet, Sor Juana Inés de la Cruz, wrote *villancicos*—popular lyrics for religious festivals—in both Castilian and Nahuatl as well as in broken Spanish meant to represent the patois of partially assimilated Africans.[13] Where Sor Juana condescended, others condemned. Thomas Gage, an English friar, found the city's Afro-Mexican women charming but complained that they corrupted the already lax morals of Spanish gentlemen.[14] Carlos de Sigüenza y Góngora, the leading Mexican intellectual of the seventeenth century, has been described by D. A. Brading as "a creole patriot who sought to endow the imperial city of Mexico with both a distinguished past and a glorious present"; nevertheless, he harbored a "thorough contempt for the Mexican populace."[15] This attitude was widely shared in upper-class circles. Like a muleteer who curses and beats his beast of burden, the elite upbraided and despised (and in fact, sometimes beat) the people who were, in the final analysis, the source of their fortunes. For the colony's economic system, also centered on Mexico City, infused by the wealth of the northern silver mines and administered by the capital's mercantile elite, ultimately depended on the labor of non-Spaniards. As one seventeenth-century viceroy admitted, "It is certain that while the Indians exist, the Indies will exist."[16]

The evolution of labor systems is central to the history of early colonial Mexico and has been described well elsewhere.[17] For our purposes, this evolution may be summarized as follows. The conquistadores had received grants of *encomienda*, the right to demand labor and tribute from designated groups of Indians. The first generation of *encomenderos* (as the grantees were known) had enormous power and prestige and enormous opportunities (not neglected) for abuse of their Indian charges. Stories of their mistreatment of the Indians, related in gruesome detail by mendicant friars and accompanied by calls for immediate reform, soon reached Spain. The friars' message fell on willing ears. It spoke to the humanitarian instincts of the crown, supposed fount of justice for its subjects. More important, it also spoke to royal fears that Mexico's encomenderos would convert themselves into permanent and fractious nobility. As John Leddy Phelan has noted, the friars' arguments were "in effect a smoke screen behind which the Crown could restrict the economic power of the colonists."[18] Throughout the first postconquest generation, the crown tightened its grip on the colony and undermined the encomenderos' strength.

A "monastic Inquisition," controlled by friars, began operating in Mexico City in 1525 and directed much of its attention to encomenderos (who were usually accused of blasphemy). After a period of political turbulence, a governmental bureaucracy began to take shape under the first viceroy, Antonio de Mendoza (1535–1550). During his administration, the crown introduced several measures designed to reduce encomendero control over the Indians. The New Laws of 1542 abolished Indian slavery, forbade new encomiendas, and limited the succession of existing encomiendas to one heir. In 1549, the crown instituted a new method of labor allocation called the *repartimiento*. Under this system, government officials drafted a proportion of the able-bodied men in each Indian community and assigned them to Spanish employers for a limited period. The encomenderos thus lost their privileged claim to native laborers. As time passed, the crown began to carry out its policy of escheating encomiendas on the death of their owners. This channeled encomienda tributes into royal coffers, further weakening the encomendero class.[19]

Yet this system too proved unsuitable in the long run. Encomenderos were now merely one voice in a chorus clamoring for more workers. Public works projects, mines, haciendas—all depended (or so it was said) on acquiring a sufficient share of repartimiento labor. But as Hispanic society became larger and more complex, the Indian population diminished. Devastating epidemics—along with ecological disruption, culture shock, overwork, and the unfortunate Hispanic policy of resettling the inhabitants of dispersed villages into central communities (*congregaciones*)—had by 1605 reduced the indigenous population to perhaps 10 percent of its pre-Columbian level.[20] The demands of a growing Hispanic sector on a shrinking pool of indigenous workers had reached critical proportions by the turn of the century. Already in 1595, Viceroy Luis de Velasco II had expressed his fears that the conservation of the Hispanic community entailed the "oppression and destruction" of the Indians. According to another observer, by 1607, the incompatibility of the Spanish and Indian repúblicas had become a colonial commonplace.[21]

The crisis in relations between the two repúblicas triggered a basic shift in the Spaniards' utilization of land and labor. In brief, the years 1570–1630 saw a major expansion of Spanish landholding and the emergence of "free" wage laborers as an essential element in the colonial economy.[22] Spanish haciendas and *obrajes* (textile workshops) came to dominate the production of goods and foodstuffs for urban centers. Though native subsistence agriculture still formed the largest sector of Mexico's economy, the Spanish were no longer dependent on community-based tribute and labor. As P. J. Bakewell remarks, "In the sixteenth century, the white community lived on the surplus produced by a vast number of Indians working in a very primitive economic system. In the seventeenth, Spaniards lived on the product . . . of an economy that was in its general outline of contemporary European design."[23]

Mexico City directed much of this economic reorganization. The city's reach was long, but its influence was most intense in the Valley of Mexico. Valley residents engaged in extensive land grabbing after 1570. By 1620, Spaniards "owned" nearly one-half of the valley's arable land. Spanish estates, of course, produced wheat for wealthy city dwellers, but they also found a market for maize among the urban poor. Mexico City's *cabildo* (municipal council) claimed in 1630 that Indians grew maize only for their subsistence needs, while the commercial supply came entirely from "rich Spaniards who have haciendas."[24] Another native product, the intoxicant pulque, also became heavily commercialized in the century after the conquest. Investigators in the 1570s found eighteen towns in the archbishopric of Mexico specializing in the sale of pulque and related products. Fifty years later, pulque marketing had become an economic necessity for many Indian villages near Mexico City.[25]

Such integration of Hispanic and Indian economies was exceptional, however. In general, Mexico's indigenous communities resisted absorption and infiltration by the Spaniards. Despite huge population losses, the interference of priests and government officials, and disruptions caused by rapacious colonials, "many villages preserved old social boundaries or established new ones and maintained a strong sense of group identity in their adjustments to the new dependency relationships imposed by colonial conditions."[26] The strength of these social boundaries (reinforced by royal policies designed to protect native communities) prevented the wholesale incorporation of Indian peasants into the Hispanic economy. Indian communities, therefore, could not fully satisfy the labor demands of Spanish *hacendados*, planters, *obrajeros*, and miners.

Forced to seek alternate sources of labor, many Spanish entrepreneurs turned to African slaves. Some 36,500 slaves arrived in Mexico between 1521 and 1594.[27] They soon became indispensable to the plantation economy of Mexico's coastal areas, where Indian population decline had been most severe. In the overall Mexican economy, however, their impact was less significant. At the height of the African influx, black slaves comprised less than 15 percent of the labor force in Mexico's major mining centers.[28] The high cost of slaves (300–400 pesos for a healthy young male) put them at a disadvantage compared to wage laborers. Furthermore, the importation of Africans was erratic, and the number of slaves available rarely matched the colonials' demand. Finally, many slaves filled highly visible but relatively unproductive roles as personal servants to wealthy Spaniards. Mexico City elites valued black slaves as status symbols and were active in their purchase: of the 20,000 blacks living in Mexico during the 1570s, 8,000 worked as slaves in the capital.[29]

Rare and expensive African slaves provided an unsatisfactory answer to Spanish labor demands. Instead, Spaniards came to rely on a group of workers who, unlike slaves, required only a minimum outlay (a daily wage) and who, unlike most Indians, had no access to resources outside the Hispanic economy. In the end, the Spanish cities, mining camps, and estates created the solution to their own labor problems. For these Hispanic centers constituted the cradle of a new population of wage laborers, composed of acculturated Indians, poor Spaniards, and castas.

Soon after the conquest Indians began to participate, with varying degrees of enthusiasm, in the Spanish economy. Hispanicization proceeded most rapidly among the caciques, many of whom became landowners and entrepreneurs. Humbler Indians migrated to Spanish cities and mining centers, became laborers on Spanish estates, or worked as muleteers or traders.[30] The importance of such naborías or gañanes grew as the scope of Hispanic economic activities expanded; indeed, the development of Mexico's mining-hacienda complex would have been impossible without increased Spanish utilization of "free" Indians. In the late sixteenth century, gañanes outnumbered black slaves and repartimiento Indians combined in New Spain's most important mining centers. Hacendados counted on gañanes to form the core of resident laborers on their estates. Their successful efforts to recruit such workers doomed the agricultural repartimiento, which was abolished in 1632.[31]

On haciendas and in mining camps and cities, Indians met and mingled with (as one landowner put it) "mestizos, mulattoes, and other servants,"[32] persons who, from birth, had belonged to neither the Spanish nor the Indian "republic." The history of miscegenation in Mexico antedates the conquest. Loyal Indian allies provided the conquistadores with mistresses; and after the fall of Tenochtitlán, some Spaniards established virtual harems. Although the church soon curbed such excesses, the continued sexual imbalance of the Spanish population ensured a high level of miscegenation. The crown did not object to Spanish-Indian unions if they were legitimized by marriage, and, legally or illegally, such unions took place on a wide scale.[33] As a result, the children of the earliest colonials were frequently biological mestizos. But in the first postconquest generation, these children were normally absorbed into either the Spanish or Indian culture—usually the former. Many conquistadores recognized their mixed-blood sons as heirs and seemed more worried over their illegitimacy than their racial status.[34]

When the term "mestizo" began to appear in the late 1530s, it referred to marginal individuals—persons of Spanish-Indian descent who were not full members of either group. Juan de Zumárraga, the first archbishop of Mexico, described them as "orphaned boys, sons of Spanish men and Indian women" who wandered through the countryside, ignorant of the law and Christianity and reduced to eating "raw meat." Zumárraga attributed their unfortunate condition to their fathers having died "in the conquest and conservation of this land" before they could be rewarded by the crown.[35] Since these boys lacked elite Spanish patrons, they could at best hope for marginal positions in a still-maturing Hispanic society; yet their physical and cultural traits kept them from full acceptance in Indian communities.

Thus, mestizos quickly joined Africans as New Spain's quintessential outsiders. Mexico's social structure was based on two fundamental principles: (1) the division between Spaniards and Indians; and (2) the maintenance of internal stability within each sphere. Spaniards believed that the castas threatened both principles. Biologically, of course, the castas did not really fit into either república. More important, they had no legitimate socioeconomic niche. The ideal community, in Hispanic political theory, was composed of faithful Christians, each performing the function appropriate to his lineage and his position in the status hierarchy.[36] Yet the castas had no preassigned place. They were not Spanish "citizens" (vecinos), nor could they claim the legitimacy of the land's original inhabitants. In short, the castas were an anomaly. Many Spaniards considered them disgusting—"low and wretched peoples."[37] Others virtually refused to recognize their existence. Antonio Vásquez de Espinosa, a priest who visited Mexico City in 1612, failed to record the presence of mestizos (though he did mention blacks).[38] Even when castas could not be ignored, they tended to be treated as a rather offensive, disorderly mass. For example, an Inquisitor's description of Mexico City in 1654, after discussing the city's Spanish and Indian communities, states, "Besides the native Indians there are many plebeians such as mestizos, blacks, mulattoes, and chinos [Filipinos], and other mixtures, whose numbers are unknown because of their confused ranks."[39]

As noted above, Spanish officials sometimes praised Indian laborers for their fundamental role in the colony's economy. In sharp contrast, castas were most commonly perceived as vagabonds, "lazy persons . . . who do not have a manual trade, nor property from which they can sustain themselves."[40] From the authorities' point of view, vagabonds were "idle" or "useless" (ociosos); they mistreated the Indians and "taught them their bad customs and idleness and other errors and vices besides."[41] Vagabonds not only failed to perform a useful function in Spanish society but disrupted Indian society as well. Most important of all, they were not under firm Spanish control. While they remained outside the pale of Hispanic society, there was no effective check on their "antisocial" behavior—behavior that might proceed beyond sporadic misdeeds to the systematic undermining of Spanish authority, perhaps even to open rebellion.[42] Many elite observers agreed that the castas were the colony's foremost partisans of insurrection. As one viceroy confided to the king, his greatest fear was that the "mestizos, mulattoes, and free blacks" would revolt and "bring after them a large part of the Indians."[43]

From the 1540s on, the Spanish crown became increasingly concerned with bringing the castas into line. The perception of a growing class of casta vagabonds gave impetus to the royal policy of erecting barriers between the two repúblicas.[44] In 1549, Charles V ordered that no castas should be permitted to receive encomiendas or hold public office without a special royal license. During the 1560s and 1570s, Spanish legislation attempted to segregate Indians from all other segments of the population. A 1563 *cédula,* repeated several times thereafter, forbade the residence of "Spaniards, blacks, mulattoes, and mestizos" in native villages. The crown pursued a similar policy with regard to cities. Indians were to live in their own barrios; work places and even hospitals were to be segregated.[45]

By emphasizing the segregation and consolidation of the Indian república, the crown in effect assigned the castas to the Spanish community. Native villages were supposed to have only Indian inhabitants, while Spanish towns contained members of all of Mexico's racial groups. A corresponding division existed in religious matters, with mendicant friars serving Indian parishes and the secular clergy attending to the rest of the populace. In Mexico City, for instance, the preconquest barrios became the parishes of San Juan Baptista, Santa María la Redonda, San Sebastián, and San Pablo, all under Franciscan supervision; the traza parish (Sagrario Metropolitano), based in the main cathedral, administered to the needs of the Spaniards and castas.[46]

This did not mean, of course, that the castas lived on an equal footing with the Spaniards. Much of the new royal legislation applied only to the former. Blacks and mulattoes, unlike Spaniards, paid tribute. The crown explicitly denied mestizos such official posts as protector of the Indians and notary public. Castas did not have the right to bear arms, an important status marker. Sumptuary legislation also attempted to define the castas' status as both non-Indian and inferior. On the one hand, casta women were forbidden to wear Indian dress (unless they were married to Indian men) on pain of one hundred lashes. On the other hand, blacks and mulattas faced confiscation of their property if they wore golden jewelry, pearls, or embroidered full-length *mantas.*[47] But colonial authorities went beyond restricting the castas' privileges; they also sought to place these anomalous groups under firm Spanish control. After the mid-sixteenth century, numerous laws attempted to monitor and limit the physical mobility of castas, particularly blacks and mulattoes.

During the early colonial period, Africans were easily the most visible and feared of the castas. The Spanish had a long history of association with Africans before the colonization of Mexico, and they had developed a severe prejudice against them. In sixteenth-century Spain, "the adjective *negro* was often a synonym for evil," and blacks "were believed to be loyal, superstitious, light-hearted, of low mentality, and distinctly in need of white supervision."[48] Spanish distrust and fear of blacks intensified in Mexico, where blacks constituted a much more important minority than they did in Spain. By the early 1570s, blacks formed by far the largest part of the castas, outnumbering mestizos by more than eight to one. Furthermore, Afro-Mexicans had highly visible roles in Mexico's economy, especially in urban areas. In Mexico City, blacks and mulattoes specialized in domestic service, but they also penetrated into the skilled trades. The ordinances of the city's craft guilds indicate that white artisans feared competition from their black counterparts. When these guilds excluded specific racial groups, they almost always (until the 1590s) singled out blacks and mulattoes. Thus, in 1570, the silk spinners refused to allow blacks and mulattoes to become apprentices; a few years later, the glovers and needle makers denied black and mulatto slaves the right to take a master's examination.[49]

But the Afro-Mexican threat to the Spanish did not consist solely of economic competition. The specter of slave revolts haunted colonial authorities, and for good reason. An alleged slave conspiracy to take over Mexico City in 1537 was followed by at least two more uprisings during the 1540s. Slave insurrections then spread to the northern mining areas, where blacks allied themselves with the still-unconquered Chichimec Indians. The possibility of such an alliance in central Mexico, where the indigenous population was most heavily concentrated, greatly disturbed colonial officials, to the point that Viceroy Velasco asked the king to curtail the slave trade.[50] He was aware of the interracial tension in Mexico City, which even travelers commented on: "The Indians and the Negroes daily wait, hoping to put into practice their freedom from the domination and the servitude in which the Spaniards keep them. Indians and Negroes hate and abhor the Spaniards with all their hearts."[51] But the viceregal warning went unheeded, and after a period of apparent quiescence, a new series of disturbances erupted in the early seventeenth century. In 1611, fifteen hundred blacks and mulattoes staged a public demonstration, marching in solemn procession past the viceregal palace and the Inquisition building with the body of a female slave whose death, they claimed, had been caused by her owner's mistreatment. Both 1608 and 1612 saw aborted conspiracies to overthrow Spanish rule.[52]

The measures taken in the wake of the 1612 conspiracy typify the Spaniards' twofold reaction to social disturbances. First, local authorities took immediate action designed to crush the rebellion and overawe future plotters, namely, the capture and punishment of the ringleaders. (In this case, thirty-five Afro-Mexicans were executed.) Second, the viceroy implemented legislation to forestall future rebellions. Most of these laws had been promulgated in the sixteenth century; however, they usually lay dormant until being activated (for brief periods of time) in moments of crisis. Nevertheless, they reveal the Spaniards' social prescription for dealing with the castas. Among other things, these laws (1) forbade castas to carry arms; (2) ordered blacks and mulattoes off the streets between 8:00 P.M. and 5:00 A.M. (i.e., during the hours of darkness); (3) banned gatherings of four or more Afro-Mexicans; and (4) required every free black and mulatto to live with a "known master" whom he could not leave without permission from a local justice.[53] In short, this body of legislation attempted to reduce Afro-Mexicans to the status of minors living under the watchful eyes of individual Spanish guardians.

At first, mestizos fared somewhat better than blacks. They did not have to pay tribute, and because of their Spanish blood, they were officially regarded as "people of reason" (*gente de razón*).[54] Efforts to bring mestizos under Spanish control were cast in paternalistic terms: the church launched programs to rescue these "sons of Spaniards . . . lost among the Indians" by gathering them into Spanish towns where they could be Christianized.[55] In the 1540s, Viceroy Mendoza, acting under royal orders, founded the Colegio de San Juan de Letrán in Mexico City. The colegio aimed at furnishing mestizos with a basic education and instruction in Catholic doctrine. Mendoza also made arrangements to house, educate, and find suitable husbands for mestiza orphans. But these institutions had very limited success: by 1579, only eighty students were attending the mestizo school, and few remained for more than one year.[56] Mexico's viceroys did little to nurture the colegio, for they shared the colonials' negative attitude toward mestizos.

As Hispanic society matured—in particular, as male colonials found it easier to marry Spanish women—the barrier between Spaniards and mestizos became less and less fluid. By 1570, illegitimate children of Spanish-Indian parentage were no longer regularly labeled "Spaniards"; instead, they were usually considered "mestizos." Indeed, as the century progressed, colonials came to regard the terms "mestizo" and "illegitimate" as practically synonymous.[57] The number of identifiable mestizos thus grew rapidly after midcentury, and they soon became associated in Hispanic eyes with Mexico's other anomalous casta groups. Royal legislation often classified mestizos with Afro-Mexicans: prohibitory regulations typically spoke of "mestizos, blacks, mulattoes, chinos, and zambos." The Spanish-casta distinction was salient in city ordinances as well. For example, a Spaniard who used fraudulent scales for weighing meat was fined twenty pesos, while a black, mulatto, or mestizo guilty of the same infraction received one hundred lashes. Mestizos, like Afro-Mexicans, were prohibited from joining most artisan guilds.[58] In addition to recognizing the Spanish-Indian dichotomy, then, the colonials perceived a biformity within the Hispanic república. On the one hand were the Spaniards; on the other, the castas. In theory, this racial principle should have neatly split Hispanic society into two groups:[59]

white	casta
Old Christians	New Christians
legitimate	illegitimate
pure blood	impure blood
honorable	infamous
law-abiding	criminal
rich	poor
noble	plebeian
nonmanual workers	manual workers

Many elements of this division did persist in the Hispanic imagination. The official stereotype of castas as illegitimate, criminally inclined, and neophytes in the faith lasted into the seventeenth century and beyond. But the complete list of opposed attributes never fully coincided. Most significant, the racial and economic aspects of the Spanish-casta division were inconsistent. In reality, not all castas were relegated to low-status occupations, nor did Spaniards hold solely prestigious positions.

A casta elite—largely mestizo in composition—first emerged in the second half of the sixteenth century. Throughout this period, Spanish officials made curious exceptions to their sweeping, increasingly severe, denunciations against mestizos. For instance, the royal cosmographer López de Velasco stated that the "greater part" of Mexico's mestizos were given over to vice, while Viceroy Martín Enríquez (1568–1580) recommended that "most" mestizos be made to pay tribute. These were not isolated or aberrant opinions; the great jurist and systematizer of colonial legislation, Juan de Solórzano y Pereira, expressed a similar ambivalence toward mestizos. He expatiated on the illegitimacy and the vices of the castas and argued that it was "unjust" to draft Indians to work in the mines while exempting mestizos and mulattoes. But at the same time, he urged that mestizos born in wedlock be given special consideration; indeed, he regarded them as eligible for grants of encomienda.[60] All of these officials more or less explicitly distinguished between "typical" mestizos—illegitimate, lazy, parasitic—and the few rational, dependable "sons of Spaniards"—mestizos who acted as allies of the colonials.

Such mestizos were particularly valuable as mediators between Spaniards and Indians. They acted as interpreters and as stewards on haciendas; they obtained positions as Indian *gobernadores* (governors) and manipulated indigenous affairs to suit their Spanish patrons.[61] After 1588, the crown, eager to further Christianization efforts among the Indians, allowed mestizos of legitimate birth to become priests. Some achieved respectable positions in the ecclesiastical hierarchy: in 1655, a mestizo friar named Tomás Manzo was chosen to head the Franciscans' Mexico City chapter.[62]

Few castas were this successful. But throughout the late sixteenth and early seventeenth centuries, the castas' prominence within the Hispanic economy increased. With the continued decline of the Indian population, the colonials necessarily became more aware of (and resigned to) Mexico's racial diversity. In urban centers such as Mexico City, the Spanish-Indian dichotomy no longer provided an adequate description of society. In particular, the desired division of labor—Spanish merchants and property owners, Indian laborers, black slaves and domestic servants—rapidly eroded. By 1644, Mexico City's Indian tributary count had fallen to 7,631, implying a population of between 21,350 and 26,700.[63] Indians now formed a minority of the laboring class and were probably outnumbered by the castas. The indigenous population was losing ground to non-Indians, literally as well as figuratively. In the 1550s, the cabildo won the right to assign property in the city's Indian sectors to Spaniards, and Spanish settlement soon spread beyond the traza's boundaries.[64] Charles Gibson has shown that changes in the city's ecclesiastical jurisdictions during the sixteenth and seventeenth centuries "represented departures from the original Indian organization and corresponded directly to subsequent changes in the city's population."[65] New parishes (Santa Catalina Mártir and Santa Veracruz) extended into the Indian barrios to serve Spaniards and castas who now lived outside the traza. Conversely, Indians moved into the central city, attaching themselves to Spanish patrons, for whom they worked as day laborers, personal servants, bakers, and so on.[66]

In some ways this process paralleled the rural movement of Indians onto haciendas, and it had a similar effect in limiting the labor supply available to other colonials. Indians employed by Spanish entrepreneurs could often evade both tribute and repartimiento requirements.[67] Spanish officials therefore sought to tap non-Indian sources of labor. In 1607, government proclamations invited "blacks, mulattoes, mestizos, and any other people" to work on the *desagüe,* the drainage canal whose laborers usually came from repartimiento drafts.[68] Increasingly, these "other people" included poor Spaniards. A 1587 cédula listed Spanish vagabonds among the unemployed who were to be placed "with masters whom they may serve or with persons who can teach them a trade." Fourteen years later, a newly promulgated labor code stated that "Spaniards of a servile and idle condition" as well as mestizos, blacks, mulattoes, and zambos should be compelled to work for a living.[69]

The existence of such impoverished Spaniards diminished the social distance between whites and castas. This process was accelerated by casta penetration into retailing, artisanry, and other trades. By the late sixteenth century, many blacks and mulattoes (free and slave alike) occupied "middleman" positions, buying—sometimes extorting—products from the Indians and reselling them in the plaza and the taverns.[70] Casta commercial activity spilled out into the streets, where ambulatory vendors sold pulque, fruit, bread, and all other manner of goods.[71] Legal barriers did little to prevent castas from entering "Spanish" trades. During the seventeenth century, for instance, Spanish surgeon-barbers fought a fifty-year battle to stop Filipinos from practicing this profession. Yet in the end, they settled for restricting Filipinos to eight shops within the city and requiring them to make an annual contribution to the barbers' cofradía.[72]

Colonial officials remained wedded to the old racial stereotypes, but they too had to recognize changing economic realities. Beginning in 1598, free blacks and mulattoes who practiced a trade were assessed two pesos annual tribute, twice the amount demanded from unskilled laborers.[73] Even diehards such as the Marqués de Gelves (viceroy, 1621–1624), who had an almost visceral hatred of blacks and mulattoes, could not impose a strictly racial formula on the city's employment structure. In 1623, he promulgated an ordinance requiring all castas to live with and serve Spanish masters; castas claiming to be legitimate artisans were ordered to present their credentials to government authorities. Forty-one mulatto, mestizo, and castizo artisans and merchants dutifully complied. (Among the artisans, eleven were masters and twenty-eight were journeymen.) What makes even this rather small number impressive is that these respondents represented only those artisans who were officially sanctioned by the gremios, many of which were on record as excluding castas. Although most casta artisans worked at relatively low-status crafts, such as shoemaker or tailor, a few had obtained entry into more prestigious guilds, for example, those of the guilders, blacksmiths, and candle makers. A mulatto named Agustín de Aguilar had even become a master gunsmith, throwing an ironic light on royal attempts to deny arms to castas.[74]

But casta artisans were only the tip of the iceberg. Within six weeks

of the original proclamation, Gelves admitted that he had underestimated
the economic contribution of the castas.

> Many of the said blacks, mulattoes, and mestizos are journeymen rather than
> examined masters, and they assist and work for the said masters, and others
> are working in other crafts and occupations in which there are no examina-
> tions or overseers, living from their honest labor; this being the case, they
> should enjoy the same [treatment] as the examined masters, for the purpose
> [of the ordinance] is to prevent their vagrancy.[75]

Once large numbers of castas became ensconced in the Hispanic economy, much of the city's social control legislation was rendered meaning-
less. Castas could not realistically be prevented from establishing their
own households, from gathering in large groups and at night, or from possessing arms. Castas with buying power daily flouted Spanish sumptuary
regulations. Gage's famous description of Mexico City's black and mulatto
women, alluded to above, stressed their ostentatious apparel.

> Nay, a blackamoor or tawny young maid and slave will make hard shift, but
> she will be in fashion with her neck-chain and bracelets of pearls, and her
> earbobs of some considerable jewels. The attire of this baser sort of people . . .
> is so light, and their carriage so enticing, that many Spaniards even of the
> better sort (who are too prone to venery) disdain their wives for them.[76]

By the early seventeenth century, the Spanish-casta dichotomy had thus
lost much of its validity. Consequently, this older model tended to give way
to yet another social dichotomy, based on cultural and economic rather
than racial indexes. We have already seen how mestizos were divided by
status and cultural affinity into a Hispanicized elite and a lower stratum
grouped with Afro-Mexicans. The new model extended a similar concept
to urban society as a whole, separating Mexico City's inhabitants into the
gente decente (respectable people) and the *plebe* (plebeians). This distinction corresponded to the division in Spain between nobles and commoners
and may be viewed as a response to the "Europeanization" of New Spain's
economy. But, in contrast to Spain, the hallmark of the Mexican plebe was
its racially mixed nature. Mexico's lower class included Indians, castizos,
mestizos, mulattoes, blacks, and even poor Spaniards.[77]

Elite colonials came to regard the plebe as a "vile rabble," marked
by "vile customs, ignorance, and irremediable vices."[78] Throughout the
seventeenth century, government officials regularly testified to the flaws
and incapacities of the commoners. The Mexico City cabildo, meeting
in 1624, described the *gente popular,* composed of "Indians, mestizos,
blacks, mulattoes, and boys," as "irrational people." The Marqués de Cerralvo, Gelves's successor, agreed with the cabildo's assessment.[79] Both Cer-

ralvo and the cabildo excluded Spaniards from the plebe. But they were eager to affirm colonial allegiance to the crown in the aftermath of Mexico City's 1624 riot. Thousands of rioters had stormed the viceregal palace and nearly murdered Viceroy Gelves, while the creole militia had proved unable or unwilling to come to his rescue.[80] Other elite commentators faced the problem of plebeian Spaniards more squarely. As early as 1607, Viceroy Montesclaros had complained about persons who although free of tainted blood were nevertheless "more incapable of goodness and honor than those who are that way by nature." By 1642, Archbishop Juan de Palafox y Mendoza included Spaniards in the plebe as a matter of course: "[The castas] and the Indians and certain lost and villainous Spaniards . . . form the people in these Provinces."[81]

As the concept of the plebe evolved, qualities originally ascribed to certain racial groups became generalized to the commoners as a whole. The cabildo labeled the gente popular, not just Indians, "irrational people"; Montesclaros claimed that some Spaniards, as well as the castas, were "badly inclined." The very appearance of general terms such as "plebe" and "gente popular"—while decrees from Spain continued to employ standard racial labels—indicates a growing creole awareness of Mexico's racially complex lower class. Yet recognition of this fact posed psychological difficulties for the wealthier colonials. Spaniards justified their domination of Mexico—and assigned rank within the Hispanic república—on the basis of lineage. Now the colonial elite found itself faced with the development of a permanent underclass of plebeian Spaniards whose behavior was no more "rational" or "moral" than that of the plebe's casta members. Some creoles reacted to this embarrassing situation by minimizing the number of poor Spaniards; those who admitted their existence and importance often displayed great uneasiness. Palafox was clearly disgusted by such "villainous" Spaniards; half a century later, the Mexican savant Sigüenza y Góngora railed against "Spaniards . . . who, in declaring themselves 'saramullos' (which is the same as knaves, rascals, and cape-snatchers) and in falling away from their allegiance, are the worst of them all in such a vile rabble."[82]

These "disloyal" Spaniards were more than a discomfiting anomaly. In elite eyes, they threatened the integrity of the Hispanic ethnic group. For, as Fredrik Barth argues, the "continuity of ethnic units . . . depends on the maintenance of a boundary";[83] and at the lower end of the social spectrum, the boundary between Spaniard and casta was eroding. As will be discussed in chapter 2, poor Spaniards and castas lived cheek by jowl, ate, drank, and socialized in the same taverns, frequented the same marketplaces, and worked in the same shops. Moreover, social intercourse led easily to sexual intercourse. Given the high level of miscegenation within the plebe, what was to prevent the descendants of Indians or even blacks from infiltrating into the Spanish group? Peninsular Spaniards already looked down on the creoles, partly because many of the latter had some Indian ancestry. Naturally, elite creoles wished to avoid (or avoid recognizing) any further "taint." They therefore needed a method of social categorization that would reinforce their sense of exclusivity. The model they developed (in part unconsciously) is known as the sistema de castas.

The sistema de castas was a hierarchical ordering of racial groups according to their proportion of Spanish blood. At its most extreme, this model distinguished more than forty racial categories, though few of these had any practical significance. The standard seventeenth-century format (there were, of course, regional variations) contained five to seven groups, ranked as follows: Spaniard, castizo, morisco, mestizo, mulatto, Indian, and black. (Castizos were the product of Spanish-mestizo unions, moriscos the children of mulatto and Spanish parents). The evolution of the sistema de castas is far from clear. Magnus Mörner notes that it "emerged slowly and gradually" but gives no specific dates. Gonzalo Aguirre Beltrán states that the sistema came into effect during the seventeenth century; John K. Chance believes that it was functioning in Oaxaca by 1630.[84] There are indications that the sistema de castas had achieved institutional form in Mexico City by the mid-seventeenth century. The parishes of Santa Veracruz and Sagrario Metropolitano began to keep separate marriage registers for the castas in 1646, and both employed the sistema's most common racial terms.[85] In short, the available evidence suggests that the sistema de castas emerged during the seventeenth century, in concurrence with, or slightly after, the gente decente-plebe model.

These two images of society were complementary. Both expressed the uneven fit between Mexico's racial and economic categories: all elites were Spaniards, but not all Spaniards were members of the elite. The gente decente-plebe model acknowledged this fact, while the sistema de castas attempted to diminish its significance. By imposing a strict hierarchy on Mexico's welter of racial divisions, the sistema assured that the "cream" would rise to the top: since poor Spaniards took their place at the apex of plebeian society, all Spaniards ranked higher than all castas. Moreover, by making finer racial distinctions among plebeians, elite Spaniards could hope to render the Spanish-casta boundary less permeable.

In theory, one's place in the racial hierarchy was based on lineage; in reality, few except for the most elite families could trace their ancestry back for several generations. The Spanish therefore stressed skin color as a guide to racial status among commoners.[86] Phenotype, of course, was not a flawless, objective standard. As Patricia Seed argues,

The laws governing the inheritance of physical characteristics . . . can produce a theoretically infinite range of colors, hair textures, and other features, but colonial Mexican society recognized only four intermediate shadings beyond the basic Black, white, and Indian. These shadings—castizo, mestizo, mulatto, and morisco—represented only a tiny fraction of the range of possible physical features. . . . The recognition of only four groups as separate depended on social selection of the relevant categories of groupings.[87]

The question of which social sector made this selection will be taken up later. But it should be noted that even elite creoles—whose interests the sistema de castas served—did not adopt this model in every circumstance. Simple stereotypes from the sixteenth century—about humble, pliable Indians, pernicious castas, and loyal creoles—persisted throughout the colonial period. Furthermore, as we have seen, local regulations (such as gremio ordinances) continued to lump castizos, mestizos, blacks, and mulattoes (and sometimes Indians) together.

Thus, the sistema de castas had limited applicability; it fell far short of covering every area of life. In Barth's terms, the sistema provided a "structuring of interaction"[88] focusing on sexual and marital relations between castas and Spaniards. Among elite Spaniards, marriage was often a weapon to promote the interests of the family. Kinship ties, centered on the extended family, were vital to the creation and transmission of wealth, status, and power in the Hispanic community. Marital alliances with the "impure" castas offered creoles few advantages. Indeed, insofar as they lowered the family's prestige, such marriages could be very damaging. Preserving creole wealth and *limpieza de sangre* (purity of blood) required endogamy. Under the sistema de castas, phenotype acted as a sieve, filtering out unsuitable candidates for admission to Spanish families.[89] The colonials also hoped that such racial pride would penetrate to the non-Spanish strata, isolating the lighter-skinned groups among the castas and further lengthening the social distance between Spaniards and Afro-Mexicans.[90]

The possibility of the plebeians uniting to overturn Spanish rule had long been a colonial nightmare—one that turned briefly into reality in 1624 and 1692. It is not surprising, then, that the supposed divisive effects of racial differences within the plebe were an article of faith for many Spanish officials. The Marqués de Mancera (viceroy, 1664–1673) reported that the plebeians' laziness, drunkenness, and other vices had created many disturbances in the past but that even more would have occurred if the commoners' "different shades had not also produced a diversity of inclinations."[91] A racial hierarchy also helped to explain the disquieting phenomenon of "successful" (or elite) castas. If moral and intellectual qualities were transmitted through heredity, those with less tainted, more Hispanic bloodlines should be superior to other castas; their success was only to be expected. Viceroy Mancera applied this reasoning to mestizos in general.

> The mestizos, sons and descendants of the Spaniards, are no less presump-tuous than the Negroes and mulattoes . . . but in a somewhat more elevated manner. Their presumption is better controlled and more subject to reason. They are proud that they have our blood in them and on various occasions have shown that they know how to carry out their responsibilities.[92]

Mancera's comments reveal how racial labels could be used to rank the economic utility of plebeians. Elite colonials despised the "lower" trades on principle but nonetheless recognized "the virtue of employing . . . the miserable poor in the exercise of the necessary arts and offices of the re-public."[93] Plebeians were simultaneously a threat to and an indispensable support for the established order. The elite tended to cast this dual nature of the urban poor in racial terms. On the one hand were the "honorable" poor—Spaniards, Indians, and some mestizos—who provided essential labor in their respective spheres. On the other hand were the castas, whose moral failings had already been established and who were natural scape-goats for plebeian misbehavior. For example, many observers charged that the castas' pernicious influence on the Indians caused the riot of 1692.[94]

Because elite Spaniards often subsumed economic categories under racial labels, their statements about Mexican social and economic life must be treated with great caution. The brute fact, which Spanish models tended to paper over, was that most Mexico City residents, regardless of racial affiliation, lived within the constraints of severe poverty. The mechanisms that maintained this skewed socioeconomic system drew little comment at the time, but they should not be ignored by a modern in-vestigator. To grasp more realistically the relationship between race and class in colonial Mexico, we must avoid the temptation to view ethnic or racial groups abstractly, out of the lived experiences and social context glossed over by elite commentary. In the next chapters, we will exam-ine the plebeians' material culture, then turn to their social relations, and finally investigate their views of society and of themselves.

2

Life among the Urban Poor:
Material Culture and
Plebeian Society

For the modern visitor to Mexico City, choking on exhaust fumes and anxiously checking ozone levels, it may be some comfort to know that pollution, in one form or another, is an age-old problem. Insalubrity plagued the colonial city as well,[1] though seventeenth-century contaminants were far less insidious than their modern counterparts. Filth and disease advertised their presence, but city authorities, lacking adequate knowledge and technical abilities, could engineer no solution. However, the wealthy could buy themselves a measure of protection: a more balanced diet, cleaner living conditions, and somewhat better health care. The plebeians stood totally exposed.

In the colonial period, popular notions of hygiene were very primitive; city residents frequently treated public thoroughfares as private garbage dumps. Major plazas and streets had mounds of trash piled in the corners, despite "their foul odors which cause disease."[2] In some instances, sewage from private residences flowed into canals through open pipes. Dead animals—dogs, cats, and even horses—were disposed of in streets and canals. During periods of epidemic disease, naked human corpses sometimes lay exposed to the sun all day before being removed by the authorities.[3]

Mexico City's location in the midst of a lake posed an additional set of difficulties—above all, the problem of flooding. The most serious flood of the colonial period occurred in 1629, leaving the city partly inundated for five years and causing a temporary population loss of many thousands.[4] After this disaster, the crown instituted a project to dig a huge drainage canal, the desagüe, thereby reducing the water level of the surrounding lakes. Work on the desagüe continued, on and off, for over a century, consuming millions of pesos and thousands of Indian laborers. Yet episodes of flooding recurred at intervals, notably, in 1648, 1675, 1707, 1732, and 1747–48.[5]

Besides their immediate dangers, these waters—"the common and continual enemy of this city," as the cabildo once remarked—took a terrible toll on the city's complex infrastructure.[6] Mexico City was tied to the mainland by several causeways, the most important being the three that followed the original Aztec pattern, "connecting the city with Guadalupe to the north, Tacuba to the west and Mexicalzingo and Coyoacán to the south."[7] Within the city, both canals and paved streets were in use, though the latter increasingly gained at the expense of the former. Still, the main canals (especially the one leading from Mexicalzingo) served as major conduits for fresh produce from nearby regions. Many smaller canals criss-crossed the city; in fact, residents sometimes found it necessary to build private bridges to connect various pieces of their property.[8] But even in this environment, potable water was not always ready to hand. Like the streets, the canals were heavily polluted by garbage and sewage, and medical authorities regarded them as "the most favorable foci for . . . epidemic disease."[9] Fresh water reached Mexico City from two major aqueducts stretching west to Chapultepec. A system of 28 public fountains and 505 private fountains—the latter intended for the homes and businesses of the wealthy—provided an adequate water supply to the traza, but outlying areas were less well served. In particular, the northern barrio of Tlatelolco lacked drinking water for much of the seventeenth century.[10]

All of the city's public works required constant attention and repair. By the late seventeenth century, it had become clear that the annual budget for this work—4,000 pesos for the upkeep of aqueducts and water pipes, plus 1,200 pesos for street cleaning—was inadequate. Surveying the condition of the city in 1696, government-appointed architects painted a sorry picture. The majority of the city's bridges, they reported, were unusable and would have to be totally rebuilt; those in better condition still required considerable repair. The canals were blocked, raising the threat of widespread flooding, not to mention disease caused by their "filthy and loathsome" refuse. They also warned that "all kinds of supplies enter through these canals, and the canoes will be inconvenienced and hindered, and unable to navigate as they do when the canals are clean."[11] The streets were in somewhat better shape, though much of their pavement was ruined. The architects estimated the costs of repairing the aqueducts alone at 35,000 pesos and put the city's total repair bill at 105,000 pesos. The crown ordered a new tax on tobacco to help fund the repair program, but this was hardly sufficient. The city government instituted a general policy of legislating against littering, finding new tax sources to pay for cleanups, and making property owners responsible for the condition of bordering streets and canals.[12] These measures also proved dismal failures. In 1704, the southern causeway, the city's longest, was found to be "useless and unpassable to coach or horse, or on foot, because of the poor condition of its pavement." In 1717, the cabildo fumed, "Since the rains, both in this and previous years, have been heavy, much damage has occurred. . . . [The city's public works] have fallen to such a miserable state that the canals are choked; most of the streets are full of trash, and their paving stones are destroyed; some bridges are damaged, and others need to be totally rebuilt. The causeways are the same."[13] Not until the 1790s did conditions improve noticeably, even in the central city. For the urban poor, an unclean, malodorous, disease-ridden environment was a fact of life.

Decent housing also eluded many Mexico City plebeians. A residential hierarchy existed in the city, providing a sensitive index to socioeconomic standing.[14] Elite families possessed mansions worth thousands of pesos. A 1713 bill of sale describes a fairly representative example of such structures.

> [The ground floor has] a suite of apartments off the main corridor, a small room, a stall for horses next to the entrance, a patio, a spacious parlor, [and] a stairway that leads to the upper story, which is divided into a main room, a bedroom, and two more parlors.[15]

This building also included a connected enclosure for raising chickens. It was valued at 3,380 pesos, by no means an extremely high price for an elite residence.

Such houses constituted a prime status symbol among the upper classes. Privately owned homes were also a cause for pride among the less wealthy. Nicolasa de Espinosa, a mestiza widow, explained that she had purchased her house and yard "with my own money, acquired with my hard work and skill, [a fact] which is public and notorious."[16] But the houses owned by artisans, petty merchants, and minor Indian nobles were humble indeed compared to the sumptuous dwellings of the wealthy. Most of the former sold for less than 100 pesos. They seldom possessed more than one story, and many had been personally constructed by their owners.[17] Those that changed hands were frequently in less than ideal condition. Don Gregorio Mancio, a royal interpreter, purchased a plot of land from two artisans which contained solely the outer walls of what had been a small house. An Indian woman named Bernarda Angelina owned a six-room building "with four rooms roofed and two unroofed," while María Dominga, a free black woman, once bought "a small adobe house composed of two ruined rooms without doors and windows."[18]

This evidence suggests that owners had difficulty keeping up their properties, which is not surprising given the urban environment described above. In some cases, home-owning castas and Indians had inherited their property and perhaps found proper maintenance beyond their means. For instance, Juan Ramírez, a mere journeyman carpenter, owned land and buildings worth 250 pesos: a pair of two-room suites, each with a door on the street, a yard, and a turfed path leading to a nearby aqueduct. But he had inherited these from his parents, who had purchased them from Don Martín Alonso, an Indian noble. Houses were often divided among heirs; in fact, it was not unusual for rooms, rather than houses, to be the unit of inheritance and sale. The mestizo Juan de la Plata inherited from his father "one-half of a small adobe house; . . . the said house is run-down and in poor condition; one-half is occupied by some Indians and the other belongs to my nephews." [19] As this example indicates, even small houses tended to be shared among families. Nicolasa de Espinosa gave half of her hard-earned house to her stepchildren. Juana de los Angeles Canales willed one apartment to her niece and two more to her adopted son. The mestiza seamstress Sebastiana Hernández left her house to a clergyman with whom she was a close friend but added the proviso that her Indian *comadre* (godmother to her child) be allowed to live "for the rest of her life" in Sebastiana's suite.[20]

Even those who possessed rooms in small, run-down buildings, however, were privileged compared to the majority of their neighbors. Few Mexico City inhabitants actually owned their own homes. Most of the traza's buildings (aside from public structures) were in the hands of the city's twenty-two convents and twenty-nine monasteries. In the late seventeenth century, the Convent of Balvanera alone rented out eighty-eight units (stores and residences) in fifty-three buildings.[21] Like privately owned residences, rented houses clearly demonstrated Mexico City's hierarchy of living quarters. Ecclesiastical rent books usually distinguished between *cajas bajas* (or *pequeñas*)—one-story dwellings—and *casas altas* (or *grandes*)—two-story structures of stone built around a central courtyard. The latter often served as apartment buildings (*casas de vecindad*). The most affluent tenants would live in the upper stories, in suites of rooms "called *viviendas* to distinguish them from the single-room apartments that were normally found on the ground floor and called *cuartos*," [22] or *aposentos*. The lower story also frequently contained a store, workshop, or tavern facing the street. Alternately, casas altas might be leased to a single person or family. Table 2.1, based on a sample of ecclesiastical rent books, demonstrates the elite status of these tenants. Persons with the honorific title *don* or *doña* formed the large majority of tenants in buildings renting for more than 100 pesos per year. Only when rents dropped below 70 pesos did the proportion of dons and doñas fall to less than one-third. Doubtless the men and women who paid such rents lived in the upper story, leaving the ground floor to their servants or employees or renting out its rooms. Thus, José de Torrez, leasing a house from the Sanctuary

Table 2.1. Ecclesiastical rentals in the Mexico City *traza*, 1660–1730

Type of Housing	Yearly Rent (pesos)	Number of Tenants	Percentage of Dons and Doñas	Average Length of Tenancy (months)
Casas grandes	300+	75	80.0	39.63
Casas grandes	100–299	289	66.1	23.01
Acesorias, viviendas, entresuelas, casas pequeñas	32–99	410	34.3	12.00
Cuartos, aposentos	Less than 32	198	8.6	9.98

Source: AGN, Templos y Conventos, vol. 87, exp. 1; vol. 103, exp. 1; vol. 160, exp. 9; Bienes Nacionales, vol. 237, exp. 3; vol. 457, exps. 1–2, 18; vol. 649, exp. 6; vol. 823, passim; vol. 1,146, exps. 3, 5; vol. 1,221, exp. 7.

of Our Lady of Guadalupe for 175 pesos a year, sublet an aposento to Josefa de Saldívar for 2 pesos monthly. The inner yard of a house owned by Antonio Ramírez, a Spanish baker, contained reed and adobe shacks (*jacales*) lodging Indians. In a similar fashion, the Convent of Balvanera rented two "ruined aposentos" in an empty lot behind a church to "a few Indians" for 2 or 3 reales a month.[23]

As the last two examples suggest, those who could not afford more than a few pesos per month for rent often had to settle for substandard housing. Residential buildings, like public works, suffered from the city's recurrent earthquakes and floods. But ecclesiastical owners were loath to lay out the necessary sums for constant repairs. Instead, they commonly allowed buildings to slowly deteriorate, periodically lowering the rent until they were no longer profitable. By this time, the structures in question might have to be "remade and rebuilt, for the most part, from the ground up, with new walls, roofs, doors, and windows."[24] Rents could then be increased up to 50 percent. Under this system of operation, casas altas sometimes remained vacant for months because of their poor condition, and the less profitable aposentos might deteriorate even further, in one case to the point that the roof threatened to collapse.[25] But, in contrast to elite dwellings, even the worst cuartos could usually find some tenant willing to pay a few reales monthly for a place to stay. A small apartment described as "uninhabitable" in May 1716 nevertheless had a tenant and (not yet repaired) was still being rented two and one-half years later. One Indian woman actually lived in a house under construction to take advantage of the low rent.[26] For the poorest housing, the owners did not always insist on regular rent collection. A man named Lázaro de los Reyes, for example, paid for his room in a casa de vecindad by "caring for the building."[27]

Despite the rock-bottom prices of the city's worst living quarters, some tenants proved unable to meet a normal schedule of payments. In the period from May 1699 to January 1703, nearly 15 percent of the rents owed to the Convent of Regina Celi remained unpaid; this amount was more than twice as great as the convent's construction costs during the same time.[28] Many of these debts were never collected, for they belonged to former tenants who had stealthily departed at night—a maneuver facilitated by their lack of bulky possessions. More scrupulous tenants unable to pay the rent left a wide variety of goods in surety, ranging from coral bracelets and necklaces to cedar chests, monachords, icemakers, and humbler goods such as chicken coops, slippers, cloaks, and other articles of clothing.[29]

A spatial analysis of central Mexico City thus reveals a vertically segregated society, divided primarily along class rather than racial lines. The wealthy dwelled upstairs, above the malodorous, disease-ridden streets and canals; the poor lived downstairs, at times bereft of protection from the elements. The residents of Mexico City's aposentos, casas bajas, and jacales formed—in particularly apt terminology—a lower class, characterized by racial diversity and, as we shall see, a hand-to-mouth existence. Lower-class homes were not strongholds to keep the outside world at bay. Plebeians lived close to the street—and close to each other.

Privacy was rare in the cramped quarters of the poor. A criminal investigation from the late seventeenth century demonstrates the easy familiarity that developed among the plebeian residents of Mexico City's apartment buildings. The investigators believed that an empty room in this particular casa de vecindad had been used to stage the nighttime robbery of an adjacent store; they therefore questioned witnesses to discover the whereabouts of both the key to this room and the key to the building's front gate. The first key, they found, had been left in the care of a mulatta named María de Salazar, popularly known as "Mary the seamstress." She, however, had been absent for much of the day preceding the robbery. When a woman had come by to inquire about renting the vacated apartment, two neighborhood girls (a Spaniard and a castiza) had shown it to her, having first entered María's empty room and borrowed the key. Nor was María in her room during the evening. Because she had quarreled with her husband, María spent the night with a friend in the building, the mestiza shirt maker Lorenza Ignacia. The two women were thus able to supply an alibi for Lorenza's brother, a prime suspect in the case; he had retired early to the apartment he shared with his sister, complaining of a toothache and head pains. As for the front gate, that had been locked late in the evening by José del Castillo, a resident tailor. Before locking up, he had asked Lucía de Medina, a mulatta widow who apparently spent much of her day at her window, whether everyone was in and had received an affirmative reply. But, José admitted, the lock was a simple bolt that could be manipulated by hand from both the inside and the outside. As one might expect, no resolution to this investigation is recorded.[30]

Failure to solve such cases was not unusual. Both the Inquisition and the Sala de Crimen had limited manpower and so relied heavily on informers. Many victims of crime took it on themselves to make preliminary investigations (*diligencias*) and then turn over the name of the suspected criminal to the authorities.[31] Obviously, this procedure provided ample opportunities for avenging insults or settling old scores by turning in one's enemies to the Inquisition or the Sala. This did indeed occur;[32] but in general, there was a widespread reluctance (particularly among plebeians) to play the role of informer. Typically, suspects exhibited illicit behavior over lengthy periods before finally being reported, often by a member of the elite. Consider the following two Inquisition cases. In 1652, a priest denounced Diego Ortiz, a blind mestizo musician, for expressing heretical opinions. Ortiz, who had a free room in the house of a Spanish captain, spent a large part of his time sitting in the patio, openly proclaiming (among other things) that Christians did not follow the true Law and that the Virgin Mary was not the mother of God. These statements were made in the presence of "Alonso Gómez, a Spanish servant in the house, and of Andrea, a free mulatta, and of Ana, a mulatta slave, and of Beatris, a Spanish girl who had been raised in this household." None of these denounced Ortiz to the Inquisition; the priest himself waited two months, perhaps because of doubts that the mestizo was sane. In fact, the Inquisitors eventually decided that Ortiz was not mentally responsible, citing his increasing obsession that mercury was growing inside his body.[33]

A still more clear-cut case of plebeian resistance to informing occurred the same year, when a mestizo named José de León was denounced for concourse with demons. José had been ejected from his dwelling when the owner discovered that he had stolen some items from the house. As he was leaving, Doña Ana de Herrera (the owner's sister-in-law) remarked, "Poor man! Where will he go now, when there is no one to help or defend him?" José responded that he would not need any help beyond that provided by a demon that accompanied him.[34] Once again, although several persons were present, the elite members of the household—Doña Ana and her sister—made the denunciation, while the servants merely seconded it. Yet José had not been popular downstairs. Gerónimo de la Cruz, a mulatto slave and coachman, claimed that he had never seen José de León "carry a rosary, nor pray, nor say 'praised be the Holy Sacrament' . . . as the custom is among Christians." Gerónimo added that the mestizo was "an evilly inclined man, a traitor with bad intentions," and a sullen drunkard who had twice attacked him with knives.[35] Nevertheless, it had apparently never crossed Gerónimo's mind to report José to the authorities.

Personal rancor may have added strength to Gerónimo's condemnation of José. But it is noteworthy that in both of these cases involving multiracial households, ethnic differences seem to have played no role whatsoever. Instead, one is more aware of a common bond among the servants, who hesitated to report illicit actions by their fellows. Some colonial administrators accused all plebeians of an unwillingness to cooperate with the civil and religious authorities, charging that they were secretly on the criminal's side. In 1716, New Spain's viceroy, the Duque de Linares, complained to the king that plebeians constantly looked for opportunities to commit robberies and that "anyone who by chance cannot carry out the deed in fact is always returning to it in his thoughts."[36]

Linares despaired of ever properly policing the commoners. Many plebeians, he reported, refused to work regularly, preferring to sponge off their friends who did have jobs. Wanted criminals could easily hide in the city's poorer quarters, where relatives, *compadres,* or simply others sharing their antipathy toward the colonial authorities would willingly shield them from the police.[37] Linares's comments reveal an uneasy awareness that a plebeian subculture had developed in Mexico City, a subculture whose norms were different from, or even opposed to, those of the dominant Spaniards. The members of this subculture were, to an uncomfortable extent, beyond the authorities' control. In this respect, they differed from the stabler group of Spanish householders, who could be easily registered and taxed, and from the Indians, who were basically the responsibility of the priests and their own gobernadores.[38] The "lawlessness" and "disorder" that elites feared in plebeians achieved highest visibility when the latter gathered in large groups, in the city's taverns and plazas.

Elite attempts to limit and regulate alcoholic intake among the poor represent an outstanding failure of Mexico City's legal system. The two major objectives of the city fathers were (1) to limit the sale of pulque to licensed taverns; and (2) to control drinking and social practices within the *pulquerías.* They accomplished neither. Pulque continued to be dispensed from street stalls and private homes. Even when pulque was banned after the riot of 1692, the viceroy allowed some to be sold in the plaza for medicinal purposes.[39] Once the ban was lifted (in 1697), Indians were allowed supplies of pulque for their own consumption. But Spaniards and castas had by this time become the most important consumers of this beverage, and many Indians were tempted to sell their pulque on the side. Court cases from the late seventeenth century testify to the prevalence of this practice. In one instance, constables investigated a casa de vecindad and found illegal skins of pulque in three separate apartments. Another case featured a slave from the provinces who explained that he had heard of how pulque could be easily obtained in certain neighborhoods of the traza.[40] Official channels of supply were contravened without much difficulty, as the story told by the mestiza Josefa de Avila shows.

I was passing by the Royal Aqueduct when I heard some men I did not know say, "Here are the *moloteros!*" I asked them, "What are the *moloteros?*" and they said, "men who sell pulque." I came to the aqueduct and saw a canoe with some out-of-town Indians who had pulque and I asked them if I could buy some. . . . They said yes, so I left and pawned my skirt and used the money to buy . . . a skinful.[41]

Even when the pulque safely made it to the taverns, the authorities' worries were far from over. Ideally, a tavern was simply supposed to dispense pulque; it was not to be a place for plebeians to congregate for hours on end. The city's thirty-six licensed taverns were segregated by gender: twenty-four for men, twelve for women. City ordinances forbade tavern owners to serve food or to allow gambling or dancing. But customary practice made a mockery of such rules. Pulquerías, in fact, fulfilled precisely the social function that colonial officials feared.

All taverns, both legal and illegal, . . . were an integral part of the social and financial life of the lower classes, serving as places of recreation where leisure hours could be spent dancing, singing, gambling, and drinking with family, friends, and lovers. They provided lodging for the homeless poor who, for free or for a nominal fee, could sleep in the back room or under the bar. They were places where the poor could easily pawn their own or stolen goods in return for money, credit, or drink. The drinking house functioned as a reassuring institution in a society subject to the anxieties of accelerating corn prices, periodic epidemics, and job insecurity.[42]

Those entrusted with policing the city, however, were not so reassured. Not that they worried overmuch about drunkenness itself, or even about occasional aberrant behavior, as when a mestizo shoemaker renounced God under the influence of alcohol.[43] Rather, they were concerned that tavern socializing encouraged a systematic breakdown of social inhibitions among the poor. For example, one priest argued that adulterated drinks (a common feature of Mexico City taverns) caused Indians "to lose their senses . . . and being [in this condition] they commit heathen idolatries and sacrifices, they fall into disputes and kill each other, and they engage in carnal, abominable, and incestuous sexual acts."[44] William B. Taylor, writing in a more modern, scholarly vein, explains that "pulquería behavior . . . approached classic disinhibition, in which a person's characteristic behavior changed, often dramatically. . . . The pulquería was a 'time-out' setting where the rules outside did not necessarily apply."[45] An insult or an argument over a gaming debt could suddenly erupt into violence; and inebriated comradeship sometimes turned into blood-soaked enmity. Ironically (and much to the displeasure of the clergy), the highest levels of violence occurred during the festive religious seasons of Christmas and Easter.[46]

Plebeians offended the religious sensibilities of the elite in other ways as well. Mexico City Inquisitors once arrested a family of blacksmiths, recently arrived from Puebla, after they held a party in honor of San Nicolás. The party-goers, it seems, had celebrated the saint's day in an overly profane manner, with popular ballads, card games, and a copious supply of *aguardiente* (cane liquor).[47] In 1691, the Inquisition reported that public crosses served as sites for popular religious festivals, including plays, bullfights, and masques. Those attending profaned these sacred symbols, committing "grave irreverences and indecencies against the same Holy Cross, under the pretext of devotion and religion, from which follows sacrilege, irreverence, and inexecrable lewdness and abuse." On religious holidays, it was common practice for "a wide variety of people" to stroll through the streets dressed as priests and perform parodies of religious ceremonies, such as confession and the laying on of hands. The Inquisitors gravely commented that these actions "caused much scandal and corruption of customs." Furthermore, since the performers operated "in the sight of everyone, especially women, they not only occasion[ed] grave damage to their own souls but also endanger[ed] the souls of those nearby."[48]

Marketplaces constituted another setting in which numerous plebeians gathered and (in elite eyes) displayed unsuitable behavior. Among Mexico City's most important markets were San Hipólito, in an Indian barrio; San Juan, in the southwestern corner of the traza; and, of course, the plaza mayor. The latter formed the commercial heart of Mexico City. The items sold there included luxury wares from Europe and the Far East, mules, horses, and fodder, textiles and clothing, and all varieties of food. The mercantile hierarchy suggested by this spectrum of goods also appeared in the plaza's architecture. After the riot of 1692, the city constructed a set of stone houses (known as the *alcaicería*) in the center of the plaza to replace the wooden booths (*cajones*) previously employed by elite merchants. The crown reasoned that each building would "be able to house a moderate family, which will reduce the risk of fire; and the increased concourse of merchants will restrain the excesses of those called . . . 'saramullos.'"[49] The cajones in the alcaicería generally rented for 200 to 250 pesos per year. In the vestibules of these stores stood smaller, wooden *cajonsillas*, whose owners paid 40 to 60 pesos annually. Finally, the plaza contained a multitude of portable stands (*mesillas*); the *mesilleros* paid between one-half and one and a half reales per week for this privilege—though some were excused from this charge.[50]

Both the stand owners and their clientele were racially mixed. Indian commerce, especially in basic foodstuffs, remained a major part of the plaza's economic scene, but the presence of castas was also marked. Indeed, in 1712, one observer commented that "all one sees in the plaza is mestizos and mestizas selling [goods]."[51] Yet in 1703, the fight against a suggested rate hike on mesillas was led by six Spaniards.[52] Like pulquerías, the plaza market served more than a commercial function. Plebeians of all races met there to eat and drink and to share in the pleasure of conversation and gossip.

Elite Spaniards had little sympathy for, or understanding of, the social benefits of such marketplaces. Off one corner of the main plaza lay the *plaza del volador*, home of the *baratillo*, or "thieves' market." This market specialized in the sale of used clothing and other secondhand merchandise and as such was of vital service to the poor. But, from the official point of view, the baratillo was merely a place where "all the vagabonds congregate"[53] and a center for the marketing of stolen goods. After the riot of 1692, Viceroy Juan de Ortega y Montañez finally persuaded the king to order the baratillo's extirpation; yet illicit sales of goods continued, and the baratillo, though never legally recognized, remained in existence.[54]

Market activity continued well into the night, when, according to government officials, plebeian insolence and misbehavior reached their height. The plaza mayor's nighttime market (*tianguillo*), reported the *corregidor* (a district magistrate) in 1681, was the site of (and excuse for) "a great concourse of men and women from all spheres . . . [including] escaped slaves, mulattoes, mestizos, Indians and even Spaniards" who gambled, drank, and fornicated with the female vendors. Even more scandalous, these activities spread from the plaza itself to the nearby cathedral cemetery. Dark nooks and corners—the street lamps were frequently extinguished—sheltered vagabonds who robbed passersby, causing "a great clamor from the victims." At least some of the thieves were armed. The corregidor stated that night watchmen had told him "many times how during their rounds they see many lewd and ugly things and they do not dare to arrest anyone because . . . they fear for their lives." The murder of a mulatto in 1700 led to a concerted attempt to close the tianguillo. The imperiled Indian vendors, however, took up a collection, hired a lawyer, and appealed to the viceroy, arguing that they fed poor famished laborers while gaining a profit for themselves, "and with that we pay the royal tribute and the tithes to our priests." They won a significant concession: those stands selling indispensable foodstuffs, such as atole, tortillas, and bread, could remain open.[55]

In the case of both the tianguillo and the baratillo, then, elite disgust at plebeian behavior gave way to economic necessity. This might indicate that the upper classes did not take the threat posed by plebeians very seriously. Yet criminal activity, runaway slaves, plebeian disdain for individual Spaniards, and even revolts were not figments of elite imaginations. One may suggest, instead, that elite reaction to moments of crisis demonstrated the inability of the ruling class—and in particular, the state—to find a collective, institutional response to the existence of a plebeian subculture. The constantly proposed remedies—the segregation of Indians and castas, the prohibition of pulque, the restrictions on taverns and markets, the denials of arms to mixed-bloods—consistently failed. As noted previously, these measures (implemented in the aftermath of a riot or conspiracy) would be observed for some weeks, perhaps months; then vigilance would relax, and the old practices would begin again, at first quietly, then more and more openly—until the next crisis brought a revival of the traditional safeguards.[56]

This cycle resulted in part from the poor's conservatism, their attachment to "immemorial custom."[57] But it also reflected divisions within the elite and conflicts between individual aspirations and the (government-defined) "common good." Thus, many wealthy Spaniards had significant investments in the production and sale of pulque; others flouted segregation laws to gain access to Indian servants and laborers, or maintained retinues of armed castas as a status symbol.[58] The weakness of institutional controls permitted greater freedom for the Spanish elite but at a price— "the license of the crowd." In daily life, the job of keeping the poor in line devolved on individual Spaniards. The ordinances requiring castas to live with and serve "known masters" should be read in this light. Each elite Spaniard was expected to control "his" castas: his slaves, servants, and employees. The elite exercised corporate control over plebeians mainly in the cultural realm, in "images of power and authority."[59] This perspective explains much of the supposedly "irrational" or "baroque" activity of upper-class creoles: the constant round of entertainments, the parade of luxurious coaches noted by Gage and other visitors, the "theatrical adulation" given to incoming viceroys, with "every form of colorful pageantry and exaggerated ceremony."[60] For, as E. P. Thompson has argued, an elite without iron control over the lower classes must rely on "cultural hegemony," expressed through visible symbols of hierarchy and elite participation in important public rituals. This provides an indirect means of social control, as opposed to brute force.

> Once a social system has become "set," it does not need to be endorsed daily by exhibitions of power (although occasional punctuations of force will be made to define the limits of the system's tolerance); what matters more is a continuing theatrical style.[61]

Government officials, in fact, often called for restraint in dealing with the poor, advocating a policy of watchful paternalism. The Marqués de Mancera suggested in 1673 that viceroys should beware the plotting of blacks and mulattoes "but without showing distrust"; he recommended "exacting their tributes with a light hand."[62] In 1697, Ortega y Montañez proposed similar treatment for the plebe as a whole. One should deal gently but firmly with the lower classes, he wrote, "demonstrating a quiet gravity and outward trust," for plebeians would "give much love, veneration, and respect to this representation, because to know integrity and rectitude overawes them."[63]

The one area in which such paternalism was stretched to the breaking point was criminal activity, particularly theft, violent crime, and collective uprisings. Crime had always been a problem in Mexico City; in the late sixteenth century, for example, murder was reportedly an everyday occurrence.[64] The state's policing powers were so weak that in the 1670s merchants on the Calle de San Agustín and the plaza del volador hired their own private night watchman.[65] Yet in the late seventeenth and early eighteenth centuries, many observers felt that crime had reached new and intolerable levels. The elite's sense of waning control over the populace led to "new criminal legislation and . . . augmented punishments, . . . probably supplemented by an increase in the number of constables."[66]

Despite these changes, however, the main outline of elite-plebeian relations held true. First, a fairly high level of crime was tolerated so long as it did not threaten the social structure. Second, government officials continued to show restraint in dealing with plebeian criminals. As several scholars have noted, Mexican justices preferred to mete out "utilitarian" punishments—such as forced labor—rather than executions or the other vindictive sentences characteristic of contemporary European jurisprudence.[67] But there was a marked exception to this rule, one that brings us back to the "theatrical" nature of elite paternalism. Plebeian insolence and disloyalty to superiors met with fierce and exemplary punishment indeed. For example, in 1672, two women (one mulatta and one black) falsely accused of having poisoned their mistress were dragged through the streets, then garroted; their bodies (with their right hands cut off) were then propped up in front of the city gallows for public display.[68]

For all their occasional bouts of extreme cruelty and their failure to understand the structural causes of urban crime, Mexico City's elite had a certain psychological insight. A plebeian subculture whose members spanned the racial spectrum and which had several foci—taverns, markets, servants' quarters, cofradías—to foment solidarity did indeed represent a breeding ground for "antisocial" behavior and a possible threat to the Spaniards' political authority. Plebeian contempt for wealthy Spaniards could easily escalate into violence, as the following Inquisition case from 1688 demonstrates.

Tomás Garfías, a master silk weaver, opened the case by denouncing a woman named Josefa (variously described as a mestiza or mulatta) and her

Spanish friend, Mariana. Both had previously been tenants of Garfías's mother-in-law, Doña Antonia de Dueñas, along with the family of Nicolás de Lezcano, a castizo bricklayer. Nicolás's teenaged daughter (considered a Spaniard) was evidently supposed to be a companion for Doña Antonia. But she quickly became fast friends with Mariana and Josefa, and the three of them "began to sleep together in one room, leaving [Doña Antonia] alone in hers, and making fun of her, calling her an old lady." The doña found this situation insufferable and ejected the two older women "for their lack of respect." After Mariana and Josefa were expelled from the house, their friendship with Manuela cooled considerably; in fact, some time afterward they returned to taunt her. At one point, Josefa pulled Manuela to the ground by her hair, causing Doña Antonia to exclaim, "What impudence for a mulatta to dare to do such a thing to a Spanish woman!" Josefa flared back, replying that she would do the same to Doña Antonia. Although this threat was not carried out immediately, Josefa and Mariana came back a few nights later and began heaving stones at the house. During this attack, an obviously drunken Josefa was reported to have shouted that she would willingly trade her faith in God for a pact with the devil and that her husband told her that he could enjoy any woman he wanted, even the viceroy's wife or the queen, but that he preferred Josefa. She capped these statements by announcing (in the delicate phraseology of one witness) "that she would soil herself on the High Pontiff."[69]

One cannot help feeling a class-based antagonism on the part of Josefa (whatever her psychological problems). The vicissitudes of her relationship with Manuela apparently had a personal basis. (This was true from Manuela's point of view also: it was the doña, not the bricklayer's daughter, who complained of Josefa's "impudence" and "lack of respect.") But Josefa's anger at Doña Antonia rapidly accelerated to stone-throwing and, on the ideological plane, disrespect for the twin pillars of Hispanic society, church and crown. How did the Inquisition react? The final outcome of the case is missing; yet it is noteworthy that the Inquisitors, like Doña Antonia, attempted to define Josefa's behavior in racial terms. In some ways, Josefa fit the casta stereotype perfectly: she was "insolent," unrooted, drunken, and possibly immoral (Garfías, among others, believed that she was not married to her "husband"). As one Inquisitor summed up the preliminary investigation,

> If there is any guilt in this case, most of it belongs to the said mulatta, Josefa; she is gravely suspect because of her status, her way of life, and her nature and caste; and although a similar presumption could be made of the said Mariana, since they live together and one seems as bad as the other, because Mariana is married and is a Spaniard, such a presumption would not have as much force.[70]

Elite Spaniards used racial status as a guide to moral qualities; the same actions could take on different meanings, depending on whether they were performed by whites or castas. Since the racially mixed plebeians were considered inherently vicious, the Spanish suspected the worst of their behavior—even when it was identical to that of the elite. Consider the issue of gambling. When Nicolás de Paniagua, a Spanish shoemaker being held by the Inquisition for blasphemy, wished to discredit the damaging testimony of his former mistress, he claimed that she was untrustworthy since "many vile people with evil ways of life—mulattoes, blacks, and mestizos—gather in her house because she has gambling there."[71] Yet gambling was widespread in Mexico City and, although condemned by some moralists, was generally accepted as a fact of life or even as a legitimate pleasure. Cockfighting reportedly entertained "every kind of vassal in this kingdom."[72] As John Leddy Phelan has pointed out, gambling formed an essential social activity of the colonial elite. Of course, the wealthy occasionally pressed their luck too far—some to the point that they vowed never to gamble again.[73] But elite objections to plebeian gambling took a different tack, one that paralleled their attitude toward tavern drinking and socializing. Gambling had a disinhibiting effect; in the words of one observer, it led to many "offenses against our Lord" and provided an additional motive for casta theft.[74]

There is no doubt that plebeians did, in fact, pawn stolen goods, including religious objects, to pay for gambling debts or to buy drinks in pulquerías.[75] Small stores and market stalls also proved convenient places to dispose of stolen merchandise, since buyers usually followed a "no questions asked" policy. Sellers could cover themselves by marketing the goods in small quantities at several different stores and by stating that they were acting as agents for the true suppliers.[76] In some cases this might even be true, for an item could pass through many hands before reaching its final retailer, a legitimate merchant. For instance, in December 1696, a mulatto slave, Juan Antonio Rodríguez, took advantage of his master's absence from Mexico City to steal a smock with silver filigree from the household strongbox. He then gave the smock to his roommate, the mulatto weaver Juan de la Rosa. This second Juan removed the filigree, melted it down, and sold it to a silversmith. He next passed the smock on to his brother Miguel, saying that "since he was without a cloak to wear outside, he [should] go and sell it; it was from a woman of the house named Doña Barbara, who had given it to him to sell." In all innocence, Miguel sold the smock to a merchant in the plaza mayor. This merchant, Don Andrés de Morales, claimed that he had not been suspicious, since Miguel "carried it publicly as [a legitimate] owner, as do many others who sell pieces of different kinds of clothes."[77]

This type of devious activity, although resented by the elite, could be tolerated. Much more frightening were sudden uprisings by the urban poor, which momentarily threatened the structure of colonial authority. Perhaps the most significant thing about these riots is how seldom they occurred. During the period under study, there were only three: the major riot of 1692, which will be discussed in detail in chapter 7, and two smaller ones in 1696 and 1715. It is important to understand that such uprisings, despite their rarity, were neither inexplicable nor irrational nor simply the products of plebeian anger and frustration in times of socioeconomic crisis. As Taylor and J. I. Israel (among others) have shown, colonial riots were patterned events that formed part of a political dialogue between rulers and ruled. They reflected the rioters' belief that the governing elite had certain obligations to the poor.[78] E. B. Hobsbawm remarks (in discussing urban riots in Europe) that from the plebeian viewpoint, "it is the business of the ruler and his aristocracy to provide a livelihood for his people. . . . Provided the ruler did his duty, the populace was prepared to defend him with enthusiasm. But if he did not, it rioted until he did."[79] Notice that this behavior does not necessarily imply any failure of allegiance to the overall system of government, symbolized by the king. Indeed, the rioters often invoked royalty: "Long live the king and death to bad government!" Rather, these revolts were an effective means of protest within the system. Riots, then, should be seen in the wider context of the relationship between plebeians and the colonial state.

Obviously, plebeians had most direct contact with the lower echelons of officialdom: *alguaciles, ministros de vara,* plaza *mayordomos,* and the like. Although there was considerable room for conflict here, a modus vivendi seems to have prevailed. To begin with, only a small portion of the city's numerous regulations were actively enforced. Certain sectors of the city seldom saw policemen, and even in the traza, "islands of freedom" existed—notably, the taverns, where (prior to 1692) constables were forbidden to enter.[80] Furthermore, certain implicit but widely understood standards regulated the behavior of minor officials, whose social rank, after all, was not that much higher than the plebeians'. At the very least, artisans did not hesitate to criticize constables to their faces for improper conduct. City residents were impatient—sometimes violently resentful—of the enforcement of laws that defied common sense. During a September morning in 1697, Don José Jiménez, one of the city's councilmen (*regidores*), confiscated some bread from a street vendor—a Spanish woman with six children—because the loaves were underweight. Some time later, as Don José was speaking with a friend in the Juzgado de la Diputación, a man burst in, shouting and demanding that the regidor explain his action. Don José pointed out the widow's violation of the law and added that he had given the bread to a poor woman; whereupon his interlocutor loudly exclaimed, "What sense did it make to give the bread to a poor woman instead of letting the widow keep it?" He then shouted that the regidor was neither baker nor judge and should not have meddled in the matter at all. Various witnesses testified that he hurled other insults—"There is no justice here for the poor!" "You are a coyote!"—while shaking his sword at Don José, before finally stamping off into the street.[81]

Although in this particular instance the aggrieved party purged his anger without spilling blood, such confrontations between officials and citizens could turn violent. Raised voices would quickly draw a crowd, which would then take sides (often against the officer). As a result, the precipitating incident would almost become lost in the more generalized conflict between the official and the crowd that denied him his authority. Sometimes the crowd did succeed in stripping its opponent of his dignity, as both sides resorted to a flurry of insults. The following case, drawn from the city's judicial archives, may serve as an illustration of these remarks. It was a case of almost comic confusion that ultimately turned ugly and ended in the imprisonment of some overzealous constables.

In the late afternoon of April 17, 1722, two ministros de vara arrived outside a pulquería to arrest Andrés Benítez, an Indian harness maker who, they had been informed, had fled a nearby obraje where he had been working off a debt. (In actuality, Andrés had been released from the obraje a few days previously when a friend had guaranteed the debt's repayment.) When Andrés emerged from the tavern, the constables arrested him and, pulling him by the arm, started to drag him to the public jail. Andrés protested his innocence forcefully along the way. Soon a crowd began to gather, causing the party of three to stop at a fountain, where a new discovery added oil to the flames. The ministros subjected Andrés to a search and found a large knife in the folds of some material he had been carrying. Technically, of course, carrying a concealed weapon was a serious offense; however, in this case, Andrés was apparently merely transporting a newly acquired knife back to his workshop. At this point, the mood of the crowd grew more hostile, and the constables' control of the situation began progressively to deteriorate. Andrés accused his captors of stealing a pair of earrings from him during their search—an accusation that they indignantly denied, stating that they were "honorable men with money in their purses." Some members of the crowd pushed forward to rescue Andrés. The knife maker Diego de la Cruz explained how Andrés had obtained the weapon; both Andrés's former master and his current landlady attempted to correct the constables' misapprehension about his status as a fugitive. But the constables refused to listen; perhaps they were inebriated, as some of the witnesses suggested. At any rate, their exas-

peration overflowed into a series of curses flung at Andrés's landlady (who
currently employed him in her sausage shop). They called her "whore, rot-
ten teeth, and other dishonest and disgusting things"; as she retreated into
her shop, they followed, taunting her. By this time, much of the crowd
seems to have dissipated, perhaps because it had become clear that any
charges brought against Andrés by these ministros—in their present condition—were unlikely to hold water. And indeed, after the constables had
escorted Andrés to jail and their behavior had become known, they were
themselves imprisoned.[82]

Here again, a potentially violent situation was resolved without blood-
shed. But government officials were not always so fortunate. The riot of
1696 began in a similar fashion, when an *alcalde* (magistrate) arrested one
Francisco González de Castro in the baratillo. As he was leading his prisoner to jail, a crowd of plebeians—joined by some university students—
began to shout abuse at the alcalde; their attempts to stop Castro's imprisonment soon flowered into a brief outburst of rioting, during which they
burned the plaza mayor's gibbet.[83] As we shall see, friction between the
poor and government officials also provided the immediate trigger for the
much greater riot of 1692.

One reason that displeasing behavior by government employees so seldom provoked violence was that plebeians could appeal (often successfully)
to higher authority. Again and again, poor Spaniards, Indians, and castas—including slaves—asked high religious and civil officials to overturn
the rulings of their underlings. But what of our earlier remarks on plebeian
disinclination to become involved with the authorities? The answer to this
apparent paradox is simple: the poor turned to Spanish officials in cases
of conflict, not among themselves but with their social superiors. When
normal patron-client relationships proved unrewarding, when an implicit
moral contract was broken, the matter was appealed to a higher "patron,"
whose role was to dispense "justice."[84]

At first glance this would appear to be a fatuous strategy, rather like
using a wolf to guard a sheepfold. But pitting one section of the elite
against another often proved effective, for several reasons. First, a legal
appeal did not need to run its full (and very likely expensive) course; both
patrons and clients employed such appeals as bargaining chips, as a means
of putting pressure on a recalcitrant party to fulfill his obligations.[85] Second, various cleavages existed within the elite. Although religious and
secular bureaucrats had strong ties—financial, social, or even marital—to
the local elite, they also exhibited a certain esprit de corps and with it, an
outlook somewhat different from that of the creole aristocracy. One may
add, without becoming bogged down in the complicated debate over the

"black" and "white" legends, that many functionaries honestly attempted to apply the law as they understood it.[86]

It is not surprising, therefore, that plebeians vigorously protested any violation of their acknowledged rights. For example, mulatto tailors who were denied a voice in gremio elections pointed out that this was illegal according to guild bylaws.[87] When regulations were not in their favor, plebeians defined their rights through appeals to "customary" practice. Indian guilders and painters were shielded from repartimiento demands because "they [had] always been exempted from personal service or the exercise of any other offices."[88] In the early eighteenth century, plaza mesilleros successfully resisted a proposed increase in their user fees, arguing against any innovation in the "custom of time immemorial."[89] Such attachment to the accepted "moral economy" could be very tenacious. When the mayordomo of a construction crew paid his workers (repartimiento Indians) only one real per day instead of the accustomed two, the Indians protested mightily; so the next day wages were restored to their normal level, and the Indians received an extra real for back pay.[90]

Indians were particularly adroit at gaining concessions from high officials, even in the face of prohibitive legislation. Thus, Francisca de la Cruz received viceregal assent for her practice of buying fruit from nearby rural areas and then selling it in the plaza, despite the fact that colonial law strongly opposed the resale of basic commodities.[91] In this sense, urban Indians were like their rural counterparts: recent research has documented the ability of Latin America's indigenous communities to manipulate the Spanish bureaucracy in their favor.[92] In the countryside, however, whole communities squared off against a handful of local officials; in Mexico City, such manipulation was perforce more individualistic. The ragged, illiterate plebeians of Mexico City were nonetheless more politically sophisticated than the rural poor. First, they had superior access to lawyers, notaries, and literate society in general. So, for instance, Tomasina Gerónima, a mestiza bigamously married to a mulatto slave, was able to arrange a forged letter "proving" that her first husband had died.[93] Second, they had a better grasp on how their rulers thought and on which psychological buttons to push.

The story of how Gracia de la Cruz, a black slave, kept her husband in Mexico City provides an outstanding example of plebeian manipulation of elites. Juan de la Cruz, a slave from Angola, had been temporarily placed in a Mexico City obraje by his master, Juan López Godines. Once there, he met Gracia and the two fell in love. While in Mexico City, Juan was under the supervision of one of López Godines's friends, Jacome Chirini; Gracia pestered him until he finally released Juan from the obraje and brought him to his house. Juan seized this opportunity to run away and marry Gracia. When Chirini decided to punish Juan by selling him out of the city, Gracia petitioned the religious authorities to disallow this, pointing out that it would violate the sacrament of marriage by preventing cohabitation. A week later, the vicar general of New Spain handed down a strongly worded ruling, forbidding interference with the couple's marital life "for any cause or reason" and prohibiting any mistreatment of Juan "by deed or word."[94] Nevertheless, some months later Chirini shipped Juan out to a rural estate. Once again, Gracia immediately took the matter to the proper authorities. The result was a lengthy case for which no resolution is recorded. But two points seem clear. First, Gracia forced Chirini to bring Juan back to Mexico City and to agree in principle to sell him to another *capitalino*. Indeed, Gracia herself was given the job of lining up a new buyer. Second, as the case progressed, Gracia's owner began to interject himself into the proceedings on Gracia's behalf; toward the end, the case became a flurry of petitions exchanged between two elite Spaniards.[95]

Plebeian willingness to appeal to high officials over such vital issues implies a degree of trust and respect for these rulers. Certainly, the religious and civil authorities believed that both the symbols of their offices and the officeholders themselves could overawe the populace; their very presence would have a pacifying effect. For instance, *diputados de elecciones* were appointed to oversee gremio elections, "so that if there are differences or disputes . . . [the deputy] can be on hand to see that they are conducted calmly; and, if they are not, to arrest those who make a disturbance."[96] When grain supplies at Mexico City's main storehouse became scarce during the last few days preceding the 1692 riot, the viceroy selected a "gowned minister" to attend the disbursement of corn "so that by his awe-inspiring presence the women who bought overeagerly and the officials who became impatient while selling should be quieted and thus bickering would be avoided."[97]

Plebeian attitudes toward religious leaders sometimes passed beyond respect through affection to veneration. Israel has shown that a string of important seventeenth-century bishops—Pérez de la Serna, Palafox y Mendoza, and Diego Ossorio de Escobar, among others—actively courted public opinion and managed to incite popular opposition to viceroys. The denouement of the conflict between Ossorio de Escobar and the viceroy, the Conde de Baños, demonstrates the extent to which plebeian sympathies could be enlisted in elite struggles. Relations between the viceroy and the bishop of Puebla had touched bottom in March 1664. In fact, Ossorio de Escobar, in fear for his life, had forsaken his normal post and taken refuge in the priory of Santa Ana outside the capital. Fortunately, a royal cédula arrived in June, ending Baños's term and naming the bishop as his temporary replacement. Baños tried to suppress the decree and expel the bishop from the colony. But news of the cédula leaked out on June 28, and demonstrations erupted in both Mexico City and Puebla.[98] At the priory a celebration began at two o'clock in the afternoon and lasted into the following morning. Baños, informed of this, "desisted in his purpose and returned to his quarters."[99] In Puebla, effigies of the viceroy and his wife were carried through the streets and publicly jeered at. The diarist Antonio de Robles sadly noted that Ossorio de Escobar failed to punish the miscreants, "and having been tolerated, the deed seems approved."[100] More expressions of plebeian displeasure with Baños were soon to follow. On the afternoon of June 29, "the conde, accompanied by his sons and an escort of guards, crossed to the archbishop's resistance to acknowledge the new viceroy, and as he returned without guard stones were thrown and he was harassed and mocked and compelled to run to safety."[101] Even three months after his disposition, the public appearance of Baños and his family at a bullfight drew "tremendous hissing and booing."[102]

One should remember that the high clergy formed a natural focal point for antigovernment sentiment not only for elite creoles but for plebeians as well. If an archbishop set himself against the viceroy, his status lent legitimacy to expressions of popular discontent. The "Church-and-King" crowd that shouted for Viceroy Gelves's blood in 1624 ("Death to this heretic viceroy!") was carrying the strategy of appealing to higher authority to its logical conclusion. The archbishop had excommunicated Gelves; surely the king (had he been present) would have deposed him.[103] The venerated cleric thus carried a heavy symbolic load as a representative of the people and might even pass into legend. The popular memory of Don Juan de Palafox y Mendoza was still strong fifty years after his departure from Mexico, when the Inquisition ruled that

> no portrait of don Juan de Palafox y Mendoza is to be possessed, painted, or sold, because of the worship and veneration given it . . . [by] vulgar and rustic people, who venerate him as a saint, burning candles before [the portrait], and placing it on altars, in locations superior to those of declared saints . . . and even of Our Lady the VIRGIN MARY.[104]

The comparison of Palafox with Mary makes clear his role as patron and intercessor.

The advantages of mobilizing the plebe were clear, but so were the dangers. For the more popular or respected the leader, the angrier the crowd would be if he betrayed them. This was the populace's quid pro quo: the patron had to earn popular support by fulfilling his duties. The viceroy, for example, was expected to maintain a supply of corn at the most reasonable price possible. In 1692, the Conde de Galve failed in this task. As Hobsbawm suggests and as events proved, the ruling elite paid a high price for this abdication of responsibility.

Rioting was the plebeians' last line of defense to ensure that their highest-ranking patrons met their obligations. But the colonial order functioned more smoothly when the plebeians did not have to employ this final resource, when their normal relations with social equals and superiors provided a bare minimum of food, clothing, and shelter. The secret of the colony's stability over some three centuries lay not in government regulations but in the dense thicket of social relationships, both within the lower classes and between plebeians and elites, that perpetuated the dominance of the Spanish aristocracy. The following chapters will examine more closely the social networks of the urban poor in New Spain's capital.

3

The Significance and
Ambiguities of "Race"

Beneath Mexico City's facade of power and authority—symbolized by the grandeur of the city's palaces and churches and by the geometrical regularity of its broad avenues—lay the messy vitality of the urban poor. Plebeian society was a reality: in the streets, marketplaces, and taverns, in servants' quarters, ramshackle apartments, and adobe hovels, the poor of all races worked, played, begged, gossiped, argued, fought, drank, gambled, made love—survived. They shared a lifestyle and, to some extent, a consciousness, notably, in their disdain toward the rules and regulations promulgated by the authorities. Yet one may wonder whether a group of this size (85% of the city's total population) did not have important internal divisions. Perhaps the elite commentators, in their disgust at the plebeians' miscegenation and lack of república, exaggerated the unity of the plebe. Perhaps the frequent outbursts of violence among the city's poor were not merely the result of drunken quarrels or the stress of daily life but indications of the fault lines in plebeian society.

One possible element of divisiveness leaps immediately to mind: racial differentiation. Was Mexico's racial hierarchy merely a figment of elite imaginations, a reflection of their own visceral fear of contamination by "impure" blood? Did a kind of "racial democracy" exist among the lower classes? Or was race, even for the poor, an "imperative" status,[1] dominating their lives and inescapably limiting their social options? In this chapter and in chapter 4, I assess the role of race in plebeian society.

Any investigation of racial differentiation within a population must begin with the question of how "race" is determined. The quotation marks are used advisedly, for race is not self-evident. Technically, a race is a subspecies, a geographically localized subdivision of a species, marked off from other subdivisions by differing gene frequencies that reveal themselves in physical or behavioral traits. Since *Homo sapiens* is a differentiated species (with particularly notable variations in skin color), may we conclude that racial divisions among human beings are genetically determined and therefore "real"? This proposition is strongly disputed by many modern biologists. Stephen Jay Gould, for example, argues that "the fact of variability does not require the designation of races."[2] He continues,

> The category ["race"] need not be used. All organisms must belong to a species, each species must belong to a genus, each genus to a family, and so on. But there is no requirement that a species be divided into subspecies. The subspecies is a <u>category of convenience</u>. We use it only when we judge that our understanding of variability will be increased by establishing discrete, geographically bounded packages within a species. Many biologists are now arguing that . . . [this practice] is not only inconvenient but also downright misleading.[3]

According to Gould, researchers (with modern computers at their disposal) increasingly prefer to study whole species, using multivariate analysis to map continuous patterns of variation over a species' geographic range. These patterns can then be usefully correlated with, for example, climatic conditions. This dynamic perspective eliminates the need (and the motive) for distinguishing subspecies.[4]

Thus, the concept of "race" has little or <u>no scientific basis</u>. Genetic differences cause differences in physical appearance (though one cannot assume a direct correspondence), but genes do not unambiguously sort human beings into separate categories. Indeed, the great variety of human phenotypes means that any attempt to draw a hard and fast line between, for instance, "blacks" and "whites" must be (from an objective point of view) largely arbitrary. Such a boundary is socially rather than biologically determined.

"Race" is a social construct. But since societies are complex, <u>it is not immediately clear who defines race and then allocates people to various racial categories.</u> In the multiethnic, inequitable society of colonial Mexico, one would assume that the dominant Spaniards would take the lead in defining racial boundaries, for "without a method for clearly distinguishing between one group and another, systematic discrimination cannot be practiced."[5] Such distinctions need not be elaborate or extremely precise; often they merely divide a society into dominant and subordinant groups. <u>North Americans have historically recognized only two major racial groups— "white" and "black"—using the rule of hypo-descent (whereby anyone with one black ancestor is considered black) to keep this dichotomy intact.[6]</u> In colonial Mexico, as discussed in chapter 2, the <u>fundamental racial division was also dichotomous.</u> To recapitulate briefly: The Spanish crown organized the colony around two "republics" (the república de los indios and the república de los españoles) and prescribed their functioning in minute detail. The Spanish-Indian distinction was based on easily recognizable physical, cultural, and religious differences. (The last two differences, in particular, virtually forced themselves on the Spaniards' attention during the conquest.)

In contrast, the social recognition of the castas as a third major sector of society was a long, drawn-out process, fueled by demographic and economic pressures in Hispanic society. Spaniards ignored the existence of the castas whenever possible. Royal legislation on mixed-bloods was in many ways an afterthought; the castas had no special tribunals, no hereditary leaders to mediate their relationship with the Spanish. They tended, in law and in fact, to form an underclass within the Hispanic community; but individual casta groups such as mestizos or mulattoes did not perform specified roles in the social organization. Why then was it necessary to make racial distinctions among these subordinate groups? What difference did it make if an individual was "black" or "mulatto"?

We might argue (following the distinguished Dutch sociologist H. Hoetink) that this necessity sprang from the existence of a "somatic norm image" in colonial Mexico. Hoetink defines a somatic norm image as "the complex of physical (somatic) characteristics which are accepted by a group as its norm and ideal."[7] In colonial societies, the dominant group eventually manages to impose its view of the ideal physical appearance on the rest of the population: "The lower-placed segment cannot, for psychological reasons, fail to view the dominant segment's physical characteristics as actually superior or to adopt this segment's standards regarding what is beautiful and ugly."[8] Thus, a subjective Spanish dislike for Negroid features would be translated into a greater "somatic distance" between Spaniard and black than, for instance, between Spaniard and mestizo. Since elite valuations of phenotypes would be adopted by everyone, a universally accepted continuum of physical types at varying distances from the somatic norm image could be constructed. "Race" would then be largely a matter of physical appearance. The problem of drawing exact boundaries would remain, but a consensus would exist on what a "mulatto" or an "Indian" looked like.

Some forty years ago, Aguirre Beltrán used Inquisition records to decipher the "clasificación colorida" of colonial Mexico. He found a strong correlation between a person's physical appearance and his racial label, one that held good even in fine differentiations within a given category. Aguirre Beltrán concluded that Mexico's racial classifications were "founded essentially on the difference in skin color" and "other anatomical characteristics."[9] More recently, however, another scholar, Dennis Nodin Valdés, has studied the same source but has reached a very different conclusion: "There was indeed a great deal of confusion about race in Mexico City during the late colonial period. . . . When individuals were required to describe themselves or others in court, their testimony was often inconsistent and contradictory."[10] Valdés found examples of three or even four different racial labels applied to the same person during the course of a trial; he therefore argued that categorization by skin color was "subject to personal whim." Indeed, according to Valdés, "there were no clearly defined standards which determined race."[11]

Perhaps a third sally into Inquisition documents—supported by information from other sources—will help us to resolve this issue. Inquisition and court cases are useful because witnesses were normally required to give racial identifications for both themselves and the subjects of their testimony. Conflicting opinions on these identifications do indeed provide, as Valdés suggests, strong evidence for the blurring of racial boundaries. But trial records can do more; we can push beyond the confusion by posing questions that place the process of racial identification in its social context. What was the relationship between the witness and the person being identified? Was the latter a friend or relative of the former, or a stranger? Does the witness mention any specific traits that helped him to make the classification? What is the purpose of the identification? Is it simply another piece of personal data, or something more? In cases in which the authorities do not demand racial labeling, do those involved supply it on their own? Can one detect a difference between elites and plebeians in the use and meaning of racial classification? These and similar questions will guide the following discussion.

Hoetink's concept of the "somatic norm image" suggests that phenotype should have been the major determinant of race in colonial Mexico City. But this hypothesis is difficult to verify empirically, since physical appearance can seldom be separated from all the other factors that might contribute to racial identity. The best real-life approximation is provided by those cases in which witnesses were expected to define the racial status of strangers. For example, while walking through the plaza mayor late one evening in 1688, Andrés Sebastián, a slave from Cádiz, came across a man—"a mestizo whom he did not know"—flogging a statue of Christ. Sebastián disclaimed any knowledge of the man's name or occupation. He described him as "about thirty years old and of good stature, [with a] long black mustache [and] hair to his shoulders."[12] The label "mestizo" was apparently based solely on the man's appearance. Similarly, a black slave and a mulatto stonecutter who attended a party near the parish church of Santa Catalina Mártir gave mutually consistent racial identifications to some of the strangers there, including three musicians: a moreno, a mestizo, and an Indian.[13]

Identifications based on appearance were not always consistent, however. When Miguel de la Cruz was imprisoned for a debt of thirty pesos in 1707, his creditor identified him as a castizo. Miguel had earlier described himself as a mestizo; and a prison official (*señor de visita*) referred to him as a Spaniard.[14] Andrés Benítez (whose scandal-provoking arrest has been described above) served briefly in the obraje of one Juan Miguel. The obrajero, who apparently had little contact with Benítez (he did not know his name), called him a Spaniard. The other witnesses concurred in labeling him an Indian.[15]

None of these witnesses explained how they decided on these racial labels. But they should probably be regarded as rough guesses rather than sure identifications based on the commonly recognized traits of each race. In the first case, for instance, the man identified by Sebastián as a "mestizo" had shoulder-length hair, which was generally considered characteristic of Indians rather than mestizos.[16] Moreover, it seems unlikely that Sebastián was concerned over whether this label was "correct"; he had no emotional stake in the matter, and his estimate of the stranger's race was after all only one item in his overall description. When witnesses wished to convince the authorities of someone's racial status, they went beyond physical characterization. Consider the case of Don Francisco Cano Moctezuma, a *curandero* denounced for fraud and witchcraft. His first accuser, María de Rodilla, said that he "appears to be an *indio amestizado*," that is, an Indian with Hispanic physical and cultural traits. A second witness, the Spanish tailor Felipe Salazar, also pointed to Cano Moctezuma's "white" features. But Salazar was eager to see the curandero prosecuted, and the Inquisition did not have jurisdiction over Indians. He therefore took the trouble to gather information on Cano Moctezuma, including his birthplace, address, and the name of his wife and relatives. But above all, Salazar "made investigations to discover if he was a mestizo and found him to be a mestizo because of his dress and mode of speech." As it happened, the Inquisitors were not impressed by Salazar's diligence, dismissing his remarks as having "little substance." Instead, they focused on yet another criterion for racial classification—the fact that Cano Moctezuma had an Indian name—and turned the case over to the Provisor de los Indios.[17]

Clearly, phenotype was not the sole guide to race in colonial Mexico City. Several criteria for racial identification existed, some of which could overrule appearance. In fact, as we move from the racial labeling of strangers to the racial labeling of friends and acquaintances, physical traits become less important, and the pull of other criteria grows stronger. Not only are the judgments of different witnesses frequently in conflict but a single witness may find it difficult to pinpoint a friend's racial status. Juana de Mesa, in denouncing a former lover to the Inquisition, described him as a "castizo or mestizo"; the accused man, Nicolás de Paniagua, succeeded in convincing the Inquisitors that he was really a Spaniard.[18] When Bernabé de la Cruz was brought before the Inquisition on charges of bigamy, the consensus of the witnesses was that Bernabé was regarded as a mestizo, although he looked more like an Indian ("tiene más aspecto de indio que de mestizo").[19]

The confusion over Bernabé's status apparently resulted from the conflict between his appearance (his facial features, his hair, possibly his dress) and his life-style (he spoke Spanish and was a painter and guilder who lived and worked in the traza). José del Castillo, who claimed that he knew Bernabé "very well," brought up yet a third criterion—genealogy—when he stated that Bernabé was the nephew of a *mestizo prieto* (one with mixed Spanish, Indian, and African ancestry).[20] This report, if verified, should have decided the question, since by strict interpretation of the sistema de castas, a person with Spanish blood could not "revert" to being an Indian. But in the end, Bernabé was judged an Indian (fortunately for him, since he thereby avoided prosecution by the Inquisition). In this particular case, physical appearance won out, aided by a major chink in Bernabé's Hispanic armor: his first marriage had been to an Indian woman and had taken place in an Indian parish. This fact seems to have had decisive weight in establishing Bernabé's Indian identity.[21]

Bernabé de la Cruz may be regarded as a man who was comfortable in both Hispanic and Indian society but who was gradually "passing" into the mestizo category until tripped up by this Inquisition investigation. It is not certain whether Bernabé actively promoted this process or merely acquiesced in it. On the one hand, he retained the distinctively Indian hairstyle (*melena*); on the other, his second, bigamous marriage was to a mestiza and was recorded in the casta marriage register.[22] He also changed his name (from Bernabé to Santiago), but this was a common practice among bigamists. The shoemaker Felipe García—"also known as Pérez"[23]—followed the same strategy when he illegally entered into his second marriage. Unlike Bernabé de la Cruz, however, Felipe had passed into Hispanic society with complete success, so complete that the Inquisitors refused to believe his protestations that he was an Indian.[24] Felipe gave the Inquisition the names of his parents, both of whom (he said) were Indians, but had to admit that he "was commonly reputed to be a mestizo and the brothers of this [witness] are reputed as such."[25]

A more convincing claim to indigenous status was registered by Micaela Francisca, still another suspected bigamist. Micaela had never known her parents, but she reported that the rest of her relatives were Indians and that "when she reached the age of reason she spoke nothing but the Mexican language [i.e., Nahuatl]" and wore only Indian dress. If she knew Spanish now, Micaela said, it was only because of the "instruction of Doña Josefa de la Barrera who, having raised her since she was very young, taught her to speak in Castilian."[26] Micaela thus relied heavily on cultural criteria—speech and dress—to prove her Indian status.

These examples suggest that no strong phenotypical barrier existed between the "mestizo" and "Indian" categories. If an Indian was willing to surrender those traits of dress, coiffure, and speech summed up in the phrase "anda como indio," he could quickly "pass" as a mestizo. The case histories examined above further suggest that such cultural adaptation was closely linked to direct participation in the city's Hispanic society and economy. Bernabé de la Cruz and Felipe García both had jobs that brought them into daily contact with people of all races and walks of life. García was a shoemaker; Cruz worked as a journeyman for a mestizo painter; Micaela Francisca had been raised by a Spanish doña, and the witnesses at her wedding were mulattoes, not Indians.[27] It seems that we must add sociocultural traits to phenotype as a determinant of racial status, particularly in the case of "Indians" and "mestizos."

What happened when different criteria for racial labeling came into conflict? Was there any widely accepted standard that provided the final word on one's racial status? The Inquisitors usually turned to parish records. In theory, an individual's race was a summary of his ancestry. The baptismal ceremony was an ideal opportunity to judge a child's parentage and assign him a racial label. For Spaniards, baptismal records provided a legally valid racial designation, accepted as a guarantee of limpieza de sangre for entry into the priesthood or the university. But, surprisingly enough, casta libros de bautismos did not specify the infant's race until the early eighteenth century.[28] Indeed, among plebeians, racial labels do not seem to have been regularly applied to nonadults. Casta wills, for instance, seldom list the race of unmarried children. Apparently, a typical casta did not receive an "official" racial classification until he first came into contact with the governmental or religious bureaucracies, that is, when he first entered the labor force[29] or married. Marriage registers therefore became the primary source for racial designations. As the case of Bernabé de la Cruz indicates, the Inquisitors found marriage records particularly useful in distinguishing between Indians and mestizos. In their view, the very parish in which marriages occurred offered strong evidence of the partners' racial identity.

But such considerations did not apply to racial divisions among the castas. How did the officiating priest tell a black from a mulatto, a mulatto from a mestizo? Did he simply look at the partners and make a decision based on their phenotypes, or did he ask them for a self-evaluation? If the latter, how closely did he investigate these claims? Evidence from the late colonial period suggests that the priests simply accepted the declaration of the parties involved. In fact, in 1815, the archbishop of Mexico asserted that "the priests do not receive juridical information but rely on the word of the parties. They do not demand proofs, nor do they dispute what they are told."[30] Though research on this matter is lacking, it is possible that seventeenth-century priests were less acquiescent and more likely to strike a balance between the partners' claims and their own perceptions. At times, the conflicting principles for racial classification became visible in the marriage register itself. The records of casta marriages had two components: (1) the main body, a paragraph containing all the basic, legally required information;[31] and (2) a summary notation in the margin giving only the names and races of the marrying couple. The racial designations in the margin and the main entry, however, were not always in agreement.[32] Both sections of the record were usually written in the same hand, so we should probably regard these cases as "editorial comments" by priests who considered the partners' racial claims unjustified. However, some clerics were so little exercised by this problem that they often failed to record the couple's race at all. Just over 22 percent of the casta marriage records in the Sagrario Metropolitano parish during the years 1680–1699 lack a racial identification for at least one of the partners. These lacunae are sometimes haphazard, sometimes systematic: for instance, one of the parish's religious officials (easily identifiable by his handwriting) habitually neglected to note the racial status of the bride.

In any case, the priests certainly did not demand evidence of the partners' parentage, nor is it clear what kind of proof the bride and groom could have offered. We must conclude, then, that regardless of their validity in the eyes of Spanish officialdom, parish records did not provide authoritative racial designations based on verified accounts of ancestry.[33]

Yet it would be quite wrong to assert that plebeians paid little attention to ancestry in determining race. It is true that when their racial status was questioned, they did not (like the authorities) appeal to parish records; but they did appeal to parentage. A quick review of the Inquisition cases discussed above shows that the accused nearly always substantiated their racial status by pointing to that of their parents. Nicolás de Paniagua, who had been variously labeled a mestizo, castizo, and mulatto, gave the Inquisitors full information on his parents, "Francisco de Paniagua, a Spaniard, a native of the city of Seville . . . who was an *oficial* making glass beads; he died twelve or thirteen years ago and is buried in the Church of the Holy Trinity," and "Clara de Riveral, a Spaniard, his legitimate wife, a native of Mexico City, who lives next to the Church of the Holy Trinity in the house of Mariana de la Cruz."[34] Felipe García provided a similarly detailed account of his parents to prove that they (and thus he himself) were Indian.[35] The presumption, therefore, was that race followed from descent. If a child's father was a Spaniard and his mother an Indian, then he was a mestizo; if both his parents were mulattoes, then so was he, and so forth.

In practice, this method of defining race was functional rather than logical, pragmatic rather than theoretically sound. After all, simple reference to one's parents could not reveal the exact proportion of one's Spanish, Indian, and African blood as required by the sistema de castas. The reconstruction of racial status demanded precise knowledge of ancestry, which seldom survived for generations, even among status-conscious Spaniards.[36] Among the largely illiterate plebeians, knowledge of ancestry was slimmer and appeals to "reputational" race (i.e., the consensus among friends and neighbors) more common. Illegitimate birth or the early death of parents could render even the simplest means for determining race problematic. We have already discussed the case of Micaela Francisca, who had no direct knowledge of her Indian parents but argued that her other relatives were "known as such."[37] An *hijo natural* might identify himself with the one parent he knew, or the one who raised him. And what are we to make of Sebastiana de Santiago, a mestiza whose son was a "chino" (Filipino)? The most sensible explanation is that the boy had adopted the racial identity of his father, despite the fact that the latter was dead or absent.[38]

Even among nuclear families, the rules of racial inheritance did not function with great precision. Inquiries about the racial status of castas and poor Spaniards seldom delved more than one generation into the past, for they could not rely on plebeian memories. To return once again to the case of Nicolás de Paniagua, the journeyman shoemaker accused of blasphemy: Nicolás gave the Inquisitors a good deal of information on his parents and siblings—even to the point of identifying one of his sister's godparents—but his knowledge of earlier forebears was extremely hazy. He was completely ignorant of his paternal grandparents and knew only that his maternal grandparents had been Spaniards living in the Mexico City barrio of Tomatlán. He could not name his grandparents or his father's brothers, though he did recall that "a Spanish woman named Juana de Soto, who lives in the barrio of San Sebastián in this city, used to call this prisoner's mother 'sister.'"[39]

Clearly, Nicolás did not belong to a close-knit family, but his ignorance of his ancestors and collateral relatives was not exceptional. In the early 1670s, an impoverished silversmith named Juan de Barrios discovered—much to his embarrassment—that his bride-to-be (whom he had already deflowered) was a relative, falling within the forbidden degree of consanguinity. The couple had to receive a special dispensation to marry.[40] In a similar case, a generation later, Juan Romero and Rosa María had already posted the banns when their family ties were disclosed: Juan's mother and

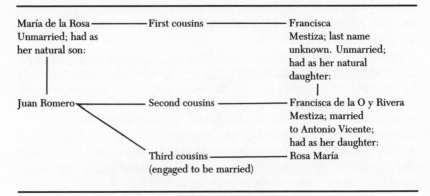

Fig. 3.1. Relationship between Juan Romero and Rosa María
Source: AGN, Bienes Nacionales, vol. 406, exp. 87.

Rosa María's grandmother had been first cousins. (See fig. 3.1). It is note-worthy that while the authorities relied heavily on information from Juan's mother in working out this relationship, even she could not remember her cousin's last name.[41]

The conflict among various criteria for racial identification, the relative unimportance of parish records, the "illogical" transfer of racial status between generations, and the vague and imprecise knowledge of ancestry all suggest that, for plebeians, lineage was not central to self-definition. But perhaps this matter may be studied in greater depth by stepping back from the emotionally saturated concept of race to investigate a more prosaic cultural artifact: names. Names are a primary symbol of the link between generations; moreover, naming children is one of the few activities in which members of even the most oppressed groups can exercise freedom of choice. Therefore, naming practices may help to reveal the family and kinship networks that allow these groups to transmit their beliefs and cultural practices over time and space.[42] They should also tell us something about how plebeians understood ancestry and kinship and how their perception of their heritage shaped their lives.

One of the most interesting conclusions to emerge from the study of plebeian naming practices is that last names seem to have been regarded as less "real" or important than Christian names. To put it simply, plebeian society was on a first name basis. In wills dictated by castas, persons are frequently referred to by their first names, with race, occupation, or nicknames added to flesh out the identification. For example, Ana de Samudio listed among her debtors "José, a mestizo," and "Antonio, a Spaniard [known as] 'the soldier.'"[43] The mestiza seamstress Sebastiana Hernández had business dealings with, among others, "an Indian named José who is a pulque seller," "a tocinera called 'la gachupina,'" and "María the nun."[44] The mulatto merchant Antonio López del Castillo held goods in pawn from "Agustín the water carrier, an Indian."[45] In all of these instances, it should be emphasized, race does not carry any great emotional weight; it simply acts as one more element of identification.

This lack of concern over surnames occurred even among those involved in more intimate relationships. A Spanish woman named Manuela (whose trials and tribulations with the Inquisition have been documented in chap. 2) lived for several months in the home of Doña Antonia de Dueñas without giving her last name to either her landlady or her roommate. Lorenzo de Torrez, a Spanish accountant, did not know the surname of the servant he seduced and later denounced to the Inquisition. The Inquisitors never found out, either, although one of the witnesses called to testify was the niece of the girl's adopted father.[46] Intergenerational remembrance of surnames also proved to be weak at times. On her deathbed, Pascuala de Santoyo could not recall her father's last name; but even she was an improvement over María de la Concepción, a fruit vendor who confessed that she had entirely forgotten both her parents' names.[47] Confusion over and ignorance of surnames could extend to living relatives, including spouses. When Gracia de la Cruz petitioned the authorities to prevent her enslaved husband from being sold out of Mexico City, she called him José de la Cruz, but according to his most recent bill of sale, he was named José Juan.[48]

This evidence casts doubt on the idea that all Mexico City plebeians had a single, "correct" patronymic. And it raises the question of how names were bestowed and what rules, if any, guided naming practices. It seems that among plebeians, surnames (like race) did not become important until one reached adulthood. During the seventeenth century, for instance, Sagrario Metropolitano's libro de bautismos de castas did not record last names for baptized infants. Nor do the full names of unmarried children often appear in casta wills. If the parent-child bond was broken when the child was still young, then, he might simply not receive a last name, employing solely his Christian name until he was forced to choose one (for instance, when he married). Francisco Hernández, an Indian servant who left home at an early age, illustrates this pattern well. Although well aware of his father's name (Gaspar Cortés), he called himself simply "Francisco" for many years, until he decided to take the surname of a co-worker.[49]

What happened in more normal circumstances? Plebeian children commonly (but not universally) drew their last names from one or more of their parents. Although a woman did not often take her husband's surname, the latter was generally the one passed on to the couple's children. (Daugh-

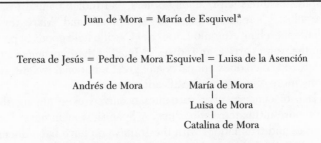

Fig. 3.2. Surname inheritance in the family of Pedro de Mora Esquivel
Source: AN, vol. 1,453, Tomás Fernández de Guevara (229), 6 September 1690, fols. 135r–137v.
[a]There were four other children, all of whom bore the surname Mora.

ters were somewhat more likely than sons to take the mother's last name instead, however.) Figure 3.2 shows a family tree (derived from the will of Pedro de Mora Esquivel, a mulatto glassmaker) in which normative naming patterns were carried out with considerable regularity. Here, the last name "Mora" descended smoothly through two generations, while Pedro himself carried a dual surname, reminiscent of a common practice among elite Spaniards. A more thorough examination of the sample of wills used in this study, however, indicates that family name patterns seldom worked themselves out so neatly. Figure 3.3 provides a useful counterweight to Pedro de Mora Esquivel's family tree. In this example, Juan Jacinto took both of his father's names, but coherence in naming practices disintegrated in the next generation: none of the children carried either parent's surname.

Unfortunately, casta wills seldom allow us to trace names for three generations with any degree of completeness. But since those writing wills usually gave their parents' names—if known—we can systematically study the transmission of surnames from one generation to the next. The (regrettably small) sample includes thirty-five cases in which both parents' surnames were known.[50] Among these thirty-five individuals, sixteen (46%) took their fathers' last name; six (17%) took their mothers' last name; one (3%) received both surnames (the example outlined in fig. 3.2); and twelve (34%) used neither parental surname. Thus, in over one-third of the cases, normative naming patterns, even liberally defined, failed to operate.[51]

Where did these names come from, if not from the parents? In one instance, the son of a slave adopted the surname of his father's owner.[52] Masters would appear to be a likely source for names of slaves, but in fact this was not the case. A sample constructed from parish records (to be de-

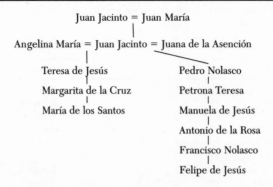

Fig. 3.3. Surname inheritance in the family of Juan Jacinto
Source: AN, vol. 782, Diego de Castilleja Guzmán (121), 19 March 1692.

scribed below) reveals that less than 6 percent of slaves used their masters' surnames. Another possible explanation for the provenance of nonparental last names is that they came from other relatives not in the direct line of descent. Undoubtedly, plebeians sometimes borrowed both first and last names from aunts and uncles, cousins, and even more distant kin. This would allow certain names to stay "in the family" even when they were not directly inherited. Figure 3.1 illustrates a possible example of this: the granddaughter of María de la Rosa's cousin was named Rosa María. But since very few records—not even wills—provide detailed information on distant relatives, it is difficult to gauge the importance of kin-derived surnames. Still, in light of the earlier discussion about the plebeians' frequent ignorance of their collateral relatives, it seems safe to say that this explanation cannot account for the bulk of nonparental last names.

Perhaps we can find a clue to the mystery in figure 3.3. When the expected naming pattern ceases to function in the third generation, patronymics are largely replaced by names with a strong religious connotation. The significance of "Jesús," "de la Cruz," and "Santos" is obvious; Pedro Nolasco was a French priest who co-founded the Mercedarian order. (Note also that both mothers had religious surnames.) Could it be that priests supplied these names or that (at least in the case of Pedro Nolasco) the child was given his saint's name? It would seem that a closer look at the most common Mexico City surnames is in order.

The following tables, based on samples drawn from the Sagrario Metropolitano parish marriage records,[53] show the most common last names for Spanish and casta men and women during the last third of the seventeenth century. Comparing the lists, one is immediately struck by (1) the diver-

Table 3.1. Most common male surnames in late-seventeenth-century Mexico City, Sagrario Metropolitano Parish

Spaniards (N=852)				Castas (N=801)			
Rank	Name	No.	%	Rank	Name	No.	%
1.	López	18	2.1	1.	de la Cruz	149	18.6
2.	García	14	1.6	2.	de los Reyes	29	3.6
3.	Pérez	13	1.5	3.	Antonio	23	2.9
4–5.	Ruíz	12	1.4	4.	Santiago	22	2.7
4–5.	Rodríguez	12	1.4	5.	García	15	1.9
6.	Castro	11	1.3	6.	Dios	13	1.6
7–9.	Fernández	10	1.2	7.	Pérez	12	1.5
7–9.	Sánchez	10	1.2	8–9.	Santos	10	1.2
7–9.	González	10	1.2	8–9.	Rodríguez	10	1.2
10.	Martínez	9	1.1	10–11.	López	9	1.1
				10–11.	Herrera	9	1.1

Source: Archivo de Genealogía y Heráldica, Sagrario Metropolitano, Libro de matrimonios de castas, roll 519, vol. 3, fol. 133v–vol. 4, fol. 68v; roll 520, vol. 5, fol. 138v–vol. 6, fol. 10r; Libro de matrimonios de españoles, 1680–1682.

gence between Spanish and casta naming patterns, and (2) the prevalence and importance of religious surnames (notably, "de la Cruz") among the latter.

In Table 3.2, we can see that only four names appear in both lists: López, García, Pérez, and Rodríguez. These names are all among the top five for Spaniards but occur toward the bottom of the casta list. The one exception is "García," the fifth most common surname for castas; only "García" and "Pérez" were used as frequently by castas as they were by Spaniards. None of the four most popular casta last names appear on the Spanish list; but their dominance among the castas of table 3.1 is astounding. Nearly one in five of the castas in this sample were surnamed "de la Cruz." Indeed, this single designation had greater popularity among castas than all top ten names put together had among Spaniards. These patterns are only reinforced when one turns to table 3.2. Here, all overlap ceases: not a single name appears on both lists. Moreover, the eight most common casta surnames (each with a religious connotation) all account for more than 2 percent of casta patronymics, easily outdistancing the most popular Hispanic last names ("Castillo" and "Espinosa" at 1.6% each).[54]

We may conclude that naming practices served a different purpose among castas than among Spaniards. Put in broad terms, a Spaniard's surname was part of his heritage, a means of linking himself to earlier generations of his family. For castas, in contrast, last names were often no more than a convenience or a bureaucratic necessity. It seems likely that

Table 3.2. Most common female surnames in late-seventeenth-century Mexico City, Sagrario Metropolitano Parish

Spaniards (N=852)				Castas (N=723)			
Rank	Name	No.	%	Rank	Name	No.	%
1–2.	Castillo	14	1.6	1.	de la Cruz	104	14.4
1–2.	Espinosa	14	1.6	2.	de la Concepción	48	6.6
3–6.	González	11	1.3	3.	de la Encarnación	38	5.3
3–6.	Ramírez	11	1.3	4–5.	María	22	3.0
3–6.	Vargas	11	1.3	4–5.	de los Reyes	22	3.0
3–6.	Velasco	11	1.3	6.	San José	20	2.8
7–8.	León	10	1.2	7.	San Antonio	16	2.2
7–8.	Mendoza	10	1.2	8.	Jesús	16	2.2
9–14.	Gómez	9	1.1	9.	Rodríguez	14	1.9
9–14.	Medina	9	1.1	10.	de los Angeles	10	1.4
9–14.	Soto	9	1.1				
9–14.	Ruíz	9	1.1				
9–14.	Torrez	9	1.1				

Source: Archivo de Genealógico y Heráldica, Sagrario Metropolitano, Libro de Matrimonios de Castas, roll 519, vol. 3, fol. 133v–vol. 4, fol. 68v; roll 520, vol. 5, fol. 138v–vol. 6, fol. 10r; Libros de matrimonios de españoles, 1680–1682.

many castas had no "official" last name until they were required to choose one when they first married. The prevalence of religious names may have resulted from priests assigning (or suggesting) such surnames to marrying couples. In this regard, it is noteworthy that the highest incidence of several religious names ("de la Cruz," "de los Reyes," and "Santiago" for men; "de los Reyes," "San José," and "Jesús" for women) occurred among the Indians, the ethnic group most closely and paternalistically guarded by parish priests.[55] (See tables 3.3 and 3.4.) With few exceptions, genuine indigenous surnames do not appear in the records. Similarly, black slaves were forced to abandon their African names and in many cases, had not had time to acquire Spanish ones. This may account for the high frequency of "de la Cruz" among them. In the sample used to construct tables 3.3 and 3.4, nearly half of the black male slaves (20 of 44) and one-third of black female slaves (9 of 29) carried this surname.

Because parish records were segregated by race, the preceding discussion has been cast in ethnic terms. But given the fact that Spaniards were, on average, wealthier than castas, one must ask whether this divergence in naming patterns reflects ethnic or class differences. Is heavy reliance on a handful of surnames a "casta" or a "plebeian" characteristic? Since the available sources rarely give the occupation or economic standing of the parties involved, this question cannot be answered directly. But perhaps it can be explored indirectly, by two methods.

Table 3.3. Most common surnames of casta men by race, Sagrario Metropolitano Parish, 1670–1672

| Name | Racial Status | | | |
	Mestizo/Castizo (N=187)	Indian (N=58)	Mulatto (N=203)	Black (N=60)
De la Cruz	16 (8.6%)	17 (29.3%)	25 (12.3%)	27 (45%)
De los Reyes	5 (2.7%)	7 (12.1%)	7 (3.4%)	2 (3.3%)
Antonio	4 (2.1%)	6 (10.3%)	3 (1.5%)	2 (3.3%)
Santiago	8 (4.3%)	8 (13.8%)	4 (2.0%)	0 (0.0%)
García	5 (2.7%)	0 (0.0%)	2 (1.0%)	1 (1.7%)
Dios	6 (3.2%)	0 (0.0%)	1 (0.5%)	1 (1.7%)
Pérez	4 (2.1%)	0 (0.0%)	1 (0.5%)	1 (1.7%)
Santos	5 (2.7%)	0 (0.0%)	2 (1.0%)	0 (0.0%)
Rodríguez	4 (2.1%)	0 (0.0%)	2 (0.5%)	0 (0.0%)
López	2 (1.1%)	1 (1.7%)	3 (1.5%)	0 (0.0%)
Herrera	3 (1.6%)	0 (0.0%)	0 (0.0%)	1 (1.7%)

Source: Archivo de Genealogía y Heráldica, Sagrario Metropolitano, Libro de matrimonios de castas, roll 519, vol. 3, fol. 133v–vol. 4, fol. 78v.

Table 3.4. Most common surnames of casta women by race, Sagrario Metroplitano Parish, 1670–1672

| Name | Racial Status | | | |
	Mestizo/Castizo (N=203)	Indian (N=78)	Mulatto (N=165)	Black (N=38)
De la Cruz	23 (11.3%)	13 (16.7%)	12 (7.3%)	11 (28.9%)
De la Concepción	13 (6.4%)	4 (5.1%)	13 (7.9%)	2 (5.3%)
De la Encarnación	12 (5.9%)	3 (3.8%)	12 (6.5%)	2 (5.3%)
María	6 (3.0%)	7 (9.0%)	0 (0.0%)	2 (5.3%)
de los Reyes	3 (1.5%)	4 (5.1%)	3 (1.8%)	1 (2.6%)
San José	5 (2.5%)	1 (1.3%)	4 (2.4%)	2 (5.3%)
Jesús	4 (2.0%)	3 (3.8%)	4 (2.4%)	1 (2.6%)
Rodríguez	6 (3.0%)	0 (0.0%)	3 (1.8%)	1 (2.6%)
De los Angeles	3 (1.5%)	2 (2.6%)	1 (0.6%)	0 (0.0%)

Source: Archivo de Genealogía y Heráldica, Sagrario Metropolitano, Libro de matrimonios de castas, roll 519, vol. 3, fol. 133v–vol. 4, fol. 78v.

We turn first to a 1689 census of the *peninsulares* living in Mexico City which has been published in the *Boletín del Archivo general de la nación*. The census numbered the city's Spanish (*gachupín*) population at 1,154. We will compare the naming patterns of these peninsulares to those of Mexico City creoles (men only, since there were virtually no female

Table 3.5. Most common surnames of *peninsulares* in Mexico City, 1689

Name	Number of Cases	Percentage of Total Surnames
1. Fernández	33	2.9
2. Rodríguez	27	2.3
3. García	26	2.3
4. González	24	2.1
5. Martínez	21	1.8
6. López	18	1.6
7. Pérez	17	1.5
8. Castro	14	1.2
9. Gómez	14	1.2
10. Sánchez	13	1.1

Source: "Gente de España en la ciudad de México, año de 1689," *Boletín del Archivo general de la nación*, 2d ser., 7, nos. 1–2 (1966): 371–406.

peninsulares in Mexico City at this time). Peninsulares provide a valuable control group because they formed an elite within the elite. The census recorded the occupation of 1,044 peninsulares: the majority (628) were merchants, while many others composed part of the civil and religious bureaucracies (132).[56] Only a few were engaged in menial tasks.[57]

Table 3.5 has two points of special interest. First, the ten most common peninsular surnames are identical (though ranked in a different order) to those listed in the "Spanish" portion of table 3.1. The creoles had to a great extent preserved the normative Hispanic naming patterns. But—this is point two—those surnames had a greater weight among peninsulares than among the creoles. Only "López" accounted for more than 2 percent of the creole surnames, while four peninsular patronymics exceeded this mark. The ten most common names totaled about 18 percent of all peninsular surnames; the figure for the creoles was 14 percent. It would seem that among creoles, the "normal" Hispanic naming patterns had been diluted. Could this have been caused by the seepage of casta last names into the creole group? Creoles were in fact more likely to have common casta surnames than were peninsulares (see table 3.6). Perhaps poor Spaniards had come to adopt the naming practices of castas, practices that might therefore best be termed "plebeian."

One way to test this hypothesis is to distinguish between Spaniards accorded the honorific "don" or "doña" and those—presumably of lower socioeconomic standing—who lacked this status marker.[58] In this instance, only the women provide a reasonably sized test group, since the uneven proliferation of this title over the years had created many more doñas (about 40% of Spanish women) than dons (less than 10% of Spanish men).[59]

Table 3.6. Most common "casta" surnames among Spaniards in late-seventeenth-century
Mexico City

Name	All Spaniards (parish records, 1680–1682) (N=852)	Percent	Peninsulares (1689 census) (N=1,152)	Percent
De la Cruz	0	0.0	1	0.1
Santiago	7	0.8	3	0.3
De los Reyes	8	0.9	1	0.1
Antonio	0	0.0	0	0.0
Dios	2	0.2	0	0.0
Santos	1	0.1	0	0.0
Total	18	2.1	5	0.4

Source: See tables 3.1 and 3.5.

If the women in table 3.2 are divided along the suggested lines, "casta" surnames are much rarer among the doñas. (See table 3.7.) Nearly one in ten non-doñas had such names, compared to fewer than one in fifty among the higher status group.

Still, even among nonelite Spaniards, names such as "de la Cruz" and "de la Concepción" did not have the preponderance that they did among castas. Many poor creoles may have clung to their patronymics as a source of pride. The construction of a racially mixed plebe took place over generations; the incomplete shift in creole naming patterns signifies a stage in the process of cultural *mestizaje*, as downwardly mobile Spaniards adapted themselves to the plebeian social milieu, influenced by—and influencing—their casta friends, neighbors, and relatives.

Plebeians, then, had only a vague knowledge of their lineage. Both elites and plebeians regarded parentage as the most important determinant of racial status; for the latter, however, lineage was not a matter of baroque complexity but merely a rough, commonsense guide to racial affiliation, to be simplified whenever possible. Consider, for example, the case of Alonso Martínez de Peralta, a Mexico City native who had moved to Texcoco early in the eighteenth century. Although the son of a mestizo and a castiza, Alonso had been taken for a mulatto by the alcalde mayor, who demanded tribute payments. Alonso appealed to the royal authorities; they sent investigators to his boyhood haunts to question the neighbors about his parentage. All of the witnesses interviewed affirmed that Alonso was a mestizo (another example of a son taking his father's status). But some went further: while recognizing that Alonso's mother was a castiza (or even a "castiza blanca"), they nevertheless stated that Alonso and his

Table 3.7. "Casta" surnames among Spanish women marrying in Sagrario Metropolitano Parish, 1680–1682

Name	Doñas (N=343)	Percent	Non-Doñas (N=509)	Percent
De la Cruz	0	0.0	8	1.6
De la Concepción	0	0.0	5	1.0
De la Encarnación	0	0.0	6	1.2
María	0	0.0	4	0.8
De los Reyes	2	0.6	5	1.0
San José	0	0.0	6	1.2
San Antonio	0	0.0	0	0.0
Jesús	0	0.0	6	1.2
Rodríguez	2	0.6	6	1.2
De los Angeles	2	0.6	3	0.6
Total	6	1.8	49	9.6

Source: See table 3.2.

"parents and brothers were never listed [as tributaries] because they were always reputed to be mestizos."[60]

Alonso's case throws light on how plebeians "solved" the problem of conflicting criteria for racial labeling. It seems that, side by side with fairly subtle racial distinctions on the individual level (based, as we have seen, on skin color and certain cultural traits), there existed a more general racial identity applied to the family as a whole. This tendency to assign families a single racial label would be reinforced if, as sometimes happened, one of the parents "passed" into the ethnic category of his or her spouse. (We will return to this point in chap. 4.)

The Martínez de Peralta episode also suggests, however, that race—even loosely defined in the plebeian manner—might yet have some significance. Race-conscious elites, after all, set the rules for tribute payment and access to employment. And perhaps plebeian society itself stopped well short of being an ideal melting pot, with Indians, for example, more likely to associate with mestizos than with mulattoes, or Spaniards maintaining a certain distance from blacks. The variety of social relationships must also be considered: interracial friendship need not necessarily translate into more intimate contacts, such as marriage. In the next chapter, we will move from the definition of race to the broader issue of race relations among the urban poor.

4

Plebeian Race Relations

On September 1, 1699, a young man named Domingo Velásquez, who wished to take holy orders, went to the Mexico City cathedral to locate his baptismal *partida*. To his embarrassment, he found his record in the register of casta baptismals. Protesting that this "was an error by the person who made the said entry," Velásquez quickly assembled three aged neighbors willing to support his claim to Spanish status. Closely echoing the other two witnesses, Bartolomé de Cárdenas, an unemployed shoemaker, stated that he had known Velásquez "since he was born and that he also knew his parents, having intimate contact and dealings with them." Cárdenas affirmed that all the members of the Velásquez family were "known and taken and commonly reputed" to be Spaniards "without any mixture."[1] Velásquez's petition was granted just two days after submission.[2]

How reliable is the data on castas found in parish records? The Velásquez incident hints at some of the complexities underlying the apparently simple act of recording a baptism or marriage. Perhaps the misplacement of his partida was merely a clerical error; but one suspects that the officiating priest deliberately set aside the family's racial claims in favor of his own judgment. As suggested previously, parish books should not be viewed as neutral or objective records but as one forum among many for the contestation and manipulation of racial identity. This is hardly surprising, given the social gulf between the participants. On one side stood the priest, perhaps disdainful of or condescending to his racially "inferior" parishioners; on the other, plebeians who were not necessarily willing to allow the church to define their racial status—or to dictate their social and moral behavior.

Plebeians sometimes mocked the symbols, rites, and festivals of the church; they also displayed a rather casual attitude toward the sacrament of marriage. In Mexico City, where females outnumbered males,[3] many plebeian women sought sexual satisfaction—and some financial security—in concubinage. Casta illegitimacy rates of over 50 percent in the second half of the seventeenth century[4] suggest the prevalence of such nonmarital unions, which constituted a primary mechanism for race mixture—above all, for miscegenation between Spanish men and casta women.[5] Moreover,

Table 4.2. Racial identification in casta marriage records, 1675–1704 (by quinquennia)

Years	Total Marriages	Marriages without One Identification	Marriages without Both Identifications	Percent of Marriages with Both Identifications
1675–1679	981	112	84	80.0
1680–1684	1,061	111	103	79.8
1685–1689	1,236	140	120	79.0
1690–1694	975	111	83	80.1
1695–1699	767	113	103	71.8
1700–1704	646	105	81	71.1
Total	5,666	692	574	77.6

Source: Archivo de Genealogía y Heráldica, Sagrario Metropolitano, Libro de matrimonios de castas, roll 519, vol. 4, fol. 141r–roll 520, vol. 8, fol. 167r.

created new racial types. The offspring of mixed marriages would not belong to either parent's race but would fall into a separate, third category. But, to return to the example cited above, Alonso Martínez de Peralta and his brothers did not find themselves placed in a distinct group formed by the mestizo/castizo combination. The friends and neighbors who identified them as mestizos apparently paid little heed to the sistema de castas' elaborate rules of racial inheritance. Racial labels, like surnames, were not precise summations of parentage. Most of the racial diversity that "should" have existed was filtered out by the sieve of social perception. Miscegenation undoubtedly produced a wide range of phenotypes, but few of these became translated into new racial categories.

Parish records confirm this conclusion: they show the consolidation of a small number of already existing ethnic categories rather than the proliferation of new ones. We will begin with the *libro de defunciones*. Figure 4.1 charts the number of casta burials in Mexico City's central parish, Sagrario Metropolitano, for the years 1672–1700. It should be pointed out that there are serious difficulties in interpreting this information. Burial registers are generally less complete than baptismal and marriage records; many of the city's poor no doubt buried their relatives "unofficially." Children are particularly underrepresented in this sample, accounting for less than 10 percent of all burials.[10] In contrast, adult women are overrepresented: slightly more than 60 percent of the castas buried were female. A final problem is that nearly one-fourth of those buried are not identified by race. (See table 4.1.) Given these difficulties, one should probably avoid drawing subtle inferences from these records, but they should furnish a rough picture of the size and demographic evolution of the various casta groups. This assessment is strengthened by the regular relationship between the specified racial categories (i.e., not including

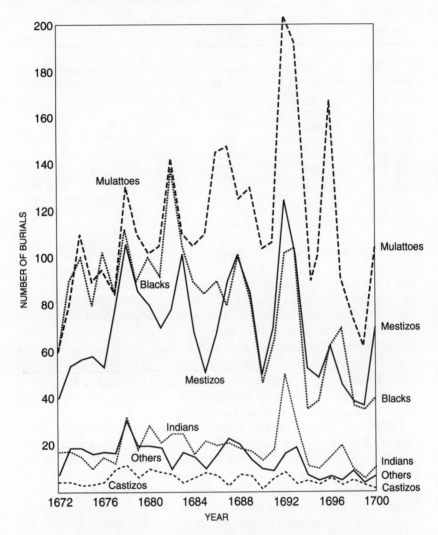

Fig. 4.1. Casta burials, by year, in Sagrario Metropolitano Parish, 1672–1700

"others"). There were always more mulatto than mestizo burials and more Indian than castizo burials. Blacks form an exception to this rule, but the decline visible in figure 4.1 was undoubtedly a real one, associated with the decreasing number of slaves in central Mexico after the mid-seventeenth century.[11] (About 63% of the blacks buried were slaves.)

By far the most striking feature of figure 4.1 is the sharp division between mestizos, mulattoes, and blacks, on the one hand, and Indians,

Table 4.3. Casta burials in Sagrario Metropolitano Parish, 1672–1700

Racial Category	Number of Burials	Percent of Total Burials	Percent of Total Burials with Racial Identification
Castizo	156	1.4	1.8
Mestizo	2,012	17.4	23.1
Mulatto	3,274	28.4	37.5
Black	2,298	19.1	26.4
Indian	532	4.6	6.1
Other	442	3.8	5.1
Unidentified	2,820	24.4	—

Source: Archivo de Genealogía y Heráldica, Sagrario Metropolitano, Libro de defunciones de castas, roll 599, vol. 1, fol. 4r–roll 560, vol. 5, fol. 45r.

castizos, and the minor categories, on the other. The first three groups accounted for about 65 percent of the burials during this period (and over 85% of the burials with racial identifications; see table 4.3). Clearly, the dominant casta groups of the late sixteenth century still held their position a hundred years later. Conversely, the intermediate categories of more recent origin are barely significant. The four hundred castas buried in an average year included only five castizos and three moriscos. Nor is there evidence that these groups were becoming more important over time. For instance, castizo burials as a percentage of total burials remained basically stable for the last two decades of the seventeenth century. This consolidation of major racial groups also appears in the Sagrario Metropolitano Parish marriage registers (table 4.4). Although the city's Indians were much more likely to be married than buried at the cathedral, mestizos, mulattoes, and blacks still comprised nearly 80 percent of all non-Spanish marriage partners.[12]

What caused this reluctance to recognize new racial divisions? In the early colonial period, the original parent populations (Indians, Spaniards, and Africans) had rapidly produced "mestizos" and "mulattoes." By the seventeenth century, however, the fragmentation of racial groups had slowed to a crawl. Why did the "mestizo" and "mulatto" categories gain such widespread social acceptance that they quickly reabsorbed any racial variants? One could argue that Mexico City's major ethnic groups corresponded to economic classes. The "mestizo" and "mulatto" labels persisted because, generation after generation, these two groups filled specific, distinctive roles in the city's economy. In contrast, the "castizo" category did not become firmly entrenched because castizos and mestizos did not have significantly different life chances.

This argument, however, has a grave weakness: recent research indicates that mestizos did not occupy "a distinct position within the social

Table 4.4. Casta marriages in Sagrario Metropolitano Parish, 1670–1704

Racial Category	Total Married	Percent of Total Partners with Racial Identification
Castizo	374	3.8
Mestizo	2,775	28.1
Mulatto	3,663	37.2
Black	1,209	12.3
Indian	1,317	13.3
Other	522	5.3
Total	9,860	100.0

Source: Archivo de Genealogía y Heráldica, Sagrario Metropolitano, Libro de matrimonios de castas, roll 519, vol. 3, fol. 133v–roll 520, vol. 8, fol. 167r.

division of labor."[13] The current study, unfortunately, cannot speak directly to this issue. It proved impossible to find the material necessary for measuring the correlation between race and occupational status. But is there some general test that can determine whether the city's racial groups were more or less analogous to socioeconomic strata? Once again, parish records can supply a rough measuring stick. As Brading and Celia Wu have remarked, burial rates are a "barometer of social disaster."[14] In periods of famine and epidemic disease, the poor, the malnourished, and the ill-housed are the most likely to die. If during years of crisis, a particular ethnic group exhibits a rise in burial rates out of proportion to that of other categories, this group probably had a lower standard of living than the rest of the population. Brading and Wu, for example, found that in León the Indians suffered far more from the ravages of hunger and disease than did Spaniards and mixed-bloods.[15]

Did such differences exist among the castas of Mexico City? Table 4.5 compares the average number of burials by race in Sagrario Metropolitano Parish during "normal" and "critical" years. The latter are the five years with the most burials from the period 1672–1700.[16] None of the racial groups in table 4.5 shows an unusually high level of vulnerability to difficult social and economic conditions. On the whole, the difference between "normal" and "critical" years was not extraordinary by contemporary standards. Studies of colonial rural parishes have shown that a famine or an epidemic could suddenly raise burial rates to three, five, or even seven times their usual levels.[17] In contrast, Sagrario Metropolitano saw a doubling of burials only once during the period under study— 1696 (587 burials as compared to 289 the year before). Several explanations for this rather small oscillation in the burial rate suggest themselves: first, Mexico City had the finest social services in New Spain, including

Table 4.5. Casta burials in Sagrario Metropolitano Parish during normal and "critical" years, 1672–1700

Racial Category	Average Number of Burials, 1672–1700 (Minus "Critical" Years)	Average Number of Burials in "Critical" Years (1678, 1682, 1688, 1692, 1693)	Increase (%)
Castizo	4.8	8.0	66.6
Mestizo	62.8	102.0	62.4
Mulatto	103.2	159.6	54.7
Black	72.5	111.4	53.7
Indian	16.6	26.6	60.2
All	363.9	561.8	54.4

Source: Archivo de Genealogía y Heráldica, Sagrario Metropolitano, Libro de defunciones de castas, roll 559, vol. 1, fol. 4r; roll 560, vol. 5, fol. 45r.

an "ever-normal" granary (the *pósito*) and a government-sponsored grain market (the *alhóndiga*).[18] In years of poor harvests, the authorities (fearful of mob violence) gave first priority to stocking city granaries. By commandeering maize supplies from the countryside, they sought to pacify the urban masses at the expense of the peasantry. At moments of severe crisis, the alhóndiga/pósito system could be stressed beyond its limits; in 1692, it faltered and ultimately failed to secure sufficient maize at low prices (see chap. 7). However, government grain policies generally protected urban consumers against complete catastrophe and in the process may also have lessened the impact of economic differences among plebeians.[19]

Second, even at the worst of times, slaves would continue to receive meager yet vital food allotments from their masters. Slave owners, after all, were hardly likely to allow their chattels to starve to death. This may account, in part, for the most striking feature of table 4.5: the supposedly "higher-status" castizos and mestizos appear somewhat more vulnerable to economic crises than do "low-status" blacks and mulattoes.[20] Given the lacunae in these burial registers, this difference may not be statistically significant. Nevertheless, table 4.5 strongly suggests that (1) the sistema de castas was not an accurate reflection of Mexico City's socioeconomic structure, or (2) the superior economic standing of mestizos and castizos was not significant enough to translate into a difference in mortality.

This last point casts an interesting light on the widely assumed economic rationale for "passing." Certainly there were some professions (such as the priesthood) that admitted a few mestizos but virtually no persons of African descent.[21] But this type of opportunity was rare. Did the prestige, privileges (e.g., exemption from tribute), and living standards of mestizos and castizos really excite envy among blacks and mulattoes? Was the connection between ethnicity and social mobility obvious and decisive enough to mold the urban poor's view of race? If so, one would expect the plebeians to have largely absorbed the racial prejudices and ranking system of the elite. They should also have engaged in extensive "passing," either to pave the way for specific advances (a new occupation) or as a general measure to improve their future prospects (and those of their children).

The issue of prejudice and discrimination among plebeians has already been addressed (albeit indirectly) in chapter 2. To recap briefly: Mexico City's traza was not segregated; multiracial households (and apartment buildings) were very common. Several kinds of social relationships, such as compradrazgo and friendship between co-workers, cut across racial lines. It also seems that overt expressions of racial prejudice seldom occurred among plebeians. The sources used in this study have failed to reveal a single example of, say, a mestizo making a racist remark about a mulatto. This, of course, is only negative evidence. Fortunately, it is possible to treat passing or—to use Seed's less value-laden term—"racial variability"[22] in a more systematic fashion. (The following observations do not apply to passing by non-Spaniards into the Spanish category but only to racial variability among castas and Indians. But unless we assume that many blacks, mulattoes, and Indians leaped directly to Hispanic status, movement up the casta hierarchy was a necessary first step.)

The technique employed to investigate racial variability was nominal record linkage between burial and marriage records. We begin by taking a ten-year sample (1688–1697) of the casta burial records for Sagrario Metropolitano Parish. We then select from the group of racially classified individuals (about 73% of the total) those who were either married or widowed and whose spouses were identified by name. This creates a list of couples in which at least one partner carries a racial label. Finally, these couples are traced to the libro de matrimonios of the same parish.[23]

The results are summarized in table 4.6. Better than one in six persons recorded here changed their racial status during their adult (postwedding) lifetime. The actual racial variability rate may have been even higher, since couples who did not remain in one parish had increased opportunities for passing. But, once again, the pattern that emerges does not seem very compatible with a society of hierarchically ranked racial groups. To begin with, note the powerful dichotomy that pervades the table. Setting aside the small chino sample, the ethnic groups fall into two sets: an "African" sector (composed of blacks, mulattoes, and moriscos) and an "Indian" sector (composed of castizos, mestizos, and Indians). For the former, the racial variability rate is 3.8 percent; for the latter, 37.2 percent. There is little movement between the sectors: the table includes only four instances of mestizo-mulatto passing (in both directions) despite the fact that they were contiguous categories in the sistema de castas.

Table 4.6. Racial variability among castas and Indians in Sagrario Metropolitano Parish

Racial Identification in Marriage Records	Number of Cases	Racial Identification in Burial Records	Number of Cases	Racial Variability (%)
Mulatto	76	Mulatto	74	2.6
		Black	1	
		Mestizo	1	
Black	27	Black	26	3.7
		Mulatto	1	
Mestizo	51	Mestizo	39	23.1
		Indian	6	
		Mulatto	3	
		Castizo	2	
		Chino	1	
Chino	10	Chino	6	40.0
		Mestizo	3	
		Mulatto	1	
Indian	7	Mestizo	5	71.4
		Indian	2	
Castizo	9	Mestizo	7	77.7
		Castizo	2	
Morisco	1	Mulatto	1	100.0
Total	181			17.7

Source: Archivo de Genealogía y Heráldica, Sagrario Metropolitano, Libro de defunciones de castas, roll 559, vol. 3, fol. 1r–vol. 4, fol. 153v; and Libro de matrimonios de castas, roll 519, vol. 3, fol. 1r–roll 520, vol. 8, fol. 17v.

Are we dealing, then, with two parallel hierarchies? If so, the castas in table 4.6 were remarkably inept at ascending the racial ladder: the majority of cases demonstrate downward rather than upward mobility. Of course, this partially results from the extreme variability exhibited by castizos, who (within the castas) could only go down. The significance of castizo passing will be taken up in chapter 6. For the moment, we will only point out that this table provides further evidence that the "castizo" category had not yet achieved full-fledged social recognition. The other group with a particularly high rate of variability are the Indians. These figures confirm the earlier discussion on the relative ease of Indian-mestizo passing. More important, the movement of both castizos and Indians into the intermediate "mestizo" category raises questions about the entire issue of upward and downward racial mobility. Indeed, the dominant trend revealed in table 4.6 is assimilation into the major racial groups. Twenty-four (73%) of the changes in racial status are either passages out of smaller ethnic groups into larger ones or transfers among blacks, mulattoes, and mestizos.[24]

This assimilationist pattern found reinforcement from the tendency

(noted above) for spouses to pass into the racial category of their partners. Seventeen of the thirty-three cases of racial mobility in table 4.6
involved this adjustment. Two husbands moved into their wives' ethnic
group, and seven wives moved into their husbands' category; in every case
but one, the nonchanging spouse was either mulatto or mestizo. In four
instances, both spouses changed their racial status in the same direction—
in three cases out of four, "downward." [25] The spouse's influence was the
strongest not when it pointed to racial advancement but when it promoted
movement into a major ethnic group. [26]

Table 4.6 thus furnishes yet another demonstration of the stability of
Mexico City's major racial categories. There is little reason to believe that
numerous castas were actively attempting to "improve" their racial status
by passing. Nor did marriage to a lighter-skinned partner necessarily help
to boost oneself or one's children into a "higher" ethnic group. Yet the
different patterns of racial variability shown by the "Indian" and "African" groups—the tendency for most passing to occur among the castizo-
mestizo-Indian triad, the infrequent movements between the mestizo
and mulatto categories—suggest that ethnic differences were nonetheless
"real." This seeming paradox can be resolved by abandoning the notion
that castas passively accepted Spanish ideas about the relative worth of different races. We have seen that castas—and plebeians in general—knew
little of their ancestry and were uninterested in the complexities of the
sistema de castas. For the vast majority of the urban poor, the material advantages of passing were limited; even the psychological benefits of racial
exclusivity seem questionable. In daily life, plebeians depended on the
assistance, friendship, and goodwill of men and women from a variety of
racial groups. Surely these bonds were more important than any desire to
have one's grandchildren move closer to the Spanish somatic norm image.

A more concrete understanding of such interracial contacts may be
gained by focusing on what Barth calls the "structuring of interaction." [27] In
measuring the assimilation between different sectors of society, not all activities have equal weight. It is more logical to create a scale, ranging from
casual contacts at one end to the most important social relationship, marriage, at the other. Marriage is the most sensitive index of social distance
as well as the primary mechanism for maintaining ethnic boundaries. [28]

Table 4.7 presents data drawn from a three-year sample of Sagrario
Metropolitano's marriage records. There are three points of particular
interest in this table: (1) all groups except castizos and black males have
endogamy rates over 50 percent, that is, Spaniards, mestizos, mulattoes,
and Indians all took more partners from within their own racial categories
than from all others combined; (2) Spaniards showed the most marked propensity for in-group marriages: the endogamy rates for Spanish men and

Table 4.7. Marriage patterns in Sagrario Metropolitano Parish, 1694–1696

Men	Women						
	Spanish	Castiza	Mestiza	Indian	Mulatta	Black	Total
Spanish	483	5	8	1	15	0	512
Castizo	1	3	6	1	3	0	14
Mestizo	6	4	90	13	18	1	132
Indian	0	1	10	27	1	0	39
Mulatto	6	5	47	10	132	7	207
Black	0	0	8	1	28	25	62
Total	496	18	169	53	197	33	966

Source: Archivo de Genealogía y Heráldica, Sagrario Metropolitano, Libro de matrimonios de castas, roll 520, vol. 7, fols. 125v–225r; Dennis Nodin Valdés, "The Decline of the Sociedad de Castas in Mexico City" (Ph.D. dissertation, University of Michigan, 1978): 35–41.

women were 94.3 percent and 97.4 percent, respectively; nevertheless, when they did choose mates from other races, they did not favor castizos and mestizos over mulattoes; and (3) the largest number of interracial marriages occurred between mulattoes and mestizos (particularly when the mulatto was the male partner).

Before attempting to draw conclusions from this table, however, we must stop to ask what factors, other than personal preference or ethnic identity, may have constrained the choice of partners. We must pay special attention to the structural characteristics of the sample. When mating is not completely random—when there is at least some tendency toward in-marriage—differences in size between racial groups, as well as the sexual balance within each group, will heavily influence the resulting marriage patterns.

> Large groups with balanced sex ratios are considerably more endogamous and less apt to intermarry than smaller groups or those with imbalanced sex ratios. More importantly, even in a relatively large group the sex with fewer potential partners may be forced to seek partners outside the group and assimilate in that fashion.[29]

A thorough analysis of marriage patterns thus calls for a statistical measure that can adjust for group size and sex ratio. We have selected Cohen's kappa (K), as recommended by Philip F. Rust and Patricia Seed.[30] Kappa has the advantage over other approaches, such as log-linear methods, of allowing us to differentiate marriage patterns by gender.[31] It compares the number of observed endogamous marriages with the number that would be expected on the basis of random mixing (given the structural characteristics of the sample). A kappa of "0" indicates the latter condition; in

Table 4.8. Conditional kappas and expected values by racial group, Sagrario Metropolitano Parish, 1694–1696

Racial Category	Men (w = 1) Ki	Women (w = 0) Ki	"Neutral" (w = 0.5) Ki	Observed Endogamous Marriages (xii)	Expected Endogamous Marriages E (xii)
Spanish	.884	.944	.913	483	425.64
Castizo	.199	.154	.174	3	11.64
Mestizo	.614	.459	.525	90	109.09
Indian	.674	.489	.567	27	31.75
Mulatto	.545	.580	.562	132	150.07
Black	.382	.741	.504	25	32.75

Source: Archivo de Genealogía y Heráldica, Sagrario Metropolitano, Libro de matrimonios de castas, roll 520, vol. 7, fols. 125v–225r; Dennis Nodin Valdes, "The Decline of the Sociedad de Castas in Mexico City" (Ph.D. dissertation, University of Michigan, 1978): 35–41.

contrast, if every possible endogamous marriage actually did take place, a kappa of "1" would be produced.

Carrying out the necessary calculations, we find that the kappa for table 4.7 is .675, indicating a very high degree of endogamy. However, it is clear that the large number of Spanish in-marriages—exactly one-half of the marriages in the table—contributes heavily to this result. The next step, then, is to find the "conditional kappas" for each racial group. By assigning different weights to the table's rows and columns, we can make the conditional kappas either sex-specific or "neutral." Finally, we can determine the number of expected marriages for the various groups, assuming the level of endogamy had been equalized throughout the sample. (See table 4.8.)

This more sophisticated approach confirms some of our earlier remarks on intermarriage. Spanish endogamy is more obvious than ever: not only is Ki much higher for Spaniards than for any other category but Spaniards are the only group for whom observed endogamous marriages exceed expected unions. The Spanish-casta social barrier stands revealed as far stronger than that between any two casta groups. Mestizos, mulattoes, blacks, and Indians all have similar (and still fairly high) levels of endogamy. But table 4.8 provides convincing evidence that group size and sex ratio did play an important role in shaping Sagrario Metropolitano's marriage patterns. With the borderline exception of Indians (their neutral Ki is slightly higher than that for mulattoes), group size is correlated with endogamy: the larger the group, the higher the conditional kappa. The same relationship can also be illustrated by a single group. Throughout the period 1670–1694, the endogamy rate for black males hovered between 46 and 57 percent. During these years, the average number of black men

Table 4.9. Casta marriage patterns in Sagrario Metropolitano Parish, 1670–1704

Men	Castiza	Mestiza	Indian	Mulatta	Black	Other	Total
				Women			
Castizo	50	61	10	31	2	20	174
Mestizo	86	778	146	161	8	72	1,251
Indian	6	111	423	25	0	19	584
Mulatto	43	408	102	1,184	84	100	1,921
Black	2	74	23	292	350	18	759
Other	13	92	29	49	6	52	241
Total	200	1,524	733	1,742	450	281	4,930

Source: See table 4.4.

married per quinquennium was 127. For the decade following 1694, this figure dropped to 63, and the endogamy rate tumbled first to 36.8 percent (in 1695–1699) and then to 25.9 percent.[32]

As for sex ratios, it is noteworthy that among castizos, mestizos, and Indians—three categories in which women outnumbered men—males were more endogamous than females. In contrast, male blacks and mulattoes outnumbered their female counterparts, and in these racial groups it was the women who displayed greater endogamy. It should be pointed out that these race-specific sex ratios were very persistent over time (see table 4.9). Their origin lay in the sexual imbalance—heavily favoring males—among imported slaves and in the tendency for Indian and mestizo men to migrate to the countryside in search of work.[33]

Of course, these structural conditions cannot explain everything. For instance, the ratio between black men and black women cannot fully account for the latter's propensity toward endogamy. Here we must include an additional consideration, slavery. The majority of black women in seventeenth-century Mexico City were slaves; by law, children inherited their mother's status. It seems likely that enslaved women would have difficulty competing in the marriage market and would usually end by marrying other slaves—who were usually black men. A closer look at a subsample of table 4.9, one that differentiates between free and enslaved Afro-Mexicans, supports this argument. Of the sixty-nine black female slaves in table 4.10, fifty-eight married black males, of whom fifty-six were slaves; only nine married mulattoes (seven slaves, two free men). Their male counterparts, however, were much more likely to marry both mulattas and free partners. This line of reasoning also helps to explain mulatto marriage patterns. If slaves were more undesirable as wives than as husbands, free male mulattoes would tend to wed relatively few blacks, marrying instead into the mestizo group. Mulattas, in contrast, would have

Table 4.10. Casta marriage patterns in Sagrario Metropolitano Parish, 1686–1690

| | | | | Women | | | | | |
Men	Castizas	Mestizas	Indians	Free Mulattoes	Mulatto Slaves	Free Blacks	Black Slaves	Others	Total
Castizos	10	12	0	4	1	0	0	5	32
Mestizos	10	152	36	21	3	0	1	15	238
Indians	1	29	131	5	0	0	0	5	171
Free mulattoes	4	57	7	120	10	4	2	12	216
Mulatto slaves	1	31	6	42	15	1	7	2	105
Free blacks	0	3	1	6	1	6	2	2	1
Black slaves	0	7	4	16	17	9	56	0	109
Others	2	18	8	6	3	0	1	8	46
Total	28	309	193	220	50	20	69	49	938

Source: Archivo de Genealogía y Heráldica, Sagrario Metropolitano, Libro de matrimonios de castas, roll 520, vol. 6, fol. 126r–vol. 7, fol. 33r.

fewer marriages with mestizos and more with black and mulatto slaves. This is precisely the pattern that table 4.10 reveals.

The above assumes that blacks and mulattas might normally be expected to intermarry. In fact, such matrimonial links between "parent" groups (blacks and Indians) and the associated intermediate groups (mulattas and mestizos, respectively) were an enduring feature of Mexico City's marriage market. When Indians (and castizos) married outside their own group, they normally wed mestizos. Similarly, when blacks married across racial lines, they almost always chose mulatto partners. Only rarely did members of the three parent groups intermarry: for the thirty-five-year period covered in table 4.9, there was not a single recorded instance of an Indian man marrying a black woman. If we divide the population into three major categories—"Spanish," "Indian," and "African"—all three display a high level of intermarriage; by this definition, over 85 percent—830 of 966—of the Sagrario Metropolitano marriages in table 4.7 were endogamous. The only significant category of intermarriages are those between mestizos and mulattoes, which still account for less than 10 percent of all marital unions.

By now it should be clear that the relations between casta groups, as revealed by marriage records, show strong similarities to the patterns of casta passing. Members of the small racial groups (blacks, Indians, and castizos) tended to both marry and pass into the larger categories. In both cases, these movements usually occurred along ethnic lines (i.e., within the broader "Indian" or "African" groups); and the mestizo-Indian link was stronger than that between blacks and mulattoes. Finally, the most important contact between these broad ethnic divisions took place at the mestizo-mulatto boundary.

This tripartite scheme is clearly superior to the racial hierarchy model as a means of conceptualizing urban society. To be sure, the data could be interpreted to conform to the sistema de castas. The latter, for example, would (quite correctly) predict relatively high levels of intermarriage and passing between castizos and mestizos, mestizos and mulattoes, and mulattoes and blacks, for these are all contiguous categories in the sistema. But the racial hierarchy model breaks down at two crucial points: (1) Spanish-mestizo marriages should have been far more common than Spanish-mulatto matches, but in fact they were not;[34] and (2) the accepted ranking of Indians just above or just below blacks conflicts sharply with the actual social distance between these groups.

Ethnicity was a social reality in colonial Mexico City. But race was a social label rather than a strictly economic one. The most intimate social relationships tended to occur among members of the same racial group. These, in turn, served as the basis for a branching network of less intimate links, which quickly penetrated into all sectors of plebeian society. Thus, a person's race might be described as a shorthand summation of his social network. In particular, mestizos and mulattoes, who formed the two largest casta groups, can be defined as persons who, while possessing Hispanic characteristics, nevertheless maintained strong ties (often including kinship) with their parent populations.

The importance of these ties to mulatto self-identity can be inferred from the demographic history of Mexico City. With the sharp curtailment of slave imports after the mid-seventeenth century, Mexico City's black population began to decline rapidly. As the number of blacks lessened, mulattoes increasingly married into the "Indian" or "Spanish" groups, and they too began to lose their identity as a separate racial category. Valdés reports that in Sagrario Metropolitano Parish, "blacks had practically disappeared from the records by the early eighteenth century. Mulattoes, who were the second most numerous of all groups in the early eighteenth century, were practically nonexistent by the early nineteenth century."[35] By 1800, the Spanish-African-Indian "triangle" had collapsed into a Spanish-Indian continuum.

Mestizos, of course, had a much larger parent group to draw on. Their close association with Indians was widely recognized, to the point that some observers refused to give the former independent status. As late as 1689, an Inquisitor could report as common knowledge that "the mestizos in this kingdom are those born of Indian women and Spanish men."[36] Casta wills affirm the importance of mestizo-Indian relationships. Mestizos were much more likely than other castas to have Indian friends, relatives, and compadres. Nor did the links between the two groups stop there: mestizos often had solid economic ties to Indians. Sebastiana Hernández, a mestiza shirt maker, is a case in point. Her personal contacts among Indians included a comadre and a close relative; in fact, Sebastiana referred to her sister as an "Indian." Perhaps Sebastiana herself had been born an Indian and had passed into the mestizo category. At any rate, these personal links no doubt aided and oriented her economic ventures, which seem to have been largely among Indians. Her will lists numerous Indian debtors: "I am owed three pesos and six reales by an Indian woman named Antonia, the wife of Juan Brito; in like manner, an Indian woman named Isabel [owes me] four and one-half pesos for a rose-colored shirt that I sold her. . . . Also, an Indian named Petrucho owes me . . . six pesos for another shirt and shorts." In addition, Sebastiana was renting out a room to an Indian woman and had lent money to a native pulque vendor.[37]

The foregoing discussion helps to explain why passing between the "Indian" and "African" groups occurred infrequently and why passing in general was not an efficacious means of social mobility. To change one's race, in most cases, meant to change one's set of social relationships. Passing was not the first step but the culmination of the social climber's strategy; it was the proof that he had successfully adjusted his social network. When racial variability took place within the broader ethnic divisions, for example, when an Indian "became" a mestizo, these adjustments might involve only a shift in emphasis: marriage to a mestiza, a more direct association with Spanish patrons, a withdrawal from indigenous communal obligations. This change certainly did not demand the severance of his links with particular Indians. In contrast, a black attempting to move into the mestizo racial group would face a more radical break with his past, entailing the construction of new and different social networks.

The children of mixed marriages, however, were in a somewhat different position, for they could choose between the social resources of their parents. One of the great puzzles of Mexico City demography is that although mestizo-mulatto unions constituted the single largest set of casta intermarriages, no widely accepted racial label ever arose to designate this combination. What happened to the children of these marriages? We suggest that they were drawn into the social network of one parent or the other, whichever was more advantageous. Despite the racial difference between husband and wife, the family as a whole would be regarded as "mestizo" or "mulatto"—just as in the case of Alonso Martínez de Peralta (see chap. 3).

Obviously, race was an extremely complex concept in seventeenth-century Mexico City. If the modern investigator finds the topic a difficult one, this is because "race" was in fact full of ambiguities and crosscut meanings. In particular, race had a different significance for the Spanish elite than for the plebe. The urban poor rejected the elite's notion of a racial hierarchy; instead, as in other areas of culture, the plebeians demonstrated their creativity by redefining "race" in a way that made sense to them and served their purposes.

But this leaves the problem of social control hanging in midair. If the elite could not impose its ideology on the castas, if they could not use race to divide and conquer the plebe, what did keep the poor in their place? We will turn to this issue in chapter 5.

5

Patrons and Plebeians: Labor as a System of Social Control

Very little is known about the laboring classes in colonial Mexican cities. The simplest questions remain unanswered. For instance, how did employers procure labor? How were workers recruited into their jobs? Historians have found copious documentation on formal labor systems, such as the repartimiento, urban guilds, and debt peonage. But too often these records contain legal prescriptions on how the system should have functioned rather than evidence of its actual operation. Even more important is the fact that urban labor markets operated on a largely informal basis. The typical urban worker—the day laborer, the domestic servant, the journeyman artisan—held no license, had only an oral agreement with his employer, received his wages in cash, and could throughout his lifetime move from one job to another without leaving a trace in any records. Even when legally binding agreements did exist, as in the case of master artisans and their apprentices, they were often unwritten. Moreover, legal formulas left large areas of work place relations unregulated, except by custom. What follows, then, will not be a systematic investigation of the Mexico City labor market. Instead, I employ a wide variety of sources to explore the everyday life of laborers, focusing on the fundamental and often complex relationship between employer and employee.

Quantitative data are sparse, though they will be presented when available. One of the great frustrations of colonial historiography is that until the very end of the period, the sources best suited for statistical analysis (such as parish registers) almost never contain data on occupation. However, in the mid-eighteenth century, the Mexico City authorities ordered a census of the traza that did include such information. This 1753 census, about three-fourths complete—has recently been analyzed by Seed.[1] Although the census date is thirty years beyond the time limits of this work, it seems unlikely that the city's division of labor would have changed radically during the intervening period. In any case, this survey, and Seed's analysis, can serve as the starting point for our discussion of labor patterns.

Table 5.1 shows the division of labor by race for adult men (not including slaves) who were employed in the traza in 1753. The occupational categories are mostly self-evident, but it should be explained that whole-sale merchants are included in the "elite" and that master craftsmen who had their own shops are classified as "shop owners" rather than as arti-sans. There are several points of interest in the table. Note that (as one would expect) casta and Indian workers were concentrated in the "artisan," "laborer," and "servant" categories, nearly splitting the first with the cre-oles and dominating the other two. As Seed points out, these occupational groups do not constitute separate economic classes; in the terminology of this study, they are all "plebeian." Instead, they represent subdivisions within a single class, based on "significant differences in their role in production."[2]

In seeking to explain the organizing principle of this division of labor, Seed draws attention to the relationship between parent and intermedi-ate racial groups. The original elements of Mexico City's population had clearly defined economic niches: the conquering Spaniards were land-holders and merchants; the Indians, unskilled workers; the blacks, slaves and servants. All three tended to persist in their original roles—even into the eighteenth century—and to transmit them to the racial groups they fathered. Thus, the majority of creoles, like the peninsular Spaniards, were merchants and shopkeepers. Although mestizos most commonly worked as artisans, they were also "more often laborers or servants than either creoles or castizos. . . . In this respect, they resembled their parent population, the Indians, more than any other group."[3] In contrast, nearly half of all mulattoes were servants, an employment pattern even more accentuated among blacks. Seed concludes that "the differences in employment be-tween mestizos and mulattoes resulted from the different economic roles of the parent groups, urban slavery on the one hand and rural agricultural labor on the other."[4]

Obviously, Seed's explanation of Mexico City's labor system is quite compatible with the discussion of race in chapter 4. There we argued that racial labels had a real meaning for plebeians because they delineated social networks. The ethnic affiliation between mestizos and Indians, for example, had a social counterpart: mestizos were more likely than mulat-toes, blacks, and Spaniards to marry or otherwise associate with Indians. If the social networks of mestizos and Indians overlapped, it is not surpris-ing that their employment opportunities did also. A young person's first entry into the labor force would depend heavily on the economic standing and social resources of his parents and relatives (both real and fictive kin). Under these circumstances, plebeian children had a strong tendency to adopt their parents' (and by extension, their racial group's) occupations. There were two reasons for this, one negative and one positive. First, poor families did not usually have the wherewithal to equip their children

88   Patrons and Plebeians

Table 5.1. Racial composition of occupational groups in the Mexico City *traza*, 1753 (with percentage distribution)

	Elite	Shop Owner	Artisan	Laborer	Servant	Total
Peninsular	35	241	12	1	1	290
Spaniards	(7.4)	(17.2)	(0.6)	(0.3)	(0.1)	(5.4)
Creole	387	1,095	1,196	34	134	2,846
Spaniards	(82.0)	(78.1)	(55.8)	(9.1)	(14.1)	(53.2)
Castizos	13	9	126	17	11	176
	(2.7)	(0.6)	(5.9)	(4.5)	(1.2)	(3.3)
Mestizos	10	21	269	83	103	497
	(2.7)	(2.3)	(12.5)	(22.1)	(10.8)	(9.3)
Mulattoes (free)	17	21	475	36	539	1,088
	(3.6)	(1.5)	(22.1)	(9.6)	(56.6)	(20.3)
Blacks (free)	0	1	1	2	23	27
	(0.0)	(0.1)	(0.1)	(0.5)	(2.3)	(0.5)
Indians	10	3	65	202	143	423
	(2.1)	(0.2)	(3.0)	(53.9)	(15.0)	(7.9)
Total	472	1,402	2,144	375	954	5,347
	(99.9)	(100.0)	(100.0)	(100.0)	(100.0)	(99.9)

Source: Patricia Seed, "Social Dimensions of Race: Mexico City, 1753," *Hispanic American Historical Review* 62 (1982): 583.

for high-status professions. Occasionally, however, a relative or compadre would come to the rescue. In his will, the mestizo Hipólito de la Cruz established a 50-peso fund for the specific purpose of teaching his grandsons to read and write. To cite another example, a loan of 200 pesos from her comadre allowed Ana Sánchez to establish a pulquería.[5] Second, parents had contacts within their own occupations that enabled them to find jobs for their children. For instance, Catalina de los Angeles, the mulatta servant of a church prebendary, managed to place both her adopted sons into service with elite Spaniards.[6]

But every act of hiring involves at least two parties: the employee and the employer. So we must add a third consideration to our discussion of job placement, elite expectations. Once a racial group became established in a given occupation—as Indians came to dominate baking; or mulattoes, domestic service—elites began to regard this as a natural state of affairs. They may therefore have purposely avoided recruiting members of other races into these jobs. It is difficult to prove this assertion for most occupations, but we do know that Spaniards were influenced by racial criteria in their selection of slaves. They always favored blacks over mulattoes, a preference reflected in price differentials: "In the 1690s black slaves sold for about twenty to twenty-five percent more than mulattoes in the same age group."[7] But if elite expectations structured the labor market, then Spanish evaluations of the castas' relative worth had a direct impact on their life chances. Could not elite racism, rather ineffectual on the ideological plane, have infected plebeian society through these hiring practices?

There are several arguments against this view. First, as mentioned above, these distinctions were not necessarily invidious. Domestic service (the province of Afro-Mexicans) and unskilled labor (dominated by Indians) had equal—and equally low—prestige and pay. (Wages for laborers were slightly higher, but their work was less steady.)[8] Second, the employment patterns we have discussed were tendencies, not absolutes. For example, many mulattoes became artisans rather than servants, sometimes achieving master status; others, as documented in these pages, rose into the merchant and shop-owner class. The existence of such upwardly mobile castas weakened the association between race and class. Finally, when considering castas who entered the "expected" occupations, one should not assume that they had passively accepted their lot in life. The city's plebeians retained a certain freedom of choice and hence a certain ability to bargain. Although their negotiating position was weak, it nevertheless existed, and they used all the resources at their command to make the best possible deal. If so many had to settle for so little, this was only a measure of the obstacles they faced.

We can begin our attempt to unravel the complexities of labor recruiting and employer-employee relations by focusing on Indian workers. The Indians are a well-documented group with a seemingly well-defined place in the economy. Undoubtedly, their main role, both in the colony as a whole and in Mexico City, was to supply unskilled labor. But for Indians living in the capital's traza, the pattern is not so clear. As Seed admits, the 1753 census was least reliable in dealing with this group. "The census takers were not interested in the Indian residents of the area they surveyed, since from their viewpoint Indians did not rightly belong there. Hence the marginal notations on many blocks: 'jacales of Indians.'"[9] Fortunately, a better source—and one within our time frame—is at hand: a series of censuses prepared in 1690–1692 by the parish priests of Mexico City's Indian barrios. These priests were required by law to keep a record of their parishioners who lived in the Spanish sector of the city. This particular set of censuses has been preserved because of its importance in the aftermath of the 1692 riot, when the viceroy ordered all the Indians living in the traza to return to their barrios. Since each parish carried out its own census, the information content varies; some do not include data on the Indians' occupations. The most complete in this respect is the census of San José Parish. Table 5.2 summarizes the occupational status of Indian male heads of households from this parish.[10] (Unfortunately, women cannot be given similar detailed treatment, because, as in other sources, their occupations are not listed, except in the case of widows.)

This table records what the 1753 census takers overlooked: the un-

Table 5.2. Occupations of Indian men from San José Parish residing in the *traza*, 1692

Laborers				Artisans	
Water carriers	33			Bricklayers	21
Porters	31			Shoemakers	19
Others	20			Hat makers	9
	—			Tailors	9
	84			Carpenters	7
Unknown					
(possibly servants)	36			Button makers	6
				Others	31
	—				—
Total unskilled workers	120			Total artisans	102
		Other Workers:	19		
		Total Workers:	241		

Source: Archivo General de la Nación, Historia 413, exp. 1, fols. 32r–40v.

mistakable presence of skilled Indian workers in the central city. (Note that this brought the Indians' economic role even closer to that of mesti-zos.) Laborers and servants, who comprised over 80 percent of all native workers in table 5.1, here account for only one-half. This difference is almost wholly attributable to the relative increase in the number of arti-sans. San José Parish alone supplied the traza with 102 craftsmen in 1692, 57 percent more than the total number of Indian artisans listed in the 1753 census. Extrapolating from the San José figures, we must conclude that there were several hundred Indian artisans living and working in the traza during the late seventeenth century. The central city apparently acted as a magnet for Indians in skilled trades. Another piece of evidence supports this hypothesis. In 1706, city authorities discovered that some fifty Indian families were living in ruined buildings near the Alameda on the western edge of the traza. When interviewed, the Indian men proved to be nearly all skilled craftsmen; fully half were bricklayers or blacksmiths, and only a handful worked as common laborers.[11]

One hallmark of the traza Indians, then, was their relatively high occu-pational status; another was their close association with Spaniards. Many Indian artisans must have been journeymen working and living with mas-ter craftsmen. The parish censuses provided a few examples of this,[12] but the practice cannot be examined in any detail since the records only rarely note the landlords' occupations. Nevertheless, one can point to several in-stances of Indians in the same trade grouping together in a single house or neighborhood. Probably these men resided either with their employers or close by their work place—which, in the traza, would definitely imply that they labored under Spanish supervision. Thus, four Indian shoemakers lived in the lower levels of the Condesa de Santiago's mansion, near one of the city's largest concentrations of *zapaterías*.[13] Francisco de la Cruz, an Indian sacristan, lived across from San Bernardo, the church where he worked.[14]

Not all Indians could make such suitable arrangements. Many had to settle for what they could find and afford: they lived in crowded tenements or "in the corrals, garrets, patios, lofts, and yards of Spaniards."[15] Their landlords, presumably, were only interested in prompt payment of the rent. The 1692 censuses, in fact, frequently mention Spanish householders such as Juan Alejo Verdugo, a royal attorney; Lic. Alonso de Ensinas, a priest; and Nicolás Bernal, a notary public—men who accepted Indian boarders although they had no direct use for their tenants' skills.[16] But even a straightforward landlord-tenant link could quickly take on additional complications. For example, while few women in these censuses have a recorded occupation, it is likely that many worked as domestic servants in Spanish *casas*, including their own residences. As noted above, it was not uncommon for tenants to fall behind in their rent payments, so that their landlords became, in effect, their creditors.[17] In addition, a Spanish householder might make a straight loan to a tenant, as did Juan de Contreras when he gave 19 pesos to "Domingo, an Indian spinner who lived in my house, . . . so he could marry."[18] Once Spaniards had an economic stake in their employees or tenants, they naturally wished to keep them in the traza under watchful eyes. (Bakery and obraje owners carried this the farthest, of course, keeping their charges under lock and key.) In so doing, however, the Spaniards became deeply involved in the process of Indian acculturation, and what began as a simply economic connection evolved by degrees into a patron-client relationship.

Living in the central city undoubtedly facilitated the Indians' Hispanicization. Traza Indians found themselves surrounded by Spaniards and castas. They worked with them: artisanry was the least segregated of occupations, employing hundreds of workers from every major racial group.[19] They socialized with them: pulquerías and gambling dens drew their clientele from all races. They lived with them: Mexico City's apartment buildings were notable for their multiracial character, and the same held true for private dwellings. Among the landlords cited above, Bernal, Ensinas, and Contreras all owned slaves; Ensinas also rented some of his aposentos to mestizos.[20] Finally, Indians married castas (though rarely Spaniards). In the late seventeenth century, 28 percent of Indian men and 42 percent of Indian women marrying in Sagrario Metropolitano (the traza church) chose casta partners.[21]

Given these conditions, traza Indians felt strong pressures to adopt the clothing, bearing, and speech of their fellow tenants and workers. Some discarded their Indian identity altogether. As a contemporary observer described the process, "Many of them take to wearing stockings and shoes, and some trousers, and they cut their hair shorter, and the women put on petticoats; and becoming mestizos, they go to church at the Cathedral."[22]

Elite Spaniards looked on Indian acculturation, in the abstract, with alarm. When the Indians mixed with the "innumerable and abject plebe" of mestizos, blacks, and mulattoes, their vices (such as drunkenness) were reinforced, while their virtues (such as humility) were lost.[23] On a practical level, Indians "hidden" in the traza could avoid many of their obligations, including tribute payments and regular attendance at the parish church. But what happened when, for example, tribute collectors came to traza Indians with their demands? They were often rudely rebuffed—by elite Spaniards. According to some records, the Indians' Spanish employers not only tried to "impede the paying [of tribute]" but actually cursed and beat the collectors.[24] Their success in obstructing the tribute gatherers can be measured by the following statistic: after 1692, when the traza Indians were briefly forced back to their barrios, annual tribute payments increased from 8,000 to 19,000 pesos.[25]

The city's parish priests also felt quite bitter over what they viewed as an unnatural alliance—almost a conspiracy—between Spaniards and Indians. The comments of Fray Antonio Guridí, from the Santiago Tlatelolco parish, deserve to be quoted at some length.

> I was a minister for many years outside this city of Mexico [i.e., outside the traza], and any Indians who were missing from the parishes that I served I found in this city . . . in various houses both of Indians and Spaniards; some fault, sir, lies with the Indians, some with the gobernadores, but most of the blame belongs to the Spanish householders of this city, who help and defend [the Indians] in their residences just to earn money from the rental of a jacal or aposento, or because of the service they get from them; this is followed by compadrazgo.[26]

Priestly attempts to rectify this situation met with strenuous opposition. The minister of San Pablo parish takes up the story.

> Even when my helpers try to take [the Indians] from the said houses, the Spaniards themselves resist them, and defend their tenants, wives, or servants, claiming to have dispensations from the Royal Audiencia, with grave penalties for those who do not obey; this causes many disputes and nightmares, and forces me to go in person; and although I take them, for each one there are two or three Spanish godparents who come to argue and quarrel, and if they do not get their way, [the Indians] flee and are hidden in their houses.[27]

Finally, to come full circle, the Spanish used these ties of friendship and compadrazgo to recruit a new generation of indigenous workers—Indian boys and girls who became servants in Spanish households and convents.[28] It is clear that elite Spaniards, in their desire to secure Indian labor, ignored their own warnings about the dangers of racial integration. Indeed, they provided valuable patronage services to draw Indians into the Hispanic economy on a more or less permanent basis.

Because of their civil status, Indians were a special case. Spanish employers may well have been unusually protective of their native workers. Yet notary records show that many Spaniards developed personal ties with their casta servants as well. In dictating their wills, they frequently demonstrated gratitude toward faithful employees by making a testamentary donation. Most of these were for small amounts and, while undoubtedly welcome, had greater symbolic than monetary importance. For instance, the churchman Don Pedro Calderón left his mulatta servant some religious artifacts, while Doña Mariana de Santander gave 25 pesos to another mulatta "who had attended me and taken care of me in my illness."[29] But some wealthy Spaniards dispensed their largesse more lavishly. Two servants of Don Francisco Guerrero—a chino and a mulatta—received 500 and 400 pesos, respectively, as well as a donation of clothing.[30] Legacies to castas of up to 4,000 pesos have been recorded (though this particular donation was subject to a legal suit).[31] Such large gifts, rather than merely tiding their recipients over a difficult period, could alter their lifestyles, providing the basis for new careers and economic ventures and thus underwriting significant social mobility. (See chap. 6 for a more complete discussion.)

However, these bequests were often deathbed gestures and perhaps should not be viewed as an accurate barometer of household labor relations. One might even suggest that some employers were motivated by guilt feelings over worker treatment and used donations as a means of redress. The fact that only one or two employees are usually singled out, however, would argue against this. Furthermore, there is other evidence that casta servants could become full-fledged clients rather than mere employees. In December 1695, the mulatto coachman Juan de Chávez appeared in court to ask for the back wages owed him by his deceased employer, Don Agustín Pérez de Villareal. As Chávez explained it, he had been employed for nearly thirteen years at a salary of 5 pesos per month. He had received one year's worth of wages but was still waiting for the balance, that is, some 700 pesos. The lawyer for Pérez de Villareal's son ridiculed this demand, saying it was not "credible."[32] Yet other such cases existed. In his will, the black artisan Andrés Escobar stated that he had served Juan de Estrada for four years but had gained less than two years' salary; Estrada still owed him over 400 pesos.[33] If these claims were in fact valid, why did Chávez and Escobar remain in their jobs, and how did they live without receiving their pay? Apparently, their employers supplied them with food, clothing, and other necessities of life. At least in the view of Chávez and Escobar, this was lagniappe rather than another form of salary. But in any case, as long as the employer functioned as a patron, as long as he took good care of his "clients," monetary rewards were a secondary consideration.

Elements of clientage infused all varieties of labor relations in colonial Mexico City. Prevailing social attitudes, as well as the exigencies of labor recruitment and control, pushed employers into the broader role of patrons. To begin with, employers bore the brunt of the day-in, day-out task of social control. The elaborate supervisory machinery of the Indian república, staffed by parish priests, native officials, and tribute collectors, had no counterpart in Hispanic society. Poor castas and Spaniards had greater freedom from supervision and control—in the eyes of the elite, the kind of freedom that led to lasciviousness, thievery, and disorder. The only curb on their social irresponsibility was the need to earn their daily bread. The elite correctly recognized this as the weak point in the armor of plebeian resistance: sooner or later they would be forced to seek out employment. For in assuming the role of worker, poor men and women acknowledged their dependence on their social superiors and thus affirmed the social order.

The work place sharply distinguished "man" from "master" and brought the two into prolonged, face-to-face contact. One should remember that even Mexico City's most "industrial" establishments were quite small. A 1670 *visita* of the city's bakeries and obrajes showed that none of the former had more than eight Indian workers, while only one of the latter had more than ten. Near the end of the century, the average labor force in Valley of Mexico obrajes (including Indians, castas, and slaves) was about forty-one.[34] The work place thus provided a unique opportunity to mold the plebeian's character. Hence the employer's duty to discipline and control his workers—either directly, through physical punishment and constraint, or indirectly, by gradually inculcating the virtues of Catholic morality, responsibility, and hard work.

The mixture of these two elements—coercion and paternalism—varied from occupation to occupation and sometimes produced results that are incongruous in modern eyes. Witness the obrajero who thoughtfully released his imprisoned workers once a day to take them to mass.[35] Perhaps the best approach to the labor systems of Mexico City is to visualize a spectrum of social control. (See table 5.3.) At one end are those systems that legally and/or physically bound a worker to his employer: slavery and debt peonage. As we proceed along the spectrum, coercion tends to give way to moral authority. By the time we reach apprenticeship, the latter is already

Table 5.3. The social control spectrum

System	Slavery	Debt Peonage	Apprenticeship	Wage Labor
Labor mobility	Permanently bound to one master	Bound until debt discharged	Bound for stipulated period	Free to change employers
Source of control	Legal ownership	Contract; physical constraint	Contract; moral authority	Wages; patronage

predominant. True, a master artisan could use corporal punishment on his apprentice, or even chain him if he had run away.[36] But the master had been granted this authority (for a limited, contractually stipulated period) by the boy's parents or guardians. In both law and community opinion, the artisan acted in loco parentis, and these punishments were salutary discipline for the apprentice. After all, the master was giving him valuable skills and training—an entrance into the adult working-day world.

Finally, at the far right of the spectrum, the element of coercion (at least in theory) disappears; and, as we have seen in the case of Indian and casta servants, employers compete for workers by offering them food, shelter, loans, compadrazgo, and so on. Thus, even for wage laborers, the employer-employee relationship seldom reduced itself to a simple cash nexus. The persistent paternalism of labor relations in Mexico City meant that employers shaped and in some instances controlled fundamental aspects of their workers' lives. But patron-client relations are never wholly one-sided. The personal, face-to-face nature of labor relations also allowed workers to put pressure on their employers. The work place was the site of continued (albeit uneven) "labor negotiations," even under the most oppressive conditions.

Let us consider slavery, the archetypal system for combining labor and social control. Under slavery, human beings were legally reduced to chattel, property that the master could treat as he saw fit. Two points should be made about slavery in colonial Mexico City. First, one must distinguish urban slavery from the plantation slavery of Brazil and the Caribbean sugar islands. The sugar planters' profits depended on imposing a debilitating work regimen on their slaves. From an accounting standpoint, the benefits of rich harvests outweighed the losses caused by the high rate of slave mortality.[37] Urban slaves did not perform any comparably vital economic function. The typical Mexico City slave was a maid, a coachman, or a personal attendant, and these roles could easily be filled by wage laborers. Indeed, as noted in chapter 4, Indians were replacing blacks and mulattoes in these occupations in the late seventeenth and eighteenth centuries. Slaves were status symbols rather than an economic necessity. Mexico City elites liked to advertise their social standing by, for example, parading around town with a retinue of armed mulattoes.[38] But after 1650, the slave trade was curtailed and slaves became more difficult to obtain.[39] Slave owners had every reason, therefore, to take adequate care of their slaves. This leads to point two: in all probability, slaves were no worse off, in a material sense, than other members of the urban poor. The burial statistics cited in chapter 4 show that blacks and mulattoes were no more (indeed, slightly less) vulnerable during periods of epidemic disease and food shortages than mestizos and castizos. Slave owners, after all, had a vested interest in keeping their property alive.

The problem with urban slavery was not that it was systematically more brutal than other labor systems. Rather, slaves suffered because they were so exposed to the vagaries of each individual master's will. A cruel master could make his slave's life a living hell. Furthermore, with some exceptions, slaves could not mobilize the Spanish legal system to defend themselves, for slavery, unlike the many forms of coerced labor that existed on the margins of legality, had the full support of the state's police power. Slave resistance thus had to take more personal forms. Violence and flight were the most drastic but also the most dangerous acts of resistance; perhaps more common were doing sloppy work, malingering, and agitating to be sold to another master. Recall the case of Gracia de la Cruz, who, when threatened with the imminent sale of her husband to another part of Mexico, took it on herself to scour the city looking for a resident buyer.[40]

This should not be seen as an absurd action: finding a "good" master was a small triumph for a slave, one of the few available given his servile condition. A slave's welfare depended in large part on establishing a rapport with his master. To avoid misunderstanding, we should emphasize that this "rapport" did not entail any personal closeness or sense of brotherhood between master and slave. Instead, it meant a greater flexibility within the exploitative, superior-inferior relationship—in the terminology used above, a reduction in the coercive element of the social control "mix," a movement along the spectrum toward paternalism and clientage.

This shift might be based on purely economic considerations. In some cases, masters apprenticed their slaves, even to prestigious artisans such as silver- and goldsmiths. As far as can be judged by contracts in the notarial records, the slave received the same treatment as other apprentices: he moved into the artisan's house and lived under his authority;[41] the artisan promised to feed and clothe the slave, to cure his illnesses, and to make him a "perfect" workman in his chosen trade.[42] When the slave emerged from his apprenticeship, he had a marketable skill that could benefit both himself and his master. The master, of course, received the bulk of the slave's earnings. As for the slave, he received the intangible benefit of status and recognition for his skills, as suggested by the case of Juan Mateo, a slave silver artisan who was popularly known as Juan de la Plata.[43] Also, particularly in those instances where the slave's master was not himself an artisan, the slave would have considerable say in the pace and nature of his work and would be relatively free from supervision.

Slave peddlers and street vendors had a similar—in some ways, greater —freedom. When Lorenzo de Cárdenas "loaned" his slave María to a Mexico City merchant as payment for a debt, the contract went into some detail on the responsibilities of the two parties if María ran away.[44] Some masters apparently allowed their slaves free rein so long as they made regular economic contributions; thus, the slave mason Francisco de Morales did not hesitate to sally forth at night to attend a fiesta.[45] Finally, to status and freedom we should add the economic benefits that accrued to slaves involved in commercial activities. They often kept part of their income themselves, to spend on extra food, clothing, and entertainment— or perhaps ultimately to buy their freedom. On the same day that José de Villalta Enríquez placed one slave in apprenticeship, he granted liberty to another, Francisca de Padilla, a mulatta who, by age twenty-three, had managed to amass 200 pesos for self-purchase.[46]

Villalta, however, did not accept Francisca de Padilla's full payment; instead, he refunded 100 pesos "to do her a good work." Such acts of kindness and generosity were rare in master-slave relationships but not unheard of. They—along with the personal freedom allowed to slaves such as Francisco de Morales—imply that feelings of trust and goodwill could develop between master and slave. One cannot hope to reconstruct the emotional life of slaves in colonial Mexico City from the existing sources; yet occasionally one catches a glimpse of devotion and loyal service to a particular master, usually through the latter's testimony: "She has attended me, served me, and taken care of me with all faithfulness."[47] More common, though still not frequent, are examples of masters who cared enough for their slaves to give them the ultimate gift—liberty. Barbara del Castillo freed her eighteen-year-old mulatta slave, Gregoria,[48] "born in my house, the daughter of my deceased slave, Josefa de Torrez."[49] This "second generation" status applied to other liberated slaves as well. In his will, Fernando Cabeza de Vaca freed two slaves, a man and a woman, both "born in his house."[50] The quasi-parental attitude expressed in freeing a slave whom one had watched grow up was made explicit when Antonia Rendón freed Miguel Márquez after "having raised him as a son."[51]

But of all the masters and mistresses cited above, Barbara del Castillo went farthest in treating her favorite slaves as adopted children. She not only freed Gregoria but provided her with a dowry of 500 pesos, later increased (thanks to contributions from two other parties) to 794 pesos. This enabled Gregoria to wed Marcos de Mesa, a militia sergeant, who estimated his net worth at 3,000 pesos at the time of the marriage.[52] In a similar fashion, Barbara del Castillo settled 557 pesos (in coin and goods) on another former slave, María de Torrez, who married a master tailor.[53]

Obviously, such social mobility was beyond the grasp of most slaves, even those who managed to obtain manumission. Cash was the language slave owners understood best; so slaves desiring freedom had to find a source of money—friends, relatives, or prospective employers. Thus, in 1681, a mulatta slave named Pascuala de los Reyes purchased her freedom by borrowing money from a Spaniard, whom she promised to serve until the debt was paid off.[54] In short, manumission often meant exchanging one master for another. There were several variations on this theme. Ana de Rivera, a free mulatta, promised to pay Juan de Aguirre and his wife 200 pesos (in installments of 1½ pesos per month) to purchase the liberty of her niece, María del Espíritu Santo. After some years of payment, another Spanish doña, Isabel de Zavala y Velasco, offered to pay the reminaing balance of 170 pesos. In return, María would come to live and work at her house and would repay Doña Isabel out of her salary at the same monthly rate.[55] By agreeing to this, Ana de Rivera in effect bound her niece to serve Doña Isabel for nearly ten years. To cite one further instance: in 1688, the cleric Don José González Ledo sold a mulatta slave, Getrudis, to Don Juan González de Noriega, with the understanding that the latter would pay his new slave 1½ pesos per month toward the purchase of her liberty. She was finally emancipated some eleven years later, in 1699.[56]

In this last example, slave and wage labor blend into each other almost insensibly. Slavery was not a unitary institution in colonial Mexico City. All masters had the same legal rights over their slaves, but in practice the slaves' situation varied enormously; and much of this variation resulted from the slaves' own efforts. They used all the weapons at their disposal, including their rapport with their masters, to make slavery tolerable and if possible, to escape altogether. The wonder is not that many failed but that some succeeded.

A similar pattern of resistance and accommodation can be found among imprisoned workers, another major branch of coerced labor in colonial Mexico City. Debt peonage is usually regarded as a rural institution, but as Gibson has pointed out, it was first used effectively in urban obrajes.[57] Although peonage was less prevalent in the Valley of Mexico than in other regions, such as the Bajío, unfree laborers made up a significant portion of the work force in Mexico City's sweatshops and bakeries.[58] In some ways, these unfortunates had less freedom—certainly less freedom of mobility—

than most urban slaves. Like slaves, they were subject at times to brutal employers who "without fear of God or their conscience[s]" inflicted severe corporal punishment.[59] However, in contrast to slaves, imprisoned workers could take advantage of debt peonage's questionable legality to manipulate their employers and increase their negotiating strength.

On July 9, 1697, an Indian baker named Juan Antonio lodged a criminal complaint against his employer, the *panadero* Antonio de la Peña. The ensuing investigation allows us to study, in some detail, the labor relations within a seventeenth-century *panadería*. Juan Antonio charged that the day before de la Peña "gave him a number of lashes all over his body with a leather whip" only because he had attempted to find a new master.[60] Interviews with a series of other Indian workers confirmed de la Peña's readiness with a whip; but the court investigators found themselves even more interested in his extremely efficient use of debt peonage as a way to retain laborers. As table 5.4 indicates, Indians who entered the panadería owing small amounts of money (as little as 10 pesos) had served de la Peña for years without being able to repay their debts. This sad state of affairs could not be blamed on the Indians' ignorance, for they clearly understood the trap into which they had fallen. Listen to the testimony of Tomás de la Cruz, explaining why he had failed to get out of debt.

> I have worked in the said panadería for three years. . . . [When I arrived] I owed the said Antonio de la Peña thirty pesos which he had given me, to be paid back by my personal service, for which I earn two and a half [reales] each day I work; one real to pay off my debt; another to buy food; and the half real in the form of a *torta*. . . . Today I owe twenty-eight pesos. . . . The days we rest or do no work because of an accident the master does not pay us a thing, nor give us a real for food or the torta, and as it is necessary to eat we ask that the real and a half which we need be added to our accounts, so most times we are in debt, and even more so when we cannot sustain ourselves with the real we receive for food.[61]

Some simple arithmetic shows the validity of Tomás's argument. Assume a six-day workweek, with Sunday off. In one week, then, a worker would earn 6 reales in cash, but he would have to pay 1½ reales on Sunday for food, so his weekly net would be 4½ reales. At this rate, it would take slightly more than one year to pay off a debt of 30 pesos. This assumes, however, that the worker had only himself to worry about. In fact, most of the bakers were married; and a week's worth of maize for a family of four normally cost about 3 reales.[62] This in itself would triple the length of time needed to retire the debt, and the baker would still face the problem alluded to by Tomás—the agricultural crises that periodically drove up the price of basic foodstuffs.[63] (The year 1697, as it happened, was just such a time of scarcity—*carestía*—and high prices.) Any kind of serious illness,

Table 5.4. Indian bakers in Antonio de la Peña's *panadería*, 1697

Name	Time in Panadería	Debt at Arrival	Original Creditor
Juan Antonio	10 years	30 pesos	Francisco Quintero (*panadero*)
Tomás de la Cruz	3 years	30 pesos	Juan Franco Corona (*panadero*)
Juan Lucas	10 years	30 pesos	Tomás Julián (*panadero*)
Felipe de Santiago	10 years	10 pesos	Tribute
Nicolás de Iglesias	12 years	30 pesos	Juan Jurado
Lázaro Joachím	1½ years	68 pesos	Juan de Mendoza
José Xuárez	3 years	30 pesos	de la Peña
Juan Tomás	5 years	28 pesos	Francisco López (*panadero*)
Nicolás Francisco	"mucho tiempo"	40 pesos	Corona
Sebastián de la Cruz	3 years	63 pesos	de la Peña
Lucas Baptista	10 days	52 pesos	"un gachupín"

Source: AJ, Penal, vol. 1, exp. 19, fols. 2r–9r.

of course, could also push the worker deeper into debt. Finally (this issue is not discussed by the Indians, but de la Peña makes a point of mentioning it) the panadería owner was the workers' chief source for the money necessary to celebrate life's most important occasions, such as baptisms and religious holidays.[64] Small wonder that the bakers found it difficult to reduce their accounts, and some fell ever farther behind. An example is Nicolás Francisco; after spending "a long time" in de la Peña's panadería, he had seen his debt increase over 70 percent, from 40 to 69 pesos.[65]

How could workers fight a system so stacked against them? Their responses strikingly resemble those of the city's slaves: some fled; some committed robbery or sabotage; but the most common tactic was to attempt to find a new employer. Bakers could not realistically hope for better wages, for 2½ reales per week was apparently the standard, city wide rate.[66] What they could expect from a new master, however, was to receive a loan of cash greater than what they already owed to their old employer. They could then pay off the latter and pocket the difference. This is what Juan Antonio had done (he received 15 more pesos) that had so angered de la Peña. It also explained, said de la Peña, why he needed to imprison "some" (according to the Indians, it was "most") of his bakery workers. If he did not keep them locked up, de la Peña complained, they would go "pawn themselves as they usually do" for additional amounts of money. He would then be faced with the unpleasant alternative of either matching the new sum of money or losing his workers.[67] Naturally, de la Peña was not presenting a disinterested point of view, but table 5.4 shows that he was probably telling the truth, while disingenuously posing as the wounded innocent. Of the eleven Indians in this table, only two had originally been de la Peña's debtors; the rest had been transferred from other creditors— in several cases from other panaderos.

De la Peña claimed that "it was not possible to obtain Indians any other way" and that looking for ever-increasing loans was "an immemorial custom among them."[68] The advantages of playing one owner off another are clear: by forcing the panaderos to advance them increasing sums of money, the bakers could accommodate growing families, pay for baptisms, funerals, and other ceremonies, and perhaps slightly improve their families' standard of living. By the same token, the bakers and obraje workers certainly benefited if they could use the legal system to ensure their freedom of mobility. Here they were less successful; imprisoned labor in obrajes and panaderías continued, despite the centuries-long opposition of the crown.[69] In the case cited above, no resolution is recorded; but a concurrent investigation of another panadería resulted in a 50-peso fine for the owner and a court order that he "treat the Indians of his said bakery well, leaving them at liberty."[70] Still, even when the system "worked," the result was that the baker fell farther into debt. The debt peon, like the slave, could seldom do better than ameliorate the terms of his exploitation.

The bakers successfully applied these tactics only because their employers found it difficult to recruit sufficient labor. The obraje and panadería owners therefore willingly sought out other procurement channels and tried to obtain casta as well as Indian workers. Some, in their eagerness to find employees, turned a blind eye to blatantly illegal practices. Antonio de San Juan, having kidnapped his mulatto nephew, managed to "pawn" him to a city bakery with no questions asked.[71] Most of those seeking additional workers, however, looked to the royal prison and its population of convicts and debtors.[72]

Debtor's prison seems on the surface such an irrational institution— how can someone pay his debt while incarcerated?—that we should take a moment to explain its logic. The key point is this: debtor's prison was not the ultimate solution for financial problems but an intermediate step designed to bring the debtor to account. The creditor used the legal system to demonstrate that he was serious about collecting the debt and to improve his leverage in the subsequent bargaining. With luck, the creditor could come away with goods in pawn, new guarantors for the loan, or even a new employee. Consider the unfortunate case of José de la Cruz, a free black resident of Mexico City. In February 1692, José found himself in debt and in prison. A 96-peso loan had fallen due, and José lacked the wherewithal to repay it, or even to buy needed clothing for himself and his family. Since his creditor, Matías de la Vega, had a written contract as proof of the loan, a debtor who was immobile and impecunious, and an obraje in need of laborers, José's fate was sealed. He agreed to "serve and work in the said obraje of Matías de la Vega, which he will occupy until repaying the ninety-six pesos of the contract plus thirty-six more pesos he has been given for clothing and other necessities."[73] Even if the creditor was not himself an obraje owner, he could still make a deal with one or request the government do so. Thus, the lawyer for Juan Cayetano Sorrilla asked that Sebastián de la Cruz, a chino who owed his client 50 pesos, be placed in an obraje or panadería until the debt was worked off. In the end, however, Sorrilla settled for a new repayment schedule.[74]

It is possible that subtle pressure from government officials influenced this decision. For while local authorities enthusiastically dispatched criminals to the obrajes, they remained uneasy about debt peonage for free subjects of the crown. Perhaps the continuing royal pronouncements against this practice gave them pause; or perhaps they felt that so mistreating a substantial proportion of the city's work force was not the best way to achieve social harmony. The city fathers preferred more paternalism in employer-employee relations. This helps to explain one of the city's most interesting programs, training juvenile delinquents in useful professions.

As Taylor has shown, the criminal justice system in colonial Mexico, favored "utilitarian" punishments over incarceration or execution. Even those found guilty of serious crimes, such as robbery or murder, were most likely to be condemned to hard labor in public works projects, presidios, or obrajes.[75] The Sala de Crimen preferred the latter option, at least for Indians. Prisoners could not escape so easily from obrajes; moreover, "they would leave with a trade and afterwards could sustain themselves through voluntary labor"—a great advantage, as (according to the Sala) Indians were "a nation little inclined to put their sons to a trade, leaving them without one until an advanced age."[76]   obrajes?

Taylor rightly calls this "an early example of criminal sentencing couched in terms of rehabilitation."[77] This proposal followed the traditional elite prescription for plebeian social control: labor under the eye of a Spanish master. Yet it is doubtful that magistrates condemning men to obrajes actually had criminal rehabilitation as a primary objective. First, many criminals already had a trade. Second, those sentenced to obrajes included Spaniards and castas. Even if a non-Indian offender did learn a trade during his sentence, he would not receive the official training and legal status that would allow him to operate within the guild system after his release. Third, actual sentences (of, for example, thieves) put less emphasis on rehabilitating the offender than on compensating the victim. Thus, Marcos Pacheco, a Spanish blacksmith, was sent in chains to a smithy for one year, until he could pay the plaintiff 20 pesos, the estimated value of the clothing Pacheco had stolen from him.[78]

The "utility" of hard labor sentences, then, lay more in their benefits than in their redeeming effect on prisoners. Nonetheless, one can find examples of the authorities making a direct effort to reform an adult convicted of relatively minor crimes. When the court condemned Luis de Garay for "dissipation" and for mistreating his wife, Tomasa de Castro, it ordered him to be "placed in a blacksmith's shop to work and to learn a trade."[79] However, while he waited in the royal prison for a master blacksmith to accept him, Luis was able to talk Tomasa into having him released. Tomasa soon regretted her decision.

> After we were together for a few days, he returned to his bad habit of gambling [our money] without giving me what I needed, and mistreating me as he used to, and now he has run away. . . . [I fear] that he will not return because of his dislike for the sentence which was not executed.[80]

Attempts at rehabilitation could backfire; the courts seldom took this chance with adults. They tended to be much more lenient with youthful offenders, however. Mexico City's Archivo de Notarías contains numerous examples of young men, convicted of minor offenses, who were placed as apprentices in various guilds. Antonio Serafín, an orphaned vagabond and sneak thief; Juan Antonio Chirinos, a mestizo arrested for vagabondage and carrying a concealed knife; Marcos de la Cruz, a mestizo orphan caught stealing a silver bowl; Nicolás de Guadalupe, an Indian found in a stand on the plaza mayor "with a girl"—none of these youths suffered whippings or imprisonment in an obraje. Instead, the court sought out artisans who would accept them as apprentices. This does not seem to have been a disguised form of imprisonment. In most instances, the youths received the same terms as any other apprentice (guaranteed by a contract); and they worked side by side with boys recruited through more normal channels. On occasion, the court-appointed guardians who handled these cases consulted their charges' occupational preferences before finding them a master.[81]

Of course, some young men found this enforced paternalism confining and reacted by running away. Yet a legal case from 1698 shows that faced with truant apprentices, the city authorities continued to value rehabilitation over punishment. On July 12 of that year, the Mexico City corregidor, Don Carlos Tristán de Pozo y Alarcón, visited the obraje of Doña Teresa Alvarez to look into the situation of two runaway apprentices being held there. Both were apprentice tailors who had escaped from their masters (in Puebla and Tlaxcala, respectively) and fled to Mexico City, where they had been captured. Don Carlos decided not to return them to their former masters, but he was still eager for them to continue their training. He asked a master tailor "to examine them to determine how much more time they needed to finish learning [their trade]. . . . The said examiner declared that they needed a year and a half to learn it to perfection." The corregidor thereupon ordered that Doña Teresa receive the boys and that their training be completed under the tutelage of "Master Pedro Antonio, head tailor of the said obraje."[82]

Why did the authorities show leniency toward such juvenile offenders? There are two possible reasons. First, Hispanic law frowned on harsh punishment for the young. The Siete Partidas sentencing instructions state that "where the party who has committed the offense is under the age of ten years and six months he shall not suffer any punishment. If he is more than that, and under seventeen, the punishment should be less in severity than that inflicted for the same offense on others who are older."[83] Second, the general notion of disciplining unruly youths through occupational training had widespread popular support, not only among elites but also among the plebeians themselves.

For plebeian parents, apprenticing a son was a positive accomplishment, for he both gained a useful skill and received discipline during a difficult period of his life. Indeed, some parents admitted that they apprenticed their sons for fear that they would otherwise "fall into vagabondage."[84] So when the government found apprenticeships for youthful offenders, the elite prescription for the lower classes met the plebeians' own perceived needs. Thus, the relatives of Nicolás de Guadalupe, the Indian boy arrested on a morals charge, actively encouraged his apprenticeship to a master tailor, complaining that Nicolás was "lazy" and "a vagabond."[85] Many lower-class parents might have wished that the government would help them provide their sons with employment. Witness the parents of Diego de los Reyes, a fourteen-year-old black, who resorted to a public appeal to "any obraje owner" who would train their "badly inclined" son— adding that they would consent to having him chained up if necessary.[86]

Plebeian parents also sought patronage and protection for their daughters. Unlike their counterparts in the upper class, plebeian women often worked for wages outside the home, and the first taste of this labor usually came in adolescence.[87] A window on the recruitment of young women into the work force is provided by two expedientes in the Bienes Nacionales branch of the national archive which contain convent records from the 1670s.[88] These records show the nuns bringing young women (mostly between the ages of ten and fifteen) into their convents as domestic servants. Several salient points emerge from a study of these expedientes. Nearly all the servants came through informal channels; only one written agreement is recorded. In some instances, Spanish doñas sent casta or Indian girls they had raised in their homes; but usually the nun and the girl's parent(s) had made the arrangement. As in the case of apprenticed boys, protection and discipline were important parental motives. In explaining how she obtained her castiza servant, one nun stated that her father "brought her to remove her from the risks of the world."[89] The parents apparently viewed these arrangements as temporary; some girls stayed only until their mothers had arranged marriages for them, and there was even an example of one *criada* being "traded" for her sister.[90] Nevertheless, while the servant remained in the convent, she was entirely dependent on the patronage of her mistress. Servants whose patrons died sometimes found it difficult to obtain sufficient food or treatment for their illnesses.[91]

Apprenticeship and domestic service gave numerous young men and women in colonial Mexico City their first work experience. But these arrangements (along with many others discussed above) also perpetuated the patron-client system. From an early age, plebeians became economically dependent on their social superiors. This limited their ability to challenge an inequitable and exploitative social system; but at the same time, it allowed a fortunate few, including some castas, access to the economic resources necessary for social mobility. Chapter 6 examines the prospects and problems facing these upwardly mobile castas.

6

The Fragility of "Success": Upwardly Mobile Castas in Mexico City

As home to the infamous "thieves' market," Mexico City's plaza del volador witnessed more than its share of crime and violence. But a particularly gruesome sight greeted early arrivals on the morning of June 28, 1698: the dangling corpse of Benito Romero, a well-known mulatto merchant. At first glance, it seemed puzzling that Romero should have hanged himself, for he was the epitome of a successful, upwardly mobile casta. Romero and his wife, Catalina de Guevara, had started with nothing, but by dint of hard work over a period of twenty years—"he with his trading, she with her enterprise of making sweets and chocolates"—they had built up considerable holdings. At the time of his death, Romero had personal possessions worth nearly 300 pesos (this total did not include conjugal property). In addition, he owned a store with goods in stock valued at 600 pesos and claimed a 50 percent share in the profits of another store whose inventory was assessed at over 4,000 pesos.[1] Since Catalina was a Spaniard, the couple easily formed social links in the Hispanic community. They had no less than three Spanish compadres; and one of Romero's Spanish friends, the priest Nicolás de Torquemada, defended the mulatto even after his suicide, calling him "a Catholic and a good Christian, fearing God and his conscience."[2]

Yet there was a dark side to Romero's success. In spring 1698, Romero became increasingly worried about his financial status, in particular, about the large debts he owed to various merchants. After struggling with his accounts for fifteen straight nights in May, to the point that his "understanding became clouded," Romero finally gave up; he closed his shop and turned to a prominent local merchant, Captain Don Juan Luis Baesa, to help him sort out his finances. With Baesa's aid, Romero reached new agreements with his creditors: one, for example, granted Romero a two-year moratorium on his debt, with payments to be spread out over an additional two years.[3] But despite the confidence his creditors had shown in him, Romero fell deeper into depression. Shortly before Romero's suicide, Torquemada found him "sick with melancholy, . . . saying that he was bankrupt and had lost his credit; and although his friends tried to calm him down, showing him what he owed and what he had, and that there remained a quantity of pesos to sustain his wife and children, nevertheless he fell into a frenzy."[4] Torquemada concluded that Romero had committed suicide while temporarily insane, driven to distraction by his business worries. Church officials concurred and permitted Romero's body to be interred in holy ground.[5]

Romero's tragedy has a double-edged message. His initial success demonstrates that Hispanic society, however hierarchical, lineage obsessed, and hostile to social climbers, was not completely closed. There were upwardly mobile castas. A former slave could become a landlady and sport a pearl necklace and bracelet; a morisca, through her "personal industry and labor," could provide her spouse with a dowry worth over one thousand pesos. A mestiza pulque vendor could support a shiftless husband and still leave several hundred pesos as an inheritance for her grandchildren. And these were all women, showing that even the combined burdens of race and gender discrimination could not completely choke off advancement.[6] But in escaping from the grinding poverty of the urban masses, upwardly mobile castas entered a world with its own uncertainties. Hard-won claims to higher status often proved insecure and fleeting. For many reasons, both personal (severe illness, an excessive fondness for gambling) and impersonal (economic recession, agricultural crises), wealth carefully accumulated over years could be lost in a brief time.[7] Romero's suicide suggests that unexpected heights could make the prospect of a fall all the more terrifying.

This chapter discusses upwardly mobile castas. The main source is a collection of some fifty wills dictated by castas and Indians. These are listed in the Appendix and have already been cited numerous times in these pages. Wills present certain problems of interpretation, most notably, because of their freeze-frame quality. The "successful" castas treated here are those who had achieved a certain economic status at one moment—the end— of a life span. Many others, such as those who obtained wealth but then dissipated it, will thus have been left out of our sample. Moreover, these documents do no more than hint at the path that the testators took to reach their final status—the twists and turns, the surprising achievements and disheartening failures that constitute an economic biography.

Despite these flaws, the wills do single out a group of men and women who accomplished what few non-Spaniards could: they escaped, at least for a while, a hand-to-mouth existence and accumulated enough assets so that their disposition became a matter of concern. Their last testaments shed light on how they did this and on other significant questions as well.

How were their economic gains, once achieved, consolidated in the face of cyclical crises, the demands of family and kin, and personal misfortune? Did these accomplishments permanently improve the status of their families? How did their success affect their relationship with both plebeians and the Hispanic elite?

At first glance, the wills do not seem to reveal any secrets for success. Several testators state with a hint of pride that they had entered adulthood bereft of goods and had accumulated their possessions solely through their own diligence and labor. However, hard work was the common lot of plebeians (if they could find employment at all); yet this seldom led to personal advancement. Their career paths resembled a treadmill rather than a stairway.

This was true even in the artisan crafts, which seemed to have a built-in ladder of ascent, from apprentice to journeyman to master. We have already seen that it was not extraordinarily difficult for a poor boy—even a casta or an Indian—to become an apprentice; in some cases, government officials actually arranged such apprenticeships as a means of rehabilitating youthful offenders. But once a young man completed his training, what were his chances for graduating from journeyman to master? Manuel Carrera Stampa, the distinguished historian of the Mexican gremios, thought that this promotion usually followed as a matter of course, although an unfortunate minority never made it.[8] Other evidence suggests that the ascent was a difficult one and that for most casta artisans, and probably for most artisans of plebeian origin, becoming a master was an unlikely proposition. For example, during the period 1712–1716, an average of only forty-three oficiales (skilled laborers) achieved master status each year. The number of new masters in certain guilds was strikingly small: just three candle makers, seven carpenters, and twelve shoemakers in a five-year period.[9] Another suggestive, though imprecise, piece of information reveals the barriers that existed between masters and journeymen: of the artisans in this study for whom relevant data are available, some three fourths of the maestros were literate, while over two-thirds of the oficiales were not.[10] Apparently these two groups were already differentiated at school age. Certainly, in studying oficiales one can often distinguish between those who will probably never go beyond journeyman status and those who are on the way to becoming masters. The latter are marked out not only by their literacy but by their social connections. A journeyman silk weaver such as Andrés de Ortega, who received a 600-peso dowry on his marriage to a Spanish lady, was clearly destined for better things.[11] Perhaps the likeliest explanation for this divergence within the ranks of the oficiales was that Ortega and those like him were the sons of master craftsmen, while the illiterate journeymen represented the plebeian recruits.

Still, one did not have to be literate, or have a family background in a craft, to become a master. What prevented an ambitious, skilled journeyman from improving his status? The obvious roadblock was money. A master needed to acquire a full set of tools (which could easily run to 100 pesos or more),[12] rent or buy a shop, and pay a licensing fee—a daunting task, unless one came into the business through inheritance. It was difficult enough for a regularly employed oficial, earning perhaps three to four pesos a week, to accumulate the necessary capital, particularly if he had a family to support.[13] To make matters worse, regular employment was by no means assured. As the term suggests, journeymen often led a peripatetic existence in their search for work.

An autobiographical sketch of Nicolás de Paniagua, the shoemaker whose contretemps with the Inquisition have been described above, may well describe the life of many seventeenth-century oficiales. After serving as an apprentice to two Mexico City shoemakers, Nicolás "left to work in different shops, where he was paid by the month, and later at the rate of an oficial." At one point Nicolás traveled to Puebla, "to see the new church," but he soon drifted back to Mexico City, where "he lived in the Calle Reloj with a friend, a pastry cook named Miguel Francisco. . . . He worked at his job, making pairs of shoes which he sold in the plaza," as well as doing piecework for various shoemakers.[14]

Nicolás had evidently settled into a satisfactory routine, but it was one that left him little chance of becoming a master even before he ran afoul of the Inquisition. He never demonstrated any burning ambition, but it is doubtful that this would have made much difference. Poor artisans were seldom able to raise themselves by their bootstraps; to ascend the economic ladder, they required an outside source of funds. Some oficiales, for example, reached business agreements with wealthy Spaniards. In January 1692, Diego de León, a journeyman candle maker, formed a company with the merchant Juan Najarros. The latter put up 2,137 pesos—137 for the necessary tools, and the rest to purchase wax. For his part, Diego agreed to manufacture and sell the candles, hiring additional candle makers as needed. Diego would receive a salary plus one-third of the profits.[15] This type of arrangement allowed a journeyman with few assets of his own to considerably augment his capital. Other artisans chose the more direct method of soliciting a loan of cash or goods, preferably with an extended period of repayment.[16]

Cash and credit, then, held the key to upward mobility. However, neither was easy to obtain in significant quantities. Paradoxically, Mexico City, the capital of a rich mining colony and the site of New Spain's mint, was cash poor. Much of Mexico's silver went to Spain, the Caribbean, and the Philippines. Moreover, because of the monopolistic structure of the transatlantic trading system, cash reserves tended to accumulate in the

Table 6.1. Possessions of Juan de Oliva y Olvera

One small adobe house
Clothing
Saints' images, including:
one image of Nuestra Sennóra de Guadalupe
one image of Christ
Various (probably household) items ("cositas")

Source: AN 750, Pedro del Castillo Grimaldo (114), 9 March 1686, fols. 38r–40r.

hands of a small elite of import-export merchants, the *almaceneros.* The resulting cash shortage was exacerbated for the urban poor by the colony's failure to produce a sufficient number of small denomination coins.[17]

It should therefore come as no surprise that even successful castas seldom had a high degree of liquidity: their assets consisted of goods rather than cash. Consider tables 6.1 through 6.3, which provide an inventory of goods (as listed in their wills) for three castas: Juan de Oliva y Olvera, a mestizo *cajonero* (store owner); Teresa de Losada, a mulatta who "washed for and served the pages of the viceroys"; and Josefa de la Cruz, the mulatta widow of a slave, who apparently engaged in small-scale commerce.

The tables illustrate the mix of possessions common in our sample (and also suggest the wide range of specificity in these wills, which frustrates attempts at quantification).[18] The most common items, listed by virtually every testator, were clothing and household goods. Religious artifacts are also prominent; apparently they were acquired once basic necessities had been met. A surprisingly large proportion of the sample—nearly half—owned real estate. Usually this consisted of a small house or plot of land; but some had multiple holdings and were, in effect, investors or landlords.

Juan de Oliva y Olvera, Teresa de Losada, and Josefa de la Cruz all had collections of worldly goods indicative of moderate prosperity. Yet their assets did not include any cash worth mentioning. In fact, both Josefa and Juan ordered that no masses be said for their souls, because of their "poverty." All three testators had outstanding debts or loans; Teresa, for instance, had borrowed money from her grandchildren to purchase her house, while Josefa had a 15-peso claim on a gachupín for two months' sustenance. But again, these transactions do not suggest access to resources sufficient to lift them to a new socioeconomic level. It is unlikely that any of them ever had more than 100 pesos in hand at a given time. Under these circumstances, they quite sensibly spent their money on the necessities and minor luxuries of life. Besides, the money spent on these purchases was not wholly irretrievable. The possessions themselves constituted a kind of reserve, since they could be pawned and thus reconverted into small amounts of cash.

Table 6.2. Possessions of Teresa de Losada

One house (rented out)
One wooden wardrobe
One large wooden chest
Plates
Saltcellars
One necklace and bracelet of pearls (50 pesos)
Earrings (worth 120 pesos each)
Four ounces of pearls (200 pesos)
Silk curtains
Silk ribbons
Six lienzos [a]
Three skirts
Three shirts
"Some paintings and items of little value"

Source: AN 776, José de Castro (119), 27 February 1690, fols. 37v–39v.
[a]Paintings of religious subjects on linen cloth.

Pawning one's possessions was a common reaction to financial difficulties. The extent of this practice may be judged from the 1699 inventory of a small Mexico City store, in which pawned goods (prendas) followed sugar and soap as the third most valuable items in stock.[19] Even relatively wealthy castas frequently had a large proportion of their property in pawn. Consider the case of Nicolás Hernández, a mestizo and sometime shop owner. At his death in 1692, he possessed "some houses of adobe and stone" in the southern section of the traza which he willed to a priest. To his granddaughter and niece he left mattresses and some paintings; but the bulk of his nonessential goods seem to have been in pawn. An ambulatory merchant held Hernández's writing desk for a 5-peso loan. Hernández had pawned an image of Christ's Resurrection to a shoemaker for 6 pesos. A spare mattress had to be redeemed from a journeyman goldsmith. Nearly all of Hernández's collection of religious artwork had passed into the hands of his creditors. In addition, Hernández had regular debts of some 60 pesos, including 20 pesos to a panadero for "bread that he gave me to supply a retail store I had" and 13 pesos to his daughter-in-law "that she lent me in reales for my sustenance." The ledger was not completely one-sided, since Hernandez was a creditor as well as a debtor: one of his tenants owed him 33 pesos in back rent. Nevertheless, he had determined to liquidate his remaining estate to meet his obligations and to make one final gesture in favor of the church: "I order that if the few goods I possess are able to satisfy and pay for my funeral and burial and some debts [I owe] . . . out of the amount left over six pesos should be given in alms to the Hospital of Señor San Antonio Abad to aid in its construction."[20]

Nicolás Hernández's life evidently alternated between bursts of eco-

Table 6.3. Possessions of Josefa de la Cruz

One bed, with two mattresses
Two woolen sheets
One bedspread
One blanket
Two black skirts
Some petticoats
Six bags for stuffing cushions
Small boxes, chairs, and tables
One big jar from Michoacán
Some paintings of different saints
One image of Nuestra Señora de la Limpia Concepción
One small saint's image
One small image of Christ
Some engravings
Two "copper things"
One harp

Source: AN 3,369, Marcos Pacheco de Figueroa (499), 12 December 1685, fols. 64r–65r.

nomic prosperity and collapse. At the high tide of his fortunes, he was wealthy enough to acquire considerable property; as his fortunes ebbed, pawning served to cushion the impact of his descent. Even so, he was at times reduced to living on charity. Perhaps Hernández was a poor businessman, or perhaps he was simply unlucky. Yet this pattern of economic oscillation appears to have been common among artisans and traders. Antonio López del Castillo, a mulatto merchant, had debts of over 400 pesos, but his debtors owed him even more. He held several items in pawn for other people but had himself pawned two pearl necklaces, a pearl and a coral bracelet, and two rings as a surety for a friend's loan.[21] Sebastiana Hernández, whom we discussed in chapter 4, had numerous debtors (mostly Indians), but her range of creditors was even wider. She had pawned many items, including a necklace to María de la Cruz, a black slave, for 8 pesos; a pair of silver table knives to a tocinero (bacon vendor) for 4 reales; and an embroidered cushion to a Spanish gentleman for 2 reales.[22]

The world inhabited by most upwardly mobile castas, the world of artisans, shopkeepers, and traders, was an insecure and volatile one. In this environment, "cash flow" is a misleading term; money dribbled in and out of one's hands in fits and starts. Petty commerce could not function on a cash-and-carry basis; credit was the essential lubricant of the economic system, even at the simplest level, such as purchases of bread, clothing, and other necessities. Consumers would run up a tab, paying when they could. Credit purchases and running accounts were common

practice among small-scale traders as well.[23] Such transactions were seldom recorded in writing. It is rare to see a loan of cash or goods worth
less than 100 pesos notarized. The creditor might receive a handwritten
IOU, but more likely, the two parties would simply conclude a quick oral
agreement. These were routine, everyday matters, casually dispatched.
Pedro de Soberón, the Spanish owner of a cacao shop, described how he
loaned money to a fellow merchant.

> Miguel de la Cruz, a mestizo servant of Bentura de la Cruz, came . . . to the
> *cacaguatería* of this witness, which is on the corner of Provincia and Calle
> Reloj, and in the name of the said Bentura de la Cruz, . . . asked for ten
> pesos, and [the witness] gave them to him, and would have given him many
> more if he had so requested.[24]

He could confidently lend this money to Bentura de la Cruz, who was (in
Soberón's words) "a man of good credit." When Bentura failed to repay the
loan after several days, Soberón assumed that he had simply forgotten and
went to remind him, only then learning that Bentura had never asked for
the money. It seems that Miguel de la Cruz, who was working for Bentura
to pay off a debt, had found an ingenious way of raising money by trading
off of his employer's reputation. At least three of Bentura's acquaintances
had fallen for this trick.[25]

Miguel's scheme throws considerable light on the world of commerce in
colonial Mexico City. His swindle worked, at least temporarily, because
he tapped the reservoir of goodwill built up by Bentura de la Cruz. The
victims, operating on their personal knowledge of Bentura, took him (as
they thought) at his word and gave him the money without question or
hesitation ("I would have given him . . . more if he had so requested"). In
the absence of legal documentation, such a reputation for trustworthiness
was a sine qua non for commercial success. Like its English equivalent,
the Spanish word *crédito* had a dual meaning, linking financial and moral
worth. Only those whose premises could be trusted, who could claim
"buena fama y reputación," gained the continuous access to credit necessary for their business dealings, hence Benito Romero's panic when he
feared he had "lost his credit."

Despite occasional abuses, this credit system worked rather effectively.
A certain level of honesty was enforced by the face-to-face relationships of
the marketplace, by the familiarity and personal links between buyer and
seller. Traders who sold goods on credit had to trust their customers not to
decamp with the merchandise; consumers, lacking receipts, had to trust
merchants not to exaggerate their debts. That is why Teresa de Losada
could calmly declare in her will, "I owe Alonso Montero, a clothier, the
amount shown in his [account] book" and why the businessman Juan de

Arenas could list several hundred pesos worth of outstanding loans secured only by oral agreements.[26]

The credit networks of modest artisans and merchants could be surprisingly extensive. Table 6.4 presents a rare and fascinating document: a list of all the people who (as of April 12, 1693) owed money to Salvador de Cañas, a master shoemaker. As in previous examples, his credit transactions were not large—most of the debts listed are under 10 pesos—but they were numerous and of several different kinds, including a running account with Juan Sánchez, onetime sales of his wares on credit, and (one assumes) straightforward loans. Of course, the most striking feature of this list is the prevalence of other shoemakers. Cañas appears as a endless fount of small loans (certainly of cash and perhaps also of tools or working materials) to his fellow artisans. Here was no formal "credit market" but a series of decisions doubtless based on Cañas's personal assessment of "Nicolás el chino," "Ambrosio el negrito," and "José, the seller of horses." How many Salvador de Cañases did Mexico City contain? We begin to glimpse the importance of credit as an integrative mechanism, the daily process of give and take, borrow and repay, promise and fulfill, that linked artisan to merchant, producer to consumer, and patron to client.

For credit networks had vertical as well as horizontal components. Salvador de Cañas's pattern of loans, in its modest way, has a clear bias. The six men singled out as vecinos—"householders" or "respectable citizens"—owed him 116 pesos, 5 reales, which represented about 40 percent of his outstanding loans. At the other end of the scale, the five people named as "journeymen shoemakers" had received only 16.5 pesos, 10 of those going to one of their number (possibly an employee of Cañas himself). It seems that Cañas preferred to deal with the relatively well off—after all, they were better risks—but he did not entirely neglect those of lower economic standing. Unfortunately, we have no corresponding account of Cañas's debts; perhaps he had none. But if he did borrow, one would expect his list of creditors to be even more skewed in the same direction. The hypothetical result would be a kind of modified middleman status.

It is easy to see why this pattern would obtain. The economic vicissitudes noted above would frequently oblige shopkeepers, merchants, and artisans to borrow. The recipient of the loan might invest it in his business by renting larger quarters, arranging for the delivery of new merchandise, refurbishing his stock of goods, or (in the case of artisans) purchasing new materials and tools. If he realized a profit from these investments, most of it would return to the creditor when the loan was repaid. The remainder would probably go for living expenses and household purchases. But who, throughout this cycle, supplied him with these goods and profited from

Table 6.4. Salvador de Cañas's credit network

	Amount	
Debtor	Pesos	Reales
Juan Sánchez, vecino de Guautitlán Adjustment of accounts	45	
Juan Carranza, likewise a vecino of Guautitlán	10	
Alonso Martínez, master shoemaker in this city	36	
Diego de Aquino, Indian, journeyman shoemaker	1	
Antonio Juárez, journeyman shoemaker in this city	1	
Juan de Olivares, vecino of this city	9	
Francisco de Rueda, also a shoemaker	4	4
Gregorio Cario, shoemaker, vecino of this city	7	
In addition, the aforesaid owes	29	5
Felipe "el cuate," shoemaker	3	5
Juan de Alegría, shoemaker	1	
Francisco de Estrada, shoemaker	8	4
José de Alegría, shoemaker	4	
Nicolás "el chino," shoemaker	4	6
Antonio "el judío," shoemaker	1	2
Juan de Bobadilla, shoemaker	1	4
Marcos Antonio, journeyman shoemaker	3	4
Juan de Tapia and Francisco Pacheco	9	
Diego Domínguez, shoemaker	5	4
Juan Ramos, shoemaker	1	4
José, the seller of horses	12	
Baltasar de los Reyes	2	5
Lucas de Santiesteban, ministro alguacil	6	
Matías, shoemaker	2	4
Juan Manuel, shoemaker	3	
Gabriel Cortés, shoemaker	2	7
Ambrosio, called "el negrito"	5	4
José de Pastrana, shoemaker	1	6
Juan Isidro, Indian aguador, 12 pesos for money, buckets that he carried off, and the costs of replacement	12	
Bernabé Mirabal, owes the value of a pair of breeches he ordered made	—	
Pascual Quintana, two pairs of shoes	1	2
Don Cristóbal de Montoya, vecino of this city	7	
Manuel de Espiñan, trader, vecino of this city, for money and work	9	
Matías de los Angeles	3	4
Pascual Quintana, journeyman shoemaker	1	2
Juan Prieto, journeyman shoemaker	10	
Antonio de Castañeda	1	
The said Antonio [sic] "el negrito" also owes	1	4
José de Pastrana	1	5

Source: AJ, Civil, vol. 58, 12 April 1693.

his expenditures? The answer, of course, is other shopkeepers, merchants, and artisans, either those from his own socioeconomic level or from the elite. Thus, the money loaned was drawn back toward the upper levels of society, closing a circle that excluded the plebeians. Only the fragments of such loans reached the lower classes—indirectly—when the original borrower paid his employees' wages or when he turned patron himself. But these "second stage" patrons would have relatively little largesse to dispense and (given the odds against prompt repayment) even less incentive to do so. As a general rule, they would lend much smaller amounts to plebeians, both in single instances and in sum, than they borrowed from elites.

There is, in fact, evidence for the existence of just such second stage patrons. We can begin with Pedro de Mora Esquivel, the mulatto glassmaker who has been mentioned earlier. Pedro was an unusually successful artisan: between his first and second marriages he managed to accumulate some 2,000 pesos worth of "real estate, tools of my profession, and other goods." He therefore had considerable resources at his disposal; indeed, when he dictated his will, his outstanding loans exceeded his debts. Even so, most of his financial transactions were with his social superiors or equals. Pedro listed two major creditors in his will, both wealthy Spaniards: a gachupín captain with whom Pedro had a running account (the amount of the debt is unspecified), and Don José de Rettes, who had loaned Pedro 200 pesos. Pedro's most important debtor was also a member of the elite, a Franciscan from Coyoacán who had borrowed 235 pesos "in confidence." Another fairly large loan (100 pesos) had gone to Nicolás de Arellano, an ambulatory vendor. His relationship to the glassmaker is unclear, but he may have been a business associate; perhaps he hawked some of Pedro's wares in the street.

Pedro's will records only three loans to people who could definitely be regarded as his social inferiors or dependents. One was not, properly speaking, a true loan: Antonio de Artiaga, one of Pedro's tenants, owed him 58 pesos in back rent. As for the other two, Pedro had advanced 71 pesos to "Diego de Asencio, a free mulatto," and 124 pesos to "Diego Martín de Barrientos, a journeyman glassmaker who works in my house."[27] This last sum was surprisingly large; it seems likely that Pedro lent Diego this money—either in friendship or as a legitimate business investment— so that the latter could establish himself in his own shop. In any case, the ratio between Pedro's credit transactions with elites (200 to 235 pesos) and those with plebeians (58 to 124 pesos) was quite small, in the range of two-to-one and four-to-one.

Few patrons displayed Pedro's generosity, however, and this differential was normally far greater. Consider the economic network of Josefa de Salas, a mulatta widow who owned several pieces of Mexico City real estate. Her business dealings with elite Spaniards involved large sums of money: she owed Don Juan de Rojas over 100 pesos and had borrowed 800 pesos from Don Juan Cayetano de Valdés. Her transactions with plebeians were on a different scale: "Francisco de Aviles, a muleteer from the town of Jalapa, owes me 23 pesos; . . . Francisco de León, a muleteer of this city, owes me about 39 pesos, the remainder of [a loan of] 55 pesos, of which he gave me the rest in reales and a piece of Brittany cloth; . . . his wife owes me 5 pesos and 5½ *tomines* for bread that I gave her on credit."[28] The will of Felipa Correa, widow of Cristóbal de Castillo, who owned a mule team, tells a similar story. Felipa realized over 3,200 pesos from the sale of her husband's animals and equipment, indicating that his business had been a profitable one. Yet the list of her debtors, also largely inherited from her husband, shows that he was far from openhanded. José de Aguilar, the mayordomo of Cristóbal's mule team, received 80 pesos worth of sacks on credit. Cristóbal also sold one of his employees a set of guns, to be paid for in installments out of his wages. Another muleteer managed to obtain a loan of 19 pesos.[29]

When people engaged in less lucrative activities, they became patrons on a correspondingly smaller scale. For instance, the financial dealings of Sebastiana Hernández, the mestiza seamstress discussed above, never exceeded 20 pesos. We may also cite, as additional examples of "third stage" patrons, two fruit vendors, María de la Concepción and José de Chavarría. The former, on her death in 1698, had debts totaling 52 pesos to merchants who had supplied her with goods; she also had various items valued at 8½ pesos in pawn with two Spanish doñas. The largest loan recorded in María's will was for 11 pesos. In addition, she had advanced 6 pesos to Francisco Platero, a muleteer, and had sold a woman named Ana Ponce a *huipil* worth 5 pesos on credit.[30] José de Chavarría's debts amounted to 75 pesos: he owed 50 pesos to Toribio Pérez, from whom he had purchased some sugarcane (though José claimed to be too impoverished to honor the debt), and 25 pesos to a plaza vendor whose name he could not recall. José listed only one debtor, a Chalco resident called Diego de Tapia, who owed him 9 pesos.[31] With these two fruit sellers, we have clearly reached the economic level where the last trickles of patronage are beginning to dry up.

So credit was widely available, but for most people, it was available only in small amounts—"emergency" loans to tide one over a crisis rather than "self-improvement" loans. The latter could be obtained only by avoiding the chain of intermediaries and tapping directly into elite purses. How did a fortunate few manage to do this? Here we run into one of the limitations of wills as a historical source. We glimpse the testators at a particular moment in time—usually (since they take the trouble to write wills) a prosperous moment. They are enjoying the fruits of their success, one of which is the buena fama y reputación that gives them ready access to extensive credit. Benito Romero borrowed 527 pesos from one Spanish merchant and went into partnership with another. When Domingo Pérez, a mulatto fish seller, settled accounts with his wholesaler, he found himself 2,000 pesos in debt. He agreed to pay this sum in annual installments of 250 pesos, which suggests that both Pérez and his creditor harbored few doubts about the mulatto's continued prosperity.[32]

In Mexico as elsewhere, nothing succeeded like success. But wills supply only fugitive hints of early struggles, of the first steps up the ladder. In fact, many testators do not even state their occupations, which must be inferred from the business transactions listed in the will. This is particularly true for women, so that the provenance of their fortunes is often puzzling. To cite an extreme example, what is one to make of the mulatta María de la Concepción, who on her marriage to a chino slave brought him a dowry of over 5,000 pesos, "acquired through my skill [*inteligencias*]?"[33]

We should not dismiss the possibility that some castas advanced (as they claimed) simply through their own merits. Trade offered an avenue in which, with luck, each profitable venture provided a stepping-stone for a further, more profitable one. Benito Romero was not alone in acquiring an impressive fortune, by casta standards, as a merchant. Juan de Arenas, at the time of his death, had at least 450 pesos in cash, a slave, a half share in a plaza cajon worth 2,000 pesos, and 19 marks of silver. Augustina de la Cruz managed to accumulate over 1,000 pesos in cash by selling pulque.[34]

Still, one suspects that ability was most often not enough, that having the right connections mattered from the start. But these connections, however well known at the time, may have largely eluded formal documentation. Those revealed in our sample of wills, then, represent only the most obvious cases. We indeed find that several of the testators, including many of the most successful, had close personal ties to Spaniards, including ties of blood. The sample included twelve known cases of first-generation castas, that is, castas who had one Spanish parent. (The sample also contains six testators descended from Indian nobility on at least one side of the family.) Of course, this Hispanic connection might not necessarily prove beneficial. A parent's ability or willingness to aid his or her child could vary considerably, depending (among other things) on the parent's own wealth and status, feelings toward the child, and racial attitudes. Furthermore, one of the primary advantages of Hispanic parentage—access to superior social networks—is extremely difficult to document, though it can sometimes be inferred.

Consider, for instance, Mateo de Aguilar, the mulatto son of a Spanish father. According to Aguilar's will, when he married he neither received a dowry from his bride nor had wealth or possessions of his own. Yet he had a prestigious occupation—he was a jeweler, working in pearls and gold—and while he did not claim master status, he was clearly successful and respected. Aguilar noted (with implicit pride) that he had been the founder and treasurer of a cofradía, and he even made a gesture of noblesse oblige, forgiving half of a debt owed him by a Spanish widow, Doña Maria de Arroyo.[35] Perhaps Aguilar succeeded strictly through his own ability; but it seems probable that his father's influence helped him gain admittance to his profession and access to the necessary patronage. Similar remarks could be made about the castizo artisan José de Tovar, a master cooper, although he had the additional advantage of distinguished Indian ancestry through his mother's family: he was the "grandson of Juan de Tovar, an Indian cacique, the discoverer of the Virgen de los Remedios."[36]

In other cases, Hispanic parents bestowed direct material benefits on their casta children. Juan de Oliva y Olvera, a mestizo clothes seller, received a house and property from his parents; his will also contained several expressions of gratitude toward his brother for financial assistance.[37] The father of Marcos de la Mesa, a mulatto militia sergeant, gave his hijo natural a share in his lucrative Philippine business ventures. (Mesa also benefited from a 794-peso dowry granted to his wife, a former slave, when her mistress freed her.)[38] In the most favorable circumstances, parental generosity could have a life-altering impact. What would the future normally hold for an illegitimate mulatta? She could anticipate a life of poverty, with a narrow and unappetizing range of occupational options: servant, washerwoman, petty trader, prostitute. But Gerónima de Vega y Vique, the illegitimate daughter of a Spanish don and a free black woman, inherited both her father's name and much of his estate: she owned houses, furnishings, cash, even slaves, including (ironically enough) two fellow mulattoes.[39]

Vega y Vique had enviable economic status for a casta, but some doors were still closed to her. It is noteworthy that she did not marry particularly well by her economic standards. Of her two husbands, one was not a Spaniard, and the other was a petty trader worth barely more than 100 pesos. Nor was hypergamy characteristic of the other successful castas mentioned above. Marcos de Mesa's wife, however large her dowry, was still a former slave. Mateo de Aguilar, as noted above, married a mulatta who brought him no dowry at all. The sample of casta wills provides more systematic data. Eliminating those who never wed, we have forty-five people who contracted a total of fifty-eight marriages. Among these, there are only five recorded cases of marriages to Spaniards.[40] This was actually a high rate of intermarriage, compared to the normal incidence of casta-Spanish unions.

(See table 4.7.) Perhaps many more sought such favorable matches. But if so, most sought in vain: hypergamy was neither the foundation of nor the capstone to the careers of upwardly mobile castas. In other words, these castas were unable to take the final, crucial step that would fully integrate them into the city's Hispanic social network and thereby guarantee them sustained participation in elite economic circles. Instead, they remained in the precarious position of second stage patrons, still dependent on the favor of wealthy Spaniards while expected to support their own relatives, employers, and servants.

Thus, at the boundaries of the elite, race took on a new importance. The most successful castas were precisely the ones who felt the full impact of Spanish racial ideology and were thus particularly jealous of their buena fama y reputación. For example, casta merchants who traveled through the countryside often felt it necessary to arm themselves; but since castas were legally prohibited from carrying weapons, they needed special permission. Their petitions to the viceroy reveal the castas engaging in one side of an implicit debate, answering unspoken accusations of laziness, immorality, and unreliability. One after another, they proclaim their record of diligent labor, their services to the community, and their tax contributions to the crown. Some present elite Spaniards to confirm these virtues.[41]

This desire for self-vindication, combined with a genuine assimilation of upper-class beliefs, also surfaces in the pious bequests featured in many casta wills. The reader will recall that plebeians often demonstrated a casual and (in the eyes of church officials) disrespectful attitude toward the Catholic religion. Elite castas tended to be more orthodox. Witness the common presence of religious artifacts among their possessions. In making out their wills, they had a final opportunity to show true devotion and Christian charity. For instance, Gerónima de Vega y Vique made the normal donations for the beautification of saints and the redemption of Spaniards captured by the Moslems; however, she also made a special contribution toward the construction and adornment of the Sanctuary of Nuestra Señora de Guadalupe. In addition, she bequeathed 200 pesos to her brother (to start him in a trade) and 100 pesos to a Spanish orphan she had raised.[42] In similar fashion, José del Valle bequeathed 100 pesos to Lic. Alonso de Ensinas, "my spiritual father," for distribution among the poor; ordered one hundred masses said for the souls of his father and himself; and, in the eventuality of his mother's death, left his estate to the cofradía of the Santísimo Nombre de Jesús in the monastery of San Agustín, where he also asked to be buried. Ana de Samudio, a wealthy mestiza widow, donated 100 pesos to aid "the procession of Jesús Nazareno [during] Holy Week" and allotted the sizable sum of 500 pesos for her burial and masses.[43] Micaela de la Encarnación entrusted her entire estate to a cleric, whom she asked to oversee its distribution "respecting the great and entire satisfaction that I have in good works of a Christian, zealous, and pious nature, and I trust that he will do all the good that he can for my soul."[44]

In distancing themselves from their plebeian counterparts, upwardly mobile castas also became more receptive to Hispanic views on race. This statement finds support in the casta requests to bear arms. None of these supplicants questioned the values of legitimacy and hereditary social status. On the contrary, two claimed descent from conquistadores, and two others said they were married to *cacicas*. Mestizos and especially castizos showed some awareness of their putative superiority over the other castas. Pascual Coronel Bocanegra, for example, pointed out, "Although . . . my mother is mestiza, I am a castizo, and I am married . . . to Juana Corres, a Spaniard."[45] Such evident regard for these fine distinctions may explain the high degree of racial variability displayed by castizos, as shown in table 4.6. It is quite possible that many of the "castizos" in this table were mestizos who had attempted to "promote" themselves but whose new racial identity was not credited by the local community. In the same vein, one can easily find examples of persons who, although listed as castas in the burial records, omitted this fact when dictating their wills.[46] As castas became increasingly associated with elite Spaniards, they naturally attempted to play down their racial standing. Some successful castas may even have passed on "Spanish" status to their children or grandchildren.

The "Spanish" label had more than prestige value. Earlier in this study we cast doubt on the utility of passing as a means of social mobility. What good would it do a black weaver to become a "mulatto"? But elite castas faced a different situation. Having reached a certain economic level, they found that the main barrier to further progress was, in fact, their race. By moving into the "Spanish" category, they gained access (for their descendants, if not for themselves) to the institutions of higher learning and the city's most important and profitable occupations. "Spanish" status offered another advantage: thanks to their social connections, Spaniards down on their luck had a safety net. For instance, Doña Antonia de Miranda, a poor Spanish woman (her mother took in clothes for washing and sewing), received 300 pesos to marry or enter a convent from a wealthy friend of the family.[47] Many of Mexico city's *obras pías* (pious endowments) also provided dowries to Spanish *huérfanas*. Similarly, Spanish boys left orphaned could frequently rely on elite sponsors to arrange entry for them into the more prestigious guilds.[48]

The materials available for this study do not permit us to estimate how frequently successful castas passed into the "Spanish" category. The castas in our sample obviously failed to make this transition. Denied the psychological and material benefits of Hispanic status, they had good reason to fear that their hard-won gains might melt away, that they or their children might slide back down the slope to penury. Pitfalls appeared on every side. A single importunate dependent could be a major drain on one's capital. The mestiza pulque vendor, Agustina de la Cruz, complained bitterly about the constant badgering she suffered from her husband, Melchor de los Reyes. After years of plying her trade, Agustina amassed some 1,000 pesos that, at her husband's request, she divided evenly between them. However, Melchor had "spent and dissipated [his share] in a brief time," failing to provide for his wife's necessities ("not even a pair of shoes"). Indeed, Agustina was forced to pay for Melchor's food and clothing. She had fallen into the habit of giving her husband 5, 6, or 7 reales each evening, knowing that he would drink and gamble them away, to avoid nightmarish "quarrels and disputes" with him. Agustina made a point of cutting Melchor out of her will.[49] In a 1672 will, the casta couple María de la Concepción and Miguel de Silva had left 600 pesos to their adopted daughter, Francisca; five years later, "having come to poverty" and having already given Francisca a hefty dowry—300 pesos in cash, over 900 pesos worth of goods—they found it necessary to revoke this clause.[50]

But at least María and Miguel were able to transfer a significant portion of their wealth to their heir. This was no mean accomplishment. The preservation of family fortunes across generations challenged even the colonial elite. A popular proverb told the story: "Father merchant, son gentleman, grandson beggar." How much greater was the difficulty for those with less wealth and fewer remedies? A mestizo shopkeeper might seek a degree of flexibility by purchasing items that could be pawned, but this was hardly equivalent to establishing an entail or putting money into a safe, income-producing investment, such as real estate.[51]

Large families posed particularly difficult problems for upwardly mobile castas. First, simply supporting a large family from day to day could prevent accumulation of capital in the first place. Second, the parents' assets, when dispersed among multiple heirs, might dwindle to insignificance. Three hundred pesos made an adequate dowry or grubstake but not when split six or seven ways. The obvious solution to these problems was to avoid children. This may seem facetious, but in fact, the castas in our sample showed a marked prospensity toward small families. The fifty testators had ninety-nine children, or two per family. (This includes both legitimate and acknowledged illegitimate children and also those who did not survive to adulthood.) This figure is somewhat misleading, for as table 6.5 shows, no fewer than sixty-two of these children came from just ten fami-

Table 6.5. Family size among casta testators

Number of Families or Individuals with:		Total Number of Children in Group of Families or Individuals
No children	20	0
1–3 children	20	37
4 or more children	10	62
Total	50	99

Source: See Appendix.

lies. The other forty testators—80 percent of the sample—had three or fewer children, with an average of just under one per family. Forty percent were childless. Given the time and place, it is extremely unlikely that they were practicing birth control. They probably wanted children (indeed, many of them adopted and raised orphans) but were unable to conceive them.[52] Thus, infertility restricted family size, with economically beneficial results, but at the cost of a different kind of deprivation.[53]

In some ways, the castas discussed here led favored lives. They lived in relative material comfort. Unlike most residents of Mexico City, they did not have to labor all day for a pittance. They retained their personal freedom: they were not bound to an owner or chained to a workbench. Most were their own bosses; some were employers. In their own neighborhoods, they were persons of some importance, the kind who ran cofradías, marched with their guilds in religious processions, and dispensed advice and small sums of cash to tenants, apprentices, and poor relations.

But if we enlarge the context, the picture changes drastically. Compared to the genuine elite, whose wealth dazzled capitalino society,[54] upwardly mobile castas had laughably small "fortunes." They could seldom accumulate enough capital to be truly secure, so they sought assistance from their superiors and thus became enmeshed in a network of patrons and clients ultimately dominated by the elite. By playing the role of middlemen, they allowed the elite to extend its reach far down the social spectrum, into areas where the labor system was ineffective, and in a less blatantly exploitative form. A mulatto trader gives succor to a widow; a Spanish foreman locks his workers into an obraje: both represent mechanisms of social control, but the former has a more humane face. Upwardly mobile castas also served as "good examples," proving that a better life was possible if one worked within the system. Nor did it seem likely that these middlemen would turn on their elite patrons. Their very "success" and respectability inhibited any direct challenge to the regime: they had too much to lose.[55]

So it proved, in the long run. But though not given to sociopolitical analyses, these castas perhaps sensed, as they daily witnessed the displays of the colonial aristocracy and the pomp and splendor of the viceregal court, that they were being used, that they supped on bread crusts and drank the dregs of the wine. On a June evening in 1692, some of them would take their revenge.

7

The Riot of 1692

In the seventeenth century, New Spain and its capital seemed to epitomize the order, stability, and continuity of the colonial system. Even in the midst of Spain's collapse as a European power, a steady stream of peninsular bureaucrats maintained an imposing and virtually unchallenged state apparatus in Mexico. Earlier scholars tended to view this as a static, even somnolent age—"the long siesta." We now know that beneath its placid surface, Mexico City witnessed a constant round of political scheming, intrigue, and alliance and counteralliance.[1] Still, the *pax hispanica* was shattered only twice, in the riots of 1624 and 1692. Both featured violence, destruction of property, and the frightening spectacle of thousands of people raging in the plaza mayor, shouting for the viceroy's blood. But the second offered a more direct and threatening challenge to Spanish authority. Recent studies of the 1624 riot suggest that it may have been encouraged by members of the elite as one move in an elaborate political struggle.[2] The riot of 1692 did not fit into any such framework of intraelite conflict, seeming rather to reflect pronounced popular anger at the wealthy and at Spanish rule in general: "Death to the gachupines!" Indeed, elite commentators were inclined to see this riot as an indigenous uprising, a *tumulto de indios*, and thus as especially alien and dangerous.

Unfortunately, the 1692 riot has not received the close scrutiny of its earlier counterpart. The few historical narratives are based, for the most part, on published accounts written by elite Spaniards. These accounts suffer from an obvious bias. But more important, they give us the views of observers and reactors rather than instigators and participants. The voices of the rioters themselves remain unheard. The following analysis of the tumulto—its causes, development, and aftermath—provides for the first time both plebeian and elite perspectives. As so often happens, the extraordinary illuminates the commonplace. The paper trail left in the riot's wake allows us to probe more deeply into seventeenth-century social relations, to discover the colonial regime's underlying strengths and weaknesses as well as the tensions within plebeian society itself.

The tumulto of 1692 has generally been viewed as a classic corn riot. It is certain that it occurred after a year of unremitting agricultural disaster. Heavy rains and flooding in June and July 1691, combined with an out-

125

break of blight, ruined both the autumn wheat and maize harvests. Mexico City residents faced shortages and price increases in both grains throughout that winter and the following spring. Indeed, maize prices in 1692 reached their highest in the century. Moreover, the riot took place in early June, precisely the time of year in which demand for maize was greatest.[3] All this argues for the centrality of grain shortages in any explanation of the 1692 riot. Yet to draw a direct line from heavy clouds and empty maize stalks to the rioting, burning, and looting of June 8, to comment (as one observer did) on "the fire into which the water was transformed by the stress of hunger,"[4] is to adapt a simplified view of causality that belittles its human subjects. A generation of research on European crowd behavior has cast serious doubts on this "spasmodic view of popular history," the idea that "we need only bring together an index of unemployment and one of high food prices to be able to chart the course of social disturbance."[5] In studying the 1692 uprising, one must give heed not only to the economic but also to the social and political circumstances—particularly since maize shortages played a curiously ambiguous role in contemporary explanations for the riot.

Few of those who gave legal testimony in the aftermath of the riot ventured an opinion on its cause. For many witnesses (especially Indians), this was no doubt part of a broader attempt to disassociate themselves from the riot, to present themselves as mere bystanders or onlookers without any special knowledge. But references to maize shortages do appear, usually attributed to someone else. Thus, the Indian porter (*cargador*) Antonio de la Cruz (who eventually went to the gallows for possession of stolen goods) claimed that he heard Indians running toward the plaza, shouting that they would burn it down "because of the lack of maize."[6] Another suspect "heard it said that the Indians of Santiago [Tlatelolco] had burned the Royal Palace and all the rest . . . [because] there was no maize for the said Indians, only for the Spaniards, all of which was told him by his wife and an Indian, Matías de los Angeles."[7] Some elite witnesses also cited maize shortages as the proximate cause of the riot, though with the clear implication that this was a superficial and inadequate cause, of less impact than the Indians' ingratitude and perfidy.[8]

As the authorities gradually recovered from the shock of June 8, an "official" explanation of the riot began to crystallize which pushed the maize shortage even farther into the background. This account placed the blame squarely on the Indians themselves. An early version appears in the instructions for the court that the court attorney (*fiscal*), Don Juan de Escalante y Mendoza, wrote three days after the riot. He argued that it was vital to "unsheath the sword of vengeance" on suspected wrongdoers, "to contain the unrestrained boldness of a people who have betrayed the faithfulness and loyalty of vassalage with an action as unjust as it was unforeseen." Normal standards of proof should be relaxed; since it was well known that the Indians were the primary culprits in the riot and the looting that followed, any Indian found with stolen goods in his possession or in his house should be convicted. Escalante y Mendoza did try to find some consolation in the hope that this outrageous behavior had been an aberration; he therefore suggested careful investigation into the possibility that the normally pacific natives had been provoked by opportunistic castas.[9]

The main elements of Escalante y Mendoza's diatribe occur again and again in reports sent to the king by the viceroy, audiencia, city council, and individual officials. The seedbed of the riot had been those dens of iniquity, the pulquerías. There the Indians' baseness and viciousness of character, normally restrained by their innate cowardice, had been unleashed by alcohol and the urgings of the castas, who hoped to profit from the resulting chaos. In these accounts, the grain shortage ceases to provide even a threadbare cloak of sympathy for the Indians; instead, it becomes yet another (and compelling) demonstration of their treachery. The basic story line—most fully developed by Sigüenza y Góngora in his well-known letter to Admiral Pez—is as follows. Central Mexico did suffer from a severe grain shortage in 1691–92, but the viceroy, the Conde de Galve, had taken heroic measures to alleviate this problem. And in fact, these measures had succeeded: according to the audiencia, maize was as plentiful in Mexico City as "in years of very abundant harvests," and grain prices there were among the lowest in the entire kingdom.[10] Sigüenza y Góngora established, at least to his own satisfaction, that Indian women were actually profiting from the situation, since they alone could meet the demand for tortillas, which they sold at a far higher price than the cost of maize. "Therefore, no other year had been more favorable for them."[11] However, in an excess of ingratitude and hypocrisy, the Indians had rioted anyway, using an alleged corn shortage as their excuse! As one cleric put it, "Our viceroy had maintained [the city] without known hunger, when the irrational resolution of the Indians brought about the unjust uprising."[12]

This "treacherous Indians" explanation (which at times, as in Sigüenza y Góngora's letter, merged into a full-fledged conspiracy theory) had obvious advantages for royal officials. First, it freed them from charges that bad government had caused the riot. Second, it resonated with long-standing beliefs shared by crown and creole alike, such as the dangers posed by racially mixed gatherings and the deleterious effects of native pulque consumption. Third, it provided obvious "solutions" through which zealous officials could prove their devotion to duty, namely, the banning of pulque and the restriction of Indians to their own barrios—both of which were rapidly, if temporarily, implemented.

Yet we must be wary of dismissing this explanation as nothing more than self-serving propaganda. The authorities did take extraordinary measures to address the grain shortage. In late 1691, the viceroy moved first to secure the maize supply from Chalco. This region, about twenty miles southeast of the capital, had long served as Mexico City's breadbasket. Its great advantage was its lakeside location, which allowed for rapid and inexpensive shipping by canoe.[13] But would the provinces' hacendados be willing to deliver the maize that Mexico City needed? Their normal practice was to stockpile and hoard their maize—for years if necessary—until they could obtain the highest possible prices. Galve refused to countenance this practice. In a series of decrees, he ordered these hacendados to sell their recent maize crop, then to open up their storehouses, and finally to dispatch the provinces' entire maize supply, beyond that needed for purposes of survival.[14] Unlike so many other edicts, these had some muscle behind them: ministers from Mexico City were sent to monitor and enforce compliance. An example of their diligence occurred, ironically enough, just before the riot. On June 6, the alcalde mayor, Pedro de la Bástida, came to Chalco in response to reports that local hacendados had been selling maize to other markets. He promptly conducted a hacienda-by-hacienda search of the district, sequestering twenty-five thousand *fanegas* of maize (about two-thirds of the haciendas' remaining store) for shipment to Mexico City, leaving behind only enough to sustain the "haciendas and poor of the province."[15]

Chalco hacendados undoubtedly dragged their feet; nevertheless, in the months following the harvest, they sent over 5,000 fanegas of maize per week to Mexico City, a rate that was maintained for most of the spring. By the end of July 1692, Chalco had delivered some 114,000 fanegas to the alhóndiga—close to 70 percent of its total supply and an unusually high figure for a poor harvest year.[16] Yet it was not enough. As early as February, the alhóndiga had begun to expand its search for maize beyond the normal channels, buying grain from Celaya, Salvatierra, Silao, and other regions and going as far afield as the Villa de León, some 150 miles from the city. These special purchases, which eventually amounted to 45,000 fanegas, far exceeded normal budgetary limits; they were financed through a donation of nearly 100,000 pesos made by the city's leading silver merchants.[17]

According to official accounts, Mexico City received 169,145 fanegas of maize between December 3, 1691, and July 26, 1692—an average of 700 fanegas per day.[18] This is an impressive figure. Enrique Florescano has estimated that during the eighteenth century, Mexico City usually consumed between 160,000 and 200,000 fanegas of maize each year and that "in the years of highest sales [i.e., years of poor harvest] the alhóndiga would sell between 110,000 and 130,000 fanegas."[19] The totals from 1692 compare favorably to these figures, all the more so since the seventeenth-century city probably had a smaller population. It would seem, then, that the Conde de Galve's measures for maintaining the maize supply were more than adequate.

But perhaps these gross figures conceal deeper problems. There are three considerations that complicate the equation between acquiring maize supplies and satisfying the needs of the urban poor: (1) demand; (2) prices; and (3) distribution. Let us consider each in turn.

Could the demand for maize simply have overwhelmed the city's supply mechanisms, despite the best efforts of the viceroy? One should bear in mind that in 1692 Mexico faced not a single but a dual agricultural crisis: both the maize and the wheat harvests failed. Wheat had been culti-vated in Mexico since the Spaniards' arrival and by 1692 had been the favored grain of the gente decente for more than a century; yet wheat production remained precarious. Like maize, wheat depended on (and, indeed, was considerably more vulnerable to) the vagaries of temperature and rainfall. Some summer (irrigated) wheat was grown but on a small scale compared with later developments. In the eighteenth century, an agricultural transformation took place in Guadalajara, the Bajío, and other regions, as hacendados invested heavily in irrigation works, storehouses, and other facilities and transferred their best land to wheat, which was now becoming a highly prized commercial crop. Even Chalco, still Mexico City's most important source of maize, produced 60,000 fanegas of wheat annually in the eighteenth century.[20]

In the 1690s, however, central Mexico had relatively small reserves of wheat, and when the wheat pest struck in the late summer, the price of the grain—already expensive compared to maize—skyrocketed.[21] Now, only the wealthiest could afford wheat bread and (according to the archbishop) "more than forty thousand in the city and its barrios ate, and sustained themselves, . . . with maize tortillas, who had not used this food be-fore."[22] The archbishop perhaps exaggerated the increase in the demand for maize, but it was certainly heavy: Sigüenza y Góngora speaks of 1,000 to 1,300 fanegas of maize sold daily in the alhóndiga by November 1691.[23] In short, Mexico City was facing an unusually high demand for maize, with the resulting depletion of reserves, and the beginnings of a crisis mentality *before* the autumn maize harvest failed. So, if Sigüenza y Gón-gora was correct in stating that the alhóndiga was distributing over 1,000 fanegas per day in November, then even if we assume the reduced maize harvest provided some alleviation, the alhóndiga supply of 700 fanegas per day from December 1691 to July 1692 may well have been insufficient. In fact, it was estimated on April 15 that the city would need 200,000 fane-gas before the next harvest, which again works out to about 1,000 fanegas each day.[24] The double blow of poor maize and wheat harvests could indeed have created a crisis so severe that the demand for maize simply outstripped the city's capacity for supply.

Of course, even abundant supplies were of little use to the urban poor if they could not afford to purchase them. The pósito and alhóndiga were designed to make sufficient quantities of maize available to consumers, but they were not mechanisms for price control. This is not surprising, considering that much of the alhóndiga's maize had not been purchased by the government but still belonged to individual hacendados, who sold it through their agents, the "encomenderos de la alhóndiga."[25] All the maize distributed by the alhóndiga on a given day was sold for a set price, but that price itself was agreed on by the various sellers and basically reflected market conditions. The alhóndiga, then, played a mediating rather than a coercive role. But the government could decree otherwise. Colonial authorities were not (to put it mildly) disposed to see free enterprise and public good as synonymous. A government role in regulating the economy was assumed: the question was how this could be done most efficaciously. As the maize crisis persisted into 1692, the Conde de Galve called for a special junta to advise him on this issue.

This junta, which met on April 29, was surely one of the most impressive gatherings of its kind in the history of colonial Mexico. Among those attending were "all the gowned ministers of the Royal Audiencia, the paymaster and royal officials, the heads of the ecclesiastic and secular cabildos, the chief prelates, and important persons from the religious orders"[26]— a veritable who's who of the colony's secular and religious leaders. The gathering commended the viceroy on having kept the city provisioned with grain "at moderate prices." The real challenge, however, would come in the succeeding six months until the next maize harvest. Two courses of action were laid before them. The first, presented by the fiscal, urged official intervention on several fronts. Ecclesiastics should use moral suasion to force their tenants to reveal hoarded maize; "rich citizens" should be compelled to pay for the transportation of maize from distant regions (such as Guatemala and Yucatán); alcaldes mayores and Indian gobernadores should require all pueblos in their districts to plant extra maize; Mexico City's corregidor should lecture the city bakers on the evils of profiteering, then install agents in the panaderías to see that they did not make underweight loaves, and finally, a price ceiling should be fixed for maize. The fiscal recommended two pesos (16 reales) per fanega.[27]

The counterproposal, written by Lic. Don Alonso de Arriaga Agüero, looked askance at most of the fiscal's recommendations but concentrated on debunking the notion of price controls. Sounding remarkably like a Hispanic Adam Smith, Arriaga stated that the price increase in maize resulted primarily from natural causes rather than price gouging. To set an artificial price ceiling (even in the doubtful event that this could be enforced) would, first, constitute an unfair blow against already overburdened farmers, and, second, encourage immediate purchases and thus the rapid depletion of the city's grain supply. The only solution, said Arriaga, was "liberty of commerce," which would allow maize prices to rise "in proportion to the calamitous state of things." Both producers and consumers would benefit: the former would of course receive greater profits, while the latter would become more disciplined purchasers, buying only what was necessary.[28]

The junta considered both reports but clearly found Arriaga's arguments more convincing. With just one abstention, they endorsed Arriaga's position and ordered dispatches sent to the relevant officials, forbidding them to

interfere with the liberty of commerce in the said grains and provisions, or with their current and common prices, or with their transportation to the places of greatest need or convenience and to the alhóndiga of the city, without prejudice to arrangements already made for its provisions.[29]

The junta expressed the hope that while this liberty of commerce might raise maize prices, it would reduce the pressure on the maize supply and "guarantee . . . the most favorable or least contrary" state of provision.[30]

In short, the junta and the viceroy deliberately allowed price increases. However sensible in broad economic terms, this policy imposed considerable and growing hardship on the individual consumer, for as maize prices continued to rise, one's ability to purchase sufficient quantities of maize sharply eroded. And maize prices did continue to climb throughout the spring. Even the special maize shipments from Celaya and other regions—the first of which arrived on March 24—did little to stem the tide. The low purchase price of the maize was counterbalanced by high transportation costs. With each shipment arriving from a yet more distant source, the price crept up inexorably from 17 reales to, eventually, 24. By the time of the riot, maize was selling at the alhóndiga for 3 to 3½ pesos per fanega.[31]

What did this mean for the urban poor? At the normal price of 9 reales per fanega[32] and given optimum conditions—that is, full employment, which itself was rather uncommon among the plebe—an unskilled worker with a family of four to feed would spend 20 to 25 percent of his salary on maize. When the price of maize tripled, as it did in 1692, this obviously placed enormous strain on plebeian families and must have forced many to the edge of starvation. The poorest went without, except for what they could scrounge, beg, or steal.[33] Some sickened and died: the number of casta burials doubled from the previous year (see table 4.5), and not everyone could afford the luxury of an "official" interment.

Thus, as maize prices continued to increase, some people were forced out of the market altogether. This may explain how the authorities were able to cope with the high level of demand—and keep the lid on popular pressures—for as long as they did. Indeed, price increases may have played a divisive role among the urban poor, precluding solidarity, separating those with a regular source of income (from employment, patrons, or kin) from the truly desperate. But as the date of the riot approached, signs of general strain multiplied. The distribution system—the system that brought maize from the hacienda to the hands of the consumer—was beginning to falter.

Difficulties first arose in the transportation of maize from outlying regions. Inclement weather had destroyed large numbers of livestock, and the resulting shortage of mules, combined with the recalcitrance of the hacendados, slowed the delivery schedules. Of the 45,000 fanegas of maize purchased (beginning on February 4) from beyond Mexico City's normal catchment area, only 18,360 had arrived in Mexico by June 8.[34] As noted above, deliveries from Chalco had also begun to go astray in the late spring. The urban poor were well aware of these problems. Descriptions of the alhóndiga on the eve of the riot speak of an "innumerable crowd," largely composed of Indian women, screaming "shameless, foul, and lewd words," quarreling, pushing, and shoving, and pressing forward until some were trampled and others suffocated, while the vendors and distributors found it almost impossible to do their jobs.[35] These are indications of people on the verge of desperation. A worried viceroy dispatched a gowned minister—Don Juan de Escalante y Mendoza, the fiscal who has already figured prominently in these pages—who, together with the corregidor, was to awe the crowd into more seemly behavior. But he could not solve the underlying problem, the grain shortages that had begun to afflict the city. On both June 8 and the day before, dozens had been turned away without getting any maize.[36]

Significantly, on both occasions groups of Indians went to protest to the archbishop and the viceroy. One of the protests failed, and the other resulted in a full-fledged riot, but both suggest that the populace held the authorities accountable for the grain shortage. In other words, this crisis was capable of generating that "moral outrage" which occurs when people "perceive their situation as the consequence of human injustice: a situation that they need not, cannot, and ought not endure."[37] This attitude was precisely what puzzled and angered the elite commentators who constructed the "treacherous Indian" thesis. Did not the Indians realize, they asked, that the viceroy had done everything humanely possible to relieve the situation? Why should the Spaniards be blamed for an act of God, quite possibly brought on by the Indians' own wickedness?

One answer to this question is provided by two letters sent to the king of Spain in July 1692. These letters present a stinging exception to the many panegyrics on the Conde de Galve. The writers, who identify themselves only as "the most loyal vassals of your majesty,"[38] lashed out at the viceroy and his entourage, compiling a catalog of their abuses: corruption (Galve "had accumulated more treasure than four [typical] viceroys in three and a half years"), tyranny, "usurping the jurisdictions of the tribunals and selling justice," forcing Indians to clean the local aqueducts at substandard pay, illegally charging a tax on livestock entering the city, and exiling to Texas anyone who opposed their schemes. Most important for our purposes, they also blamed inflated grain prices on the viceroy, his "creatures," and his supporters on the April junta, who were "full of adulation and half-crazed with avarice." The "free commerce" decree had been a sham, for the viceroy and corregidor had engrossed the maize and wheat supply and were using their monopoly to increase prices by as much as 100 percent. The authors also suggested that by getting silver merchants to finance some maize purchases, the conde had freed up official monies for speculation in the lucrative Peru and Pacific trades.[39]

How valid were these accusations? If the alhóndiga account books are accurate, then at least some of these charges (e.g., the price-fixing of maize from Celaya) must be false. However, similar practices were far from uncommon, and it is unlikely that anyone versed in the intricacies of bureaucratic infighting would manufacture such charges out of whole cloth. In any case, many people believed that the viceroy and other officials were profiting from the grain shortage. The "loyal vassals" claimed that "no one was ignorant of these matters" and added that one cleric had said that those in charge of supplying and distributing the grain supply should be hanged. Anti-Spanish and antiviceroyal pasquinades appeared both before and after the riot,[40] and during Easter a sermon preached in the cathedral apparently condemned the viceroy's handling of the crisis, since Sigüenza y Góngora said that it "imprudently" confirmed popular suspicions. On the very day of the riot, as Galve attended morning mass, "a not very indistinct murmur arose among the women . . . as he entered the church: they were execrating and cursing him in an ugly fashion attributing the shortage of corn and the high price of bread to neglect and poor management on his part."[41]

The alhóndiga shortfall on June 8, therefore, took place after months of apprehension, at a time when maize prices had reached the highest level in decades and against a backdrop of widespread suspicion concerning the motives and actions of the authorities—including the corregidor, who was present when the grain market closed. It is noteworthy that the one hundred fifty or so persons who had received no maize proved mistrustful and unwilling to leave the alhóndiga; the fiscal actually had to show them the empty storage bins upstairs before they would depart. Even so, Escalante y Mendoza had no premonition of the bloody events to follow. He described the scene at the alhóndiga as "peaceful," apparently believing that he had mollified the crowd with the (somewhat hollow) promise that they would be served first the next day.[42]

As Escalante y Mendoza was returning from the storerooms, he came across an Indian woman lying unconscious on the stairs. Her friends said she had fainted in the crush around the grain market. Having taken her pulse and assured himself that she was in no great danger, the fiscal ordered his servant to bring the woman some wine; then he made his way home. A short time later, an angry group of Indians appeared in front of the archbishop's palace, complaining of their mistreatment at the granary and demanding justice. They bore the corpse of a woman who, they said, had been killed at the alhóndiga. According to Escalante y Mendoza, this "corpse" was the very same woman he had encountered quite alive only a few minutes before.[43] The Indian protest that triggered the riot, therefore, had been fraudulent from the start.

The issue of the alleged corpse marks the first point of contention between our two main sources on the riot—observers, usually Spaniards and often members of the elite, and participants (or suspected participants), mostly plebeians and non-Hispanics. Since their division corresponds, in large part, to significantly contrasting views of the tumulto—the riot as conspiracy versus the riot as spontaneous event—it is worth pausing to evaluate this macabre incident. Was the woman really dead? Did her alleged mistreatment "cause" the riot?

Fortunately, we have two thorough accounts of the incident, one from each perspective. Miguel Gonzales, the mestizo shoemaker whose confession is perhaps the best participant source on the riot, generally supports the Indians' contention that the woman was dying, if not already deceased. He explained that he was in the plaza, chatting with some men, when several Indians passed by, carrying

> an Indian woman whose head was covered by a manta. . . . They said she was going to die and that she had been cudgeled at the alhóndiga, from which they carried her toward the Cathedral, . . . toward the cemetery where there was a Dominican padre who removed the manta and spent a brief period of time with her. . . . I don't know if he confessed her, I only heard it said that if she had been near his convent he would have given her last rights. . . . From there . . . they went to the archbishop's house, and behind them went many Indians and people of other castes [calidades] and myself.[44]

Sigüenza y Góngora was not an eyewitness to these events, but he assiduously gathered whatever information he could find on the riot. His version quickly summarizes the march through the plaza and cemetery (and says nothing of the Dominican father) so as to concentrate on the scene at the archbishop's door. Note the cynical and sarcastic tone of this quotation, in contrast to Miguel Gonzales's tempered, rather sad recollections.

> Two young students who were there came up close to the Indian woman that was being carried. One of them addressed these particular words to the other, "Say, look how that poor dead woman is sweating!" The other approached her as he could and answered, "This woman's not very dead for she's blinking a little and is swallowing saliva!" "What do you know about dead people, you stupid dogs of students?" said an Indian woman who heard their conversation, "Now all of you in Mexico City will be dead like she is!" . . . An honest fellow who was there related this to me and he assured me . . . that not only what the students said was true but that shortly before he heard the "dead" woman tell them to carry her well. Well, this is what the Indians are like![45]

We might, by assuming that the woman was seriously injured but not dead, effect at least a partial reconciliation of these accounts. What is more significant, however, is that their divergence narrows precipitously as they move on to the next stage of the story. Both describe how the Indian claimants, rebuffed at the archbishop's door, moved on to the viceroyal palace and renewed their protest there. And what of the dead woman? As the scene shifts back to the plaza, she fades completely from view. Neither Gonzales, nor Sigüenza y Góngora, nor indeed any other account of the riot ever mentions her again. Nor was the body of a woman found on the plaza after the riot was over, though of course the woman (after having served her purpose?) might have been taken to her home. All this suggests that the true nature and extent of her injuries was, in a sense, beside the point. We must look instead to the realm of symbolism to find the root of these contending perspectives and the failure of communication that triggered the riot.

On the conspiracy interpretation, the entire incident—particularly the parading of the body through the plaza—had been a deliberate attempt to incite a riot.[46] Seen in this light, the similar protest of the day before looks like a trial run, with the Indians perhaps deciding that they needed an extra element—a corpse—to whip up public fury. But if this was the Indians' intent, they apparently miscalculated. The "many" people who followed the body to the archbishop's residence probably amounted to no more than a few dozen. Lucas Gutiérrez Cabiedes, who owned a cacao store on the plaza, estimated the crowd of protestors at "fifty or sixty persons of different races, the majority Indian men and women."[47] According to eyewitness accounts, even when they returned to the plaza, they numbered fewer than two hundred. For example, Francisco de Medina, a mulatto slave serving in a plaza shop, recalled that there were "one hundred fifty Indians, mestizos and mulattoes among them, and also four or five Spaniards."[48] Only after the Indians began to throw stones did the size and heterogeneity of the crowd rapidly increase.

The Indians' actions make more sense if placed in the context of the patron-client system discussed in chapter 2. The protesters resorted to the traditional process of appealing their grievances to a higher authority. The alleged mistreatment of this Indian woman was not an isolated incident but merely the latest in a series of outrages. For instance, just two days before, another Indian woman had been severely whipped by alhóndiga officials. Miguel Gonzales, in fact, claimed that he had been discussing this very subject—with complete strangers—when the Indian procession arrived at the plaza,[49] indicating that popular resentment of the authorities was very near the surface. (The Sigüenza y Góngora quote, if nothing else, captures the anger of the protesters.) The government had failed to supply maize at a reasonable price; alhóndiga officials had mistreated poor women; the populace had grown increasingly suspicious and mistrustful of the viceroy's goodwill: what could be more natural than to appeal to the viceroy's ecclesiastical counterpart, especially given the archbishop's reputation as "the Almoner" and friend of the poor?[50] Even the bearing of a body in procession had popular precedent: Mexico City's blacks had done the same thing in 1611 to protest the murder of a slave.[51]

But the Indians found no surcease at the archbishop's house. He refused to see them; his servant delivered a court dismissal, telling them (according to one version) "to go to the Palace and let the Viceroy give them justice."[52] Under the circumstances, this must have been particularly galling advice. Still, the Indians made their way to the viceregal palace—and here they were once again rebuffed, once again denied access to legitimate authority. This was the last straw: frustration and anger exploded into violence.

As it happened, the viceroy was not in the palace; in celebration of the Octave of Corpus Christi, he had attended religious services at the friary of San Agustín, then retired to the church of San Francisco, just off the plaza. Sigüenza y Góngora writes that "his great piety saved his life,"[53] but it is possible that his presence might have averted the riot altogether. The crowd turned to violence only after its peaceful appeals had been ignored. The riot began because the authorities had unwittingly closed off the channels of communication that acted as a safety valve for plebeian discontent.[54] No more is heard of the "dead" woman after this point because this specific abuse is subsumed into a larger one: the denial of dialogue.

Of course, in the riot's aftermath, the authorities would not admit such an explanation. Elite commentators refused to acknowledge this default; indeed, this refusal was the cornerstone of the conspiracy theory. Every reasonable measure to combat the grain shortage had been taken. The people should have been grateful, not resentful. They should not—could not—have expected further dialogue. Their protests were all a ruse. They had planned a riot from the beginning, cunningly choosing a festive day when their betters' attention would be distracted.[55]

As suggested above, the timing of the riot's events makes any conspiracy theory doubtful. We can, in fact, point to the moment—shortly after 5:30—when the crowd's attitude changed from one of respectful if importunate protest to one of contempt. After the crowd was denied entrance to the palace, some of its members began to taunt the palace guard, "to make fun of the soldiers who were at the door, many of the said Indians making gestures with their cloaks."[56] Another witness made the bullfighting analogy explicit, stating that "the Indians provoked the soldiers, acting the bullfighter [toreando] with their mantas, one red, another blue, and another black."[57] The message implicit in this image—the luring of a seemingly overpowering creature to its destruction—must have seemed ominous to the soldiers inside the palace.

The palace guard was in no shape to handle this situation. Because it was a religious holiday, only a minority of the one-hundred-man garrison was in place, and many of them were off-duty, whiling away their time at gaming tables. With many of the officers absent, the normal chain of command was disrupted, which left the soldiers reluctant to take decisive action in the crucial early moments of the riot. Moreover, as events would show, the soldiers were desperately short of powder and ammunition.[58] Perhaps the protesters sensed this weakness; perhaps they suddenly grasped the immense gap between the power that the palace guard represented and the power that it actually possessed. In any case, as if continuing their "come out and fight" theme, the crowd began to throw stones at the palace. The guard responded to this implicit challenge. Some fifteen or sixteen Spanish soldiers, swords unsheathed, charged into the crowd, driving them back to the middle of the plaza; but the soldiers were quickly stopped and forced to retreat by barrages of rocks. A second sortie some minutes later met the same fate. Meanwhile, "at every moment the number of rioters grew," as Indians, castas, and even Spaniards streamed into the plaza from every direction; soon the crowd numbered in the thousands. The soldiers made a fateful decision: to prevent the rioters from storming the palace, they closed and barred all the doors, posting sentries inside each entrance. But the fury of the crowd found other outlets: within minutes, these doors had been set aflame.[59] In half an hour, perhaps less, a traditional protest had changed into a full-fledged riot. The resounding crash of stones and the flickering of firelight proclaimed this metamorphosis.

From this point on, the task of unraveling and explaining the events of June 8, 1692, becomes more difficult. Not only do these events take on a new complexity but the sources become more contradictory; in particular, the dichotomy between elite observers and plebeian participants reasserts itself even more strongly. For instance, as described by the Royal Audiencia, the riot displayed an almost Aristotelian regard for the unities of time and space, with the evening's events playing themselves out in linear fashion over the space of three hours, like acts in a play. First, the rioters set the palace aflame; then "the rabid fury of such evil people unslaked by this atrocious act, they went on to set fire to the ayuntamiento buildings"; next they burned and sacked the merchants' shops; and they intended to burn the house of the Marqués del Valle until they were dissuaded by two prelates. Finally, "their irrational barbarity satisfied," they departed.[60] From ground level, however, a far different picture of the riot emerges, less straightforward and more nightmarish. In the trial records, the riot itself tends to dissolve into a stream of chaotic incidents, a series of largely unrelated episodes.

If the modern scholar struggles to find meaningful patterns in these records, the challenge facing Mexico City judges was more daunting still. While undoubtedly sharing the predilections of their class, they could not take so Olympian a view of the riot, since they had to grapple with the facts as they presented themselves in court testimony. By way of illustration, consider an issue of consummate interest to the Spaniards—the leadership of the riot. As Taylor suggests, "Colonial Spaniards . . . could not conceive of a political movement that did not have a leader who planned and directed it."[61] But as the authorities gathered evidence, the harvest of suspects was disappointingly meager. Though closely questioned on this matter, few eyewitnesses and ever fewer participants implicated specific individuals as leaders of the riot. Even when they did, their testimony was usually not corroborated. And in the Spanish legal system, a single accusation, however convincing, did not suffice for conviction. Normally, court authorities built their cases slowly but systematically, gradually accumulating formally attested and mutually supportive testimony from numerous witnesses, until the evidence became so overwhelming that the defendant had little choice but to confess. Testimony on the riot was, in comparison, confused, partial, fragmented—a blurred snapshot rather than a careful portrait painted during many sittings. At the same time, public pressure forced the courts to try and sentence suspected criminals quickly, to discourage other potential rebels. Given these conditions, the judges did countenance torture to obtain confessions as well as the death penalty for those participating in the riot, both fairly rare practices.[62] But, to their credit, they tried to maintain a reasonable standard of evidence. Furthermore, they recognized that men in desperate circumstances will often tell their listeners what they want to hear.

Felipe de la Cruz is a case in point. Felipe, along with four other Indians, had been caught red-handed while setting fire to a viceroyal balcony. In his confession, he stated that he had overheard pulquería conversations among various cargadores who were planning to riot and burn the palace. Moreover, he claimed to have actually seen two of the plotters, named Juan Chino and Agustín, setting fires during the riot.[63] The judge thought so little of Felipe's "revelation" that he condemned him to death without bothering to question him further—an action for which he was later chided by the fiscal.[64] Still, the case was not reopened, and no other evidence ever turned up to support Felipe's rather transparent attempt to save his skin.

Much more plausible was the testimony of José Ramos, an Indian cargador arrested while fleeing Mexico with suspicious coins in his purse. (They were suspicious because they were full pesos rather than the reales and half-reales that unskilled laborers earned.) At first Ramos denied any knowledge of the riot, but under torture he admitted that he had witnessed Indian leaders provoking the rebellion,[65] testimony that he reaffirmed the next day.

As Ramos told the story,

On the afternoon of the riot the Indians gathered behind the palace. . . . The first to meet were about eight Indians from the barrio of Santiago [Tlatelolco], all with capes [i.e., members of the Indian nobility]; at about five o'clock they were complaining that maize was expensive and that they had gone without any that afternoon. Many others began to gather, coming from different places, and Lorenzo, an Indian from Santiago, . . . son of one of the current alcaldes of the said barrio, was the one who provoked the talk about the lack of maize, and everyone who was there said with one voice, "Let's go burn the palace."[66]

Ramos named several other Indians who were present, including two sons of the governor of Santiago Tlatelolco.

Ramos did not provide the ideal conspiracy story from the Spanish point of view: he said nothing about long-range planning for the riot, and the maize shortage played an uncomfortably prominent role as a motive. Yet his story did suggest that the protest at the archbishop's residence had been a charade or a diversion and that the Indians, incited by their own leaders, had made the Spaniards' ruin their objective from the start. Alas,

Ramos proved better at implicating malefactors than at identifying them. Presented with sixty Indian suspects, he could identify only one, a small-time tailor. Once again, the authorities dropped the matter for lack of evidence, although Ramos, convicted of theft, received a relatively light sentence of two years service in an obraje.[67]

Other witnesses presented alternative candidates for mob leader. Don Diego de Navarijo, secretary to the audiencia, testified that the crowd in front of the archbishop's palace had been stirred up by a "mestizo achinado" wearing a green mourning cloak, who urged his listeners "to swear to Christ that all these cuckolds, these fine gentlemen who do nothing but ask for paper and throw [people] into obrajes, have to die."[68] Juan de Velasco, a Spanish carriage maker, encountered a group of Indians in the Calle de Toledo, led by the shoemaker José de los Santos. A rather gruesome figure—he was one-eyed and crippled in both legs, which forced him to walk on his knees—Santos had an evil reputation and a tongue to match. Velasco reported him shouting, "Let's go to the palace and kill these cuckolds." When the Spaniard attempted to intervene, the Indians threw stones at him, then departed with a veiled threat: "Now we know you."[69] According to eyewitnesses, Santos popped up in several other places near the plaza, always using the same firebreathing language. "Now these cuckolds have to die, the time has come, Spaniards!" "Death to these cuckold gachupínes, we have to kill them all!" And, to an interfering Spaniard, "Go on, get away Spaniard, and be glad I haven't killed you!"[70]

Navarijo's mestizo, if he really existed, escaped, but Santos was enmeshed in the coils of Spanish justice and delivered to death. Of all the suspected ringleaders, only Santos was identified by multiple witnesses, allowing prosecutors to compile the kind of solid, well-attested case that they liked. Within two months, the shoemaker was duly tried, convicted, and executed. There is little doubt that Santos did, as he confessed, participate in the riot, but his role as a "convoker and leader of the Indians" (the official charge) is certainly open to question. On the face of it, Santos was an unlikely choice to captain a march on the plaza. (Of course, he could have been carried by his "followers," but none of the witnesses mention this.) And, for a man with a serious handicap, Santos displayed miraculous mobility. As his attorney unavailingly pointed out, Santos was sighted in five different locations at the same time.[71] A better explanation would be that a process of transference had taken place. The witnesses had seen Santos in or near the riot and had picked him out as the "leader" precisely because he was so striking a figure, so unforgettable—and perhaps, in some instances, because they were aware of his reputation as a troublemaker. Velasco recognized him and knew that he had lived in the Calle de Merced; another witness was a former employer, who claimed that Santos was a man of "evil inclination, without respect for anyone," and that it was public knowledge among shoemakers that this Indian "had killed his mother with a dagger or a blow."[72] Santos was, in short, exactly the kind of man who would do and say what they had accused him of: he was a perfect scapegoat.

Other accused leaders showed at least some of the shoemaker's traits. First, they were readily identifiable: witness Ramos's caped Indian officials or Navarijo's unusually attired mestizo achinado. ("Achinado" probably denoted striking features or dress.)[73] José de los Santos himself stated that when he arrived at a bridge leading to the plaza, he saw a tall, shirtless mulatto, waving a banner—actually a manta tied to a pole—"as if he were leading the people."[74] Second, they were "natural" leaders of a riot. Spaniards found it credible that Indian nobles could command a large native following or, alternately, that castas had planned and provoked the entire uprising. Finally, with the exception of the nobles, they were the right social type. All castas were suspected of criminal leanings (as were frequenters of pulquerías), and in the specific case of the mestizo achinado, Velasco stated that he had seen him before in the baratillo, which was tantamount to calling him a thief and a scoundrel.

Unfortunately (from the Spanish point of view), these men had one other thing in common: they were no more than minor figures operating on the fringes of the riot. On the evidence, they could not be accused of actually supervising or coordinating the night's activities. They had been seen before the riot (the Indian nobles, the mestizo achinado), or on the way to the plaza (José de los Santos), or on the outskirts of the plaza after the riot was well under way (the shirtless mulatto). During the riot proper, however, they went unnoticed. If they did lead the rioters—or even throw rocks and set fires themselves—they did so under a cloak of anonymity.

For at the heart of the riot, confusion reigned. Occasionally, a recognizable figure would loom up out of the crowd: Miguel Gonzales, for example, claimed he saw his Indian landlord,[75] and there were vague references to the widespread presence of tailors, hat makers, and shoemakers.[76] But for most observers, the rioters were a faceless and largely uncomprehensible mass. Sigüenza y Góngora's letter, although it mentions no individuals, does at least try to distinguish the activities of the castas and Indians and to estimate the crowd's size, which he places at more than ten thousand when the fires began. Most other elite Spaniards, however, limited themselves to a few contemptuous words describing the rioters as "a mob," "a great mob," "a multitude of riffraff," "an infinity of people," "consisting of Indians and plebeians," "or Indians along with another very base kind of people called mestizos."[77] Some simply stated that "the city" had risen.[78]

Perhaps we should expect no more from men stupefied with amazement or fully engaged in fighting, fleeing, or putting out fires—all the while assaulted by an earsplitting din. The noise was both indescribable and menacing. The single most common term used to describe the riot was *ruido;* and the roar emanating from the plaza, outpacing any rumor or runner, first alerted the residents that something strange and terrible was taking place. They rushed in thousands to its source—many, already suspecting what they would find, came armed with rocks and sticks— and added their voices to the cacophony. Stones rained against the palace doors; these blows, and the crashing and splintering of wood, were clearly audible on the far side of the plaza: Sigüenza y Góngora compared the sound to "more than one hundred drums of war played together."[79] Soldiers discharged harquebuses from the palace rooftop, maintaining fire even after they ran out of bullets.[80] The cathedral bells tolled, and at least some were grateful for a familiar sound amid the chaos.[81] Above all else rose the "confusion and shouting" of the rioters, who "worked their hands and their mouths with equal fervor."[82] The whistles, the curses, the screams, the shouts (which one witness compared to the cries of spectators at a bullfight)—for many, these blended into an unintelligible uproar. The mulatto Pedro de la Cruz, for instance, testified that he "saw many people, most of whom appeared to be Indians, who were shouting [but] he could not perceive what they were saying."[83] Others claimed to make out phrases, usually some version of the traditional "Long live the king and death to bad government!" Perhaps they only heard what they expected to hear; but it is also quite possible that the crowd, drawing on the same expectations, knew that this was the "correct" cry. Several defendants testified that Indian rioters ordered them to shout this and that they obeyed in fear for their lives.[84] Furthermore, the phrase—particularly in the variants that witnesses recorded—seems accurately to reflect the rioters' anger at royal officials for their betrayal of trust, their abuse of authority, their denial of dialogue. "Long live the king and death to this cuckold [a reference to the viceroy]!" "We have to put an end to this, these cuckolds have to die!" "Down with the Spaniards and the 'Gachupines' . . . who are eating up our corn!" "Death to the Viceroy and his wife! Death to the Corregidor!"[85] These shouts, while fitting within the traditional framework, tend to point to specific problems—the mishandling of the maize shortage—and specific culprits—particularly the viceroy. The preference for "cuckold" (*cornudo*) as a term of abuse, also notable in the statements attributed to José de los Santos, is not accidental but rather contains an implicit political message. By impugning the manliness of the viceroy and of the Spaniards in general, it questioned their right to command respect and deference: men who could not control their own women were hardly fit to rule over the entire colony.

The Spaniards, taken aback by the suddenness and scope of the riot, knew the crowd was angry. But, at least in the early stages of the tumulto, they understood little else. Don Diego de Navarijo, who gives one of the most thorough accounts of the riot, at least up to the moment that his vantage point, the royal jail, was set on fire, echoed many other witnesses in admitting that he heard "neither specific voices nor words but only confusion and shouting" and that "he did not know who the principal [rioters] were nor what motives the Indians had for rebelling beyond the shortage of maize."[86] Even the viceroy, who received a stream of reports at the Convento de San Francisco, was largely in the dark. Don Juan de Serecedo, arriving at San Francisco after seven o'clock, found the conde and his advisers still puzzled over "who the rioters were and what their motive was, because no one knew."[87]

If Spanish observers found the crowd incomprehensible, they nevertheless were in broad agreement about the sequence of events—until, that is, the rioters began to cart reeds and matting from the plaza shops to the palace doors and set them on fire. From this point on, the narrative drive of the Spanish accounts starts to falter. Individual accounts do not lose their linearity, but their perspective becomes narrower, more fragmented; in many cases, personal safety now becomes the observer's main concern. The various reports are also increasingly difficult to reconcile. Events cannot be so easily placed in time; for example, did the archbishop enter the plaza, in an unavailing attempt to placate the rioters, before or after the fires started? Time itself seems to expand or contract, depending on the witness. Sigüenza y Góngora describes the fires occurring in a specific order—first the palace, then the cabildo, and finally the plaza shops—over a lengthy stretch of time, perhaps as much as an hour and a half. The Mariscal de Castilla, however, reports that all three had started to burn in the time it took to go to San Francisco and back; Escalante y Mendoza, contracting events even more, says that they were set aflame simultaneously.[88]

I suggest that these contradictions do not result simply from confusion in the heat of the moment. They reflect a genuine change in the nature of the riot. At the beginning, it had a straightforward logic, based on the desire of a small nucleus of protesters to confront and demand justice from the authorities. This brought thousands to a focal point, the doors of the palace. But they achieved no resolution there, either peaceful or violent. They found their hopes for dialogue frustrated, their early attack repulsed. When we pull the evidence together, it is clear that the riot now evolved into something different—a multisided attack on the symbols of Hispanic power. Even as Serecedo received viceregal instructions to reconnoiter the plaza, a group of Indians scaled the facade of the palace and attempted to enter the main balcony; others set fire to the cabildo; still others broke into the plaza stores; a few may already have been heading for home with their loot.[89]

Like a river whose natural channel is blocked, the riot overflowed its original boundaries and found new outlets for its pent-up energies. In the process, the crowd lost its focus and fragmented into smaller groups. Spanish accounts of the riot are strained because they never fully abandon the idea of a unified crowd. They attempt to fit simultaneous events into a linear framework, to depict dispersed actions as part of an orchestrated scheme.

Sigüenza y Góngora provides a good example in his account of incendiary activities at the cabildo.

> Since the Palace was already burning on every side, they [the rioters] passed on to the municipal buildings, where the Corregidor was living, in order to do the same thing. The fact that neither he nor his wife were at home saved their lives. His coach was the first thing that they rushed upon and to which they set fire. And while this was being consumed by the flames, they dragged it rolling about through the whole plaza in triumph. While some were engaged in this and in killing the mules afterwards which were pulling the coach in a frenzy because it was on fire, others brought huge piles of *petates*, reed grass and boards up to the offices of the Public Scribers, the Cabildo where the bound books and judicial records are kept, the office of the Deputation, the public Granary, the public jail and, lighting them all at the same time, the flames exceeded those of the Palace because of being more continuous.[90]

The language implies that the rioters shifted their attention, en masse, to the cabildo, consciously choosing it as the next target for destruction. That is, Sigüenza y Góngora presents us with a single-minded crowd engaged in coordinated actions directed toward specific ends; yet what he actually describes is a variety of activities carried out by different groups at the same time. This internal tension perhaps explains why his prose becomes so clotted in his final, extremely lengthy sentence.

Spanish accounts, then, tend to depict the crowd as a vast octopus, a single will with many outreaching tentacles.[91] But the rioters—once the palace was set on fire—may have more closely approximated a hydra, the multiheaded beast of classical lore. If we recognize this possibility, if we disaggregate the crowd, then much of what is puzzling and murky about the Spanish accounts comes more sharply into focus. For instance, we have already noted the authorities' unsuccessful attempts to identify the leadership of the tumulto. Witnesses nominated several different candidates—a problem in itself—but corroborating evidence was not forthcoming. The likeliest explanation is that these witnesses had not seen leaders of *the* riot but riot leaders, "little chiefs" (*cabecillas*), such as José de los Santos's flag-waving mulatto, who rallied (for brief periods) groups of rebels and looters. These groups may not have been large. Those who saw Indians moving toward the plaza sometimes spoke of "bands" or "troops" (*tropos*) of no more than eight or ten.[92] In the riot proper, each focus of activity apparently included a core of "activists," surrounded by others who, alternately exalted, confused, or amazed, shifted between opportunistic participation, milling about, and simple gaping.

The multiheaded nature of the crowd could also explain the variations heard in the basic cry, "Long live the king and death to bad government!" as well as how Spanish witnesses got close enough to hear these shouts in such detail.[93] The crowd, far from densely packed, was surprisingly permeable, even at the height of the riot. Although some Spaniards claimed to have been thrown back by a solid phalanx of rioters,[94] many others describe themselves entering into the plaza and moving among the crowd without impediment, except for threats and the occasional stone thrown in anger.[95] The movement in and about the palace itself was impressive. Don Juan de Serecedo entered and left the palace on three separate occasions, the last two times bringing guns and ammunition to the palace guards. The court ladies managed to escape via an adjoining building and rejoin their mistress at San Francisco. The prisoners in the public jail, choking on the smoke from the rising flames, broke out of their cell and presented themselves to the warder, offering to do whatever he asked. They later joined the wheelwright Juan de Velasco and five soldiers to make a sortie into the plaza, catching and killing an Indian incendiary.[96] The survival of these people suggests a distracted or divided crowd, for surely a concerted assault by ten thousand rioters would have overwhelmed the poorly armed palace defenders, already stretched to the limit in guarding multiple entrances and putting out fires. Escalante y Mendoza recognized the Spaniards' narrow escape: the mercy of God, he said, had awakened the greed of the rioters, turning them toward robbery and away from their "malicious desire to burn the entire city."[97]

A final advantage of disaggregating the crowd is that it brings us closer to the participants' own view of the riot. Participant accounts tend to view the riot not as a single event with a specific trajectory but as a succession of more and more chaotic scenes. The confession of Miguel Gonzales, the mestizo shoemaker, mirrors the disintegration of the crowd's direction and purpose. He provides a coherent account of the opening moments of the riot, some of which has been quoted above. He notes the attempts to see the archbishop and the viceroy, the beginning of the stone throwing, the growth of the crowd, the sortie of the palace guard, the closing of the doors, the musket fire from the roof, and the wounding of some of the rioters. Finally, Gonzales himself began to take part in the shouting and

rock throwing. This moment, the beginning of Gonzales's active participation, which coincides with a new phase of the riot, the burning of the
palace ("the rest of the people began to set fire to the door of the jail"),
marks a turning point in his narrative.[98] Now, as his account proceeds, his
vision progressively narrows. At first, he talks about the crowd or "people"
(gente), but then he shifts to specific individuals and finally to his own
larcenous activities.

Once the palace had started to burn, Gonzales heard the people say,
"Let's go now to the house of the corregidor!" He hung back among the
tlaquesquales, the reed-built market stalls of the Indians, hoping to use
them as cover against the musket fire from the palace roof. But these stalls
were now being dismantled and their material used to feed the palace
fires. So, shortly thereafter, he

> went toward the house of said corregider . . . and saw that all the doors of the
> said house and the alhóndiga were already burning, and standing watching
> this, he saw that the rioters [*los del ruido*] were breaking open the padlocks
> and prying off the shingles of a clothing store [*cajón de ropa*] . . . in front of
> the alhóndiga and that having opened it, different men entered it, and so did
> the confessant.[99]

The men, including a mulatto prieto, were pulling down clothing from
shelves and filling their pockets from a strongbox on the floor. Gonzales
grabbed three fistfuls of coins and stuffed them into his shirt front; then,
spotting some clothes piled up on a counter, he "took whatever he could
carry in his arms" to a nearby bridge. There he met an Indian woman,
who begged him for a shirt "for the love of God." Gonzales left the clothing in her keeping and went back to raid a different cajón, returning with
another armful of clothing. The two then made off with their booty to his
mother's house. Gonzales left the clothing there but kept the cash on his
person, though he did lend two pesos to a friend, José, so the latter could
get a cape out of hock.[100]

José de los Santos's story follows a similar pattern. Attracted by the
"ruido y voces" of the rioters, de los Santos arrived in the plaza to find a
diverse group of castas and Indians, led by the aforementioned flag-waving
mulatto. This cabecilla caught de los Santos and forced him to shout "Long
live the king and death to bad government!" and then to feed the flames of
the already-burning ayuntamiento. All this he did "out of fear." But then,

> he saw that they were busying themselves with the fire and this witness was
> able to get away from them. . . . He went toward a narrow little store facing
> the ayuntamiento where he saw many persons whom he did not recognize,
> but they appeared to be mulattoes, mestizos, Indians, and many others, who
> were sacking the said store and taking the clothing in it, and throwing it out
> on the plaza.[101]

He entered the store and said to the looters, "Friends, give me something, I am a poor man," and two mulattoes each gave him some cloth (one a piece of gingham, the other a manta), which he took to his house.[102]

In both accounts, once flames began to spread around the plaza, the narrator becomes engrossed in the less collective, more individualistic activity of burning and sacking cajones. Each presents himself as an opportunist, a latecomer to a scene in which the normal rules have been turned upside down. Although the unity of the crowd has begun to dissolve, a free-for-all, carnivalesque atmosphere remains. The "celebrants" at any given cajón are a diverse lot, best described by the Indian cargador Antonio de la Cruz: "a great number of Indian porters, mestizo hat makers, ragged mulattoes, along with many women, Indian, mestizo, and mulatto, all stealing."[103] Cruz joined in wholeheartedly, having already gained some experience: his first move had been to loot his employer's shop.

The rioters shared, if only briefly, a feeling of brotherhood that cut across racial lines and pitted the plebeians against the wealthy. A poorly dressed Spanish youth was heard to proclaim that "he was not on the side of the Spaniards but of the Indians, calling them *compañeros*."[104] Mulatto looters gave some of their booty to José de los Santos, an Indian and a "poor man"; Miguel Gonzales allowed a mendicant Indian woman to become his accomplice. The mestizo hat maker, José Martínez, described himself, another mestizo, and a black man parceling out stolen cash "in good fellowship."[105] Meanwhile, the looters taunted their betters, joking that "the Conde de Santiago is dividing up his goods!" or jeering, "Filthy Spaniards, the merchant fleet has already come. Go on, sissies, to the shops and buy your ribbons and hair-switches."[106] Some shop owners tried to preserve their property by looting their own shops, while others, seeing that they were helpless to stop the looters, gave them an ironic blessing: "Go to it and good luck to you!"[107]

This reign of goodwill would be short-lived, however. The sudden access of wealth temporarily broke through the patronage structure that created competition among plebeians. Quite simply, there was enough for everyone: the original looters, latecomers like Gonzales and de los Santos, even passive recipients of generosity such as Gonzales's Indian accomplice. Yet from the beginning, there had been countercurrents. Some employees looted their shops, but many others guarded them.[108] Some plebeians cared for those wounded in the plaza and took them to hospitals, convents, or even their own homes; but others carried opportunism to an extreme by ambushing the heavily laden looters as they fled.[109] The glow of fellowship was rapidly disappearing, along with the rioters themselves. For the looting marked the last stage of the tumulto,[110] further and finally dispersing the riot's energy, as the participants made their way home, clutching their prizes. Now isolated individuals again, they exchanged their celebratory boldness for caution and furtiveness. Gonzales, for example, hurried to the apartment where his mother lived.

> He asked his mother, Tomasa de la Concepción, . . . for the key, and she did not want to give it to him, and the confessant told her to take that clothing he was carrying, that he could not travel with it because he would be risking his life, and his mother told him in that case she would take it and to slip it under the door.[111]

Many others pursued similar strategies: they left stolen clothing with friends, relatives, or even strangers; they crept back into their houses, trying to avoid the prying eyes of neighbors, claiming that they had only witnessed the riot, or at most, that they had "found" goods lying in the streets.[112] This fearful secrecy marked an ironic coda to the night's activity.

Still, they had good reason to be afraid, for a violent backlash was already taking shape. As mentioned above, the Spanish reaction to the riot had never been wholly passive and defensive. Spaniards moved among the crowd or escaped through it. The archbishop made a failed attempt to appeal to the rioters' consciences; the Conde de Santiago even led a charge into the crowd, albeit with unhappy results, as he was felled and knocked senseless by a stone.[113] Now, as the crowd began to disperse, the Spaniards grew bolder—though their counterattack, like the riot itself, was disorganized and disparate. Shortly after seven o'clock, armed Spaniards—as individuals or in small groups—began to venture into the plaza to take vengeance.[114] Don Juan Pérez Merino and Don Antonio de Deza y Ulloa each led bands of men who cut a swath though the plaza, "giving them [the rioters] . . . the punishment they merited, killing and wounding everyone [they] could given the extreme confusion of that night."[115]

Meanwhile, various clergymen tried, with some success, to pacify the crowd with moral suasion rather than swords. Reportedly, the church *provisor*[116] and treasurer, the latter holding the Holy Sacrament, dissuaded rioters from burning the palace of the Marqués del Valle.[117] Calming the aroused passions of the Spaniards proved more difficult, however. Priests and friars, for example, attempted to intervene with Deza y Ulloa on behalf of the now-vulnerable rioters: "They begged me not to harm them with different exclamations, to which I responded . . . that I was going to punish such enormous irreverence . . . and I continued to skirmish through the plaza."[118] Echoes of Spanish fury reached the outskirts of the city. Three Indians returning from the San Juan barrio were warned to get off the streets immediately, because Indians were being killed ("han matando a los naturales").[119]

The Spanish backlash delivered the coup de grace to the tumulto. At six o'clock, "the Indians were owners and masters of the plaza"; by ten o'clock, "there was no longer a single thief" there.[120] The plaza was now eerily empty, save for the bodies of the dead and wounded. The riot had run its course in a few brief hours, leaving behind vast destruction and smoldering Spanish anger.[121]

As the riot petered out, the viceroy and his advisers could at last clearly assess the situation and formulate a coherent response. Galve's plan aimed at (1) resolving the immediate food shortage; (2) preventing the further spread of the fire; and (3) organizing a large temporary militia. The most pressing concern was to ensure Monday's maize supply. Even before the riot ended, Galve had sent a city councillor to Chalco with instructions to secure all the available maize and dispatch it to Mexico City by canoe. Francisco de Sigüenza (the brother of Carlos) received orders to "convey and escort" any maize arriving along the road from Celaya. By noon Monday, the two men had delivered over one thousand fanegas to the alhóndiga.[122] The viceroy also sent an official to inspect the city's panaderías; but their largely indigenous work force seemed little affected by the riot. Indeed, the bakers responded to the crisis by producing an extra large quantity of dough.[123]

At least in the short run, combustion proved a sterner adversary than hunger. Mexico City, of course, had no fire-fighting equipment as such, no effective means to douse the flames, which were now visible from nearby haciendas. The fire had to burn itself out over the course of several days. The best the Spaniards could do was to set up firebreaks to prevent the flames from spreading.[124]

Spanish authority had been ravaged along with the palace, the cabildo, and the merchant's shop. To stem plebeian insolence and forestall future revolts, the Spaniards needed to summon up a credible military presence forthwith. The viceroy assigned Don Luis Saénz de Tagle, one of the city's wealthiest silver merchants,[125] the task of raising a merchant militia. Traveling door to door in the dead of the night, the newly appointed captain met with an enthusiastic response. By four o'clock Monday morning, more than two hundred armed men had assembled in the plaza.[126] Saénz de Tagle gave them a free supply of powder and ammunition. He proudly told the viceroy,

> Having learned that your Excellency had ordered the companies paid I replied that the merchant militia need not cost his Majesty even one peso, and I publicly said that he who needed pay should come to my house for it, that I would give it to him from my own funds, and everyone responded unanimously that all they wanted was to serve his Majesty.[127]

The artisan guilds, beginning on Monday with the tailors, also contributed militiamen. In addition, the viceroy issued a general call to arms,

asking "all the vecinos" of the city to enlist in temporary militia companies. The Conde de Santiago took command of these units, which by the
end of June had taken regular (and permanent) form. They consisted of
two companies, whose members served on a rotating basis, each company
maintaining twenty-five men on duty at any given time. Those forced to
absent themselves from their normal work received a daily wage: six reales
for cavalrymen, four reales for infantrymen.[128]

That first morning, the soldiers—whatever their symbolic impact—took
little direct action beyond combating fires and escorting the viceroy to
his new quarters in the palace of the Marqués del Valle. Nevertheless,
one group of soldiers, headed by Don Francisco de la Cueva, caught several suspects near the plaza in the hours before dawn. All of them—
two Indians, a mestizo, an Afro-Mexican, and a Spaniard—were carrying bundles or baskets of clothing; one of the Indians also had a hammer
(which Cueva interpreted as a weapon). Later, at 8:30, the same soldiers
responded to "information that a quantity of clothing could be found in a
house on the Calle de Aguila . . . and having broken down the door and
searched the aposento, they found a bundle of clothes beneath a bed and
an Indian on the roof whom they arrested."[129]

These actions—the easily aroused suspicions, quick arrests, and readiness to violate private property to recover stolen goods—set the pattern
for Spanish retaliation. The search for rioters and looters would become
systematized the next day, Tuesday, when the viceroy placed a guard on
the wounded men who had entered city hospitals since the riot, posted
sentries on the roads out of town, and dispatched soldiers to search Indian
barrios.[130] Arrests proliferated, as Spaniards pounced quickly on any evidence of wrongdoing. The most common targets were plebeians—especially Indians—who possessed suspiciously fine goods or clothing. For
example, Lorenzo de los Reyes, publicly sporting a new green cape, found
himself in jail when he fell apart under questioning.[131] A few suspects,
grown wise too late, were caught digging holes in their gardens (or even
in a public dunghill) to cache their treasures.[132] Spaniards also regarded
flight from the city as an admission of guilt.[133] At their worst, the authorities were indiscriminate, apprehending an entire group for the guilt of a
single member; in one instance, officers swept down on a set of jacales and
jailed everyone they found there, including such innocent bystanders as a
traveling shoe repair man and a visiting tailor mending a pair of hose.[134]

Yet most often the Spaniards found their suspicions verified, perhaps
because the arresting officers (like Francisco de la Cueva) frequently acted
on inside information. Many citizens enthusiastically cooperated with the
authorities or indeed took action on their own. Consider the story of how
Andrés Dávalos, a royal secretary, came to the aid of María de Villagrán.

On Tuesday, June 10, Villagrán had called out to Dávalos as he passed her home. Through tears, she explained that on the night of the riot, a mulatto (later shown to be Antonio de Arano) had given her daughter Juana some clothing, charging her to guard it until he returned. Dávalos decided to stay in the house, hoping to catch the mulatto. He did come, shortly after seven o'clock, but when the overeager Spaniard invited him in, Arano (perhaps startled by an unexpected masculine voice) fled. He returned early the next morning, however, after Dávalos had left, rushing into the house, brandishing a dagger, and making threats, until Villagrán, in fear for her life, gave him his package. When Dávalos discovered what had happened in his absence, he tracked Arano to a nearly church. Then, "disguising himself," he managed to talk Arano into coming out; thereupon he apprehended the mulatto and forced him to lead the way to his house, where Dávalos found the fruits of robbery inside a mattress.[135]

Other vecinos stopped short of capturing the culprit but did take on (as we have seen in chap. 2) the traditional task of *haciendo diligencias*, gathering information and evidence. The cheek-by-jowl existence of apartment dwellers lent itself particularly well to such activities, which evinced an unusual disregard for the sensibilities of those under suspicion. In one casa de vecindad, several neighbors had seen the casta artisan, José Martínez, enter the building at eight o'clock on the night of the riot with a package beneath his cape. Martínez explained that it contained a few worthless items belonging to his mother. But, their suspicions aroused, three Spanish residents took it on themselves to search Martínez's room the next day. When he refused to give them the key to his strongbox, they broke it open.[136] In another instance, Baltasar de Coca, a shop owner, had traced stolen clothing to the apartments of the Casa de Comedias. In the patio, two Spanish women listened to his tale and suggested that he search the rooms of the mestizo brothers, Juan de Dios and Antonio Ramos. As in the previous example, the search did not go unrewarded: in a "dark corner," Coca found three pieces of fine cloth, various petticoats, and other goods, all from his cajón. Putting on a brave front, Dios and Ramos demanded a receipt![137]

The campaign against the rioters did not depend on the Spaniards alone. The riot and its aftermath threw the fault lines of plebeian society into stark relief. Just as some Spaniards sided with the crowd, some plebeians and castas sided with the elite. The defenders of the palace included several convicts and at least one free black.[138] Under the circumstances, they had little choice but to cooperate; however, others willingly and eagerly struck a blow against the rebels. Two slaves, Ignacio de Colón and Agustín de la Cruz, saw a wounded Indian making off with a well-filled manta while giving the traditional antigovernment cry; Colón unsuccessfully tried to take the manta, then decided on a simpler expedient: "He hit him once or twice on the head with a stick" and placed the now unresisting Indian in his master's obraje.[139] Mulatto soldiers, already organized into professional units, were among those who kept the peace in the riot's aftermath. The citizen militias, given their provision for daily wages, certainly contained journeymen, artisans, and other workmen, and the viceregal proclamation that established these companies specifically invited "mulattoes and mestizos" to join.[140]

This decree probably reflected the widespread belief that the riot had been largely an indigenous uprising. Clearly, the authorities singled out Indians for special attention,[141] and in the face of sweeping and often indiscriminate arrests, they may have felt particularly vulnerable. One event indicative of Indian edginess occurred in the early morning of June 12. Residents of an apartment building near the Royal Hospital were surprised by a sudden shower—of clothing. The clothes had been thrown from the roof by Indians,[142] apparently to dispose of potential evidence or at least to prevent the stolen goods from being linked to any particular individual; this would give the authorities a prima facie case as leverage to obtain a confession, the disclosure of more names, and a widening circle of indictments.

The threat of betrayal was omnipresent. Under the pressure of an investigation, neighborliness, ethnic solidarity, even friendship went by the boards. The most piteous cases were those who, frightened by the experience of arrest and questioning, unwillingly betrayed their nearest and dearest.[143] More commonly, the accused deliberately informed on others, to shift the blame and soften their own sentences. Baltasar de Coca's diligencias, which merged into a broader official investigation, provide an excellent example of how these stresses multiplied and ultimately tore apart the close-knit community of a casa de vecindad. Although Coca had gathered evidence against two mestizo brothers, most of those arrested were Indian. The finger pointing began almost immediately, as the witnesses struggled to explain away stolen clothing found in their rooms.

Juan Esteban claimed that he was merely a visitor from Toluca, staying temporarily in the apartment, and that he had not seen or heard anything (thereby implicitly casting blame on his landlord).[144] Juan de Santiago declared that his brother had brought the stolen merchandise to his apartment. A more complex set of accusations and counteraccusations involved an Indian couple, Miguel Jiménez and Pascuala de los Angeles, Miguel's brother, Nicolás Jiménez, and his former lover (and friend of Pascuala), Sebastiana Francisca. Miguel and Pascuala both claimed that Sebastiana had left the damning bundle of clothing in their rooms and then run away. Sebastiana told a more convoluted (and to the Spanish court, more believable) story. She and Nicolás had left the plaza when the riot began to heat up and had gone to his brother's house. A quarrel ensued, so they left; but Nicolás had come across some newly enriched Indians and robbed them in turn, bringing his ill-gotten gains back to Miguel. According to Sebastiana, Miguel and Pascuala were lying in an attempt to shield Nicolás.[145] This story of taking goods from Indian looters was a popular last-ditch defense; Juan de Dios, one of the mestizos originally accused by Coca, used it as well.[146] Fearful, perhaps, of similar disclosures—or fabrications—the remaining Indians living in the Casa de Comedias fled the very day of the arrests.[147]

A series of viceregal decrees supported and strengthed the Spaniards' divide-and-conquer strategy. On June 9, the Conde de Galve ordered that no more than four Indians could walk the streets together; this antiriot measure most likely also aimed at isolating perpetrators for easier arrest and interrogation. The viceroy also forbade the purchase of goods from anyone "Indian, black, mulatto, or Spaniard" who was not "commonly [*notoriamente*] known as a merchant, under pain of two years [exile] in the Philippines for Spaniards, and for those of *color quebrado* [i.e., castas] two hundred lashes and two years in an obraje."[148] Looters now found themselves trapped with goods that they could not dispose of and with which they could not afford to be caught.

This dilemma is best illustrated, once again, by Miguel Gonzales. The reader will recall that Gonzales took his booty from the cajones to the home of his mother, Tomasa de la Concepción, who rather unwillingly agreed to keep it. By the next day, when her son had returned with his wife, her doubts had grown. Tomasa refused to accept money from Gonzales and tried to give the clothing back. Gonzales finally told her his story— although he put his actions in the best possible light, saying that he had taken the money from a mulatto thief and had picked up a few pieces of clothing lying on the ground. But Tomasa was still uneasy; she had learned that soldiers and clerics were searching for stolen items and had heard that the robbers and looters would be excommunicated. On Tuesday, she insisted that her son take the clothing and turn it over to the Jesuits. Gonzales complied, carrying as much as he dared—some stockings, a manta, a shawl—and leaving them with the gatekeeper at the Jesuit church. But he refused to make another such delivery: "there were so many soldiers about," "the neighbors were watching him, he could not be seen" with suspect clothing. Indeed, although he did not tell his mother, Gonzales had already decided to leave the city "for fear of being imprisoned." On Wednesday, having heard nothing further from her son, Tomasa took the rest of the clothing to a priest, Lic. Alonso de Ensinas.[149] Plebeians thus succumbed to Spanish authority. The strength and unity so briefly captured on the night of June 8 had ebbed away, leaving them exposed and vulnerable. External threats—avenging soldiers, prying neighbors, untrustworthy friends—were compounded with internal doubts. If guilt and fear plagued Tomasa de la Concepción, a mere accessory whom the Spanish did not even prosecute, what can we say about the feelings of prisoners on trial for their lives? Most tried to save themselves somehow—by denying their involvement, by claiming they were drunk,[150] or by admitting to lesser offenses. However, a few—Gonzales notable among them—favored the prosecutors with complete, detailed confessions, answering, elaborating, talking until their words had condemned them to death, and then going on, as if they needed to explain their actions less to their captors than to themselves. They seemed surprised, in retrospect, by their own boldness and unable to come to terms with what they had done.[151]

Even as the arrests and investigations proceeded, the first executions took place. On June 11, just three days after the riot, the court handed down death sentences for three Indians caught in the act of setting fire to the palace. (A fourth man, Francisco Gregorio, also found guilty, had died in prison.) Their execution, carried out later that day, was a public ritual, carefully choreographed as a demonstration of the terrible majesty of the law, a dramatic reassertion of Hispanic power. A few nights before, the social hierarchy had been shaken; in the words of a Carmelite friar, "We have seen [the Indians] so shamelessly come to lose respect for the Spaniards, that they could think of raising a rebellion; of exciting sedition, of setting fire to the *cajones* in the plaza, of sacking and burning the cabildo! And what is most amazing, they had the insolence to set fire to all parts of the Royal Palace! In Mexico City, the head of the great and powerful Mexican Empire!"[152] Now, the legal authorities would present a species of counter-theater, "the world turned right side up again," publicly reclaiming the city beginning with the "contested space" at its heart—the plaza mayor.[153]

The condemned men, "in the midst of a squadron of the royal palace guard . . . on foot with their hands tied behind their backs, accompanied by many priests, . . . arrived at the plaza mayor of the city in front of the said royal palace, where three poles had been placed to which the said Melchor de León, Felipe de la Cruz, and Nicolás de la Cruz were tied, and by the voice of Diego Velásquez, public crier, . . . the sentence was pronounced."[154] Before a "concourse of many people"—assembled for a far different purpose than the crowd of June 8—the three men each received a musket shot in the back of the head. Their skulls were, quite literally, blown apart, "broken in pieces so that no form of head [*forma de cabezas*] remained." Then, along with the body of Francisco Gregorio, they were hanged on the plaza gallows, newly mounted after being burned

Table 7.1. Sentences for riot participants

Sentence	Number	Percentage
Capital punishment	15[a]	17.4
Corporal punishment	13	15.1
Labor service	4	4.7
Corporal punishment and labor service	25	29.1
Public humiliation	2	2.3
Public humiliation and exile	1	1.2
Absolved	26	30.2
	86	

Source: AGI, Patronato, leg. 226, no. 1, rs. 3–15.
[a]Includes five condemned men who died in prison and whose corpses were publicly hanged.

in the riot: Gregorio by the neck, the others by their arms. As a final, grisly reminder of the price of rebellion, their right hands were chopped off and displayed on poles in city squares.[155]

The courts continued to operate with remarkable dispatch. The seven-week trial given to José de los Santos (see above) was quite exceptional; nearly all the other suspects had been tried and sentenced by June 27.[156] The trial of a dozen Indians charged with rioting and looting—to cite one example—achieved a Solomon Grundy-style efficiency: arrests and interrogation on Tuesday, corroborating evidence on Thursday, further testimony on Friday, additional corroboration on Saturday, sentencing on Wednesday.[157] And this procedure set no record. Two Indians and a mestizo, also charged with looting, were arrested (at 10 A.M.), tried, and sentenced the same day.[158]

Working at this pace, the courts could hardly retain the scrupulous attention to detail and careful consideration of circumstantial evidence that characterized the Spanish judiciary. The trial records clearly show that possession of stolen goods counted as sufficient proof of larceny; similarly, any wounded man brought to city hospitals in the riot's aftermath was considered a participant—no "spectator" or "innocent bystander" category existed. Attorneys for the accused had no time to build an adequate defense, and in any case, their objections were generally given short shrift.

The sentences handed down were exceptionally severe. Table 7.1 demonstrates the infrequency of relatively mild punishments, such as public humiliation or fines. Among noncapital convictions, more than one-half included corporal punishment, with one hundred lashes as a minimum, two hundred as the usual quota. The single most common penalty was a combination of flogging and forced labor service, from two to ten years in duration. Even more striking are the fifteen death sentences—ten if we exclude those "hanged" after death—meted out by a legal system that might normally see years pass between executions. Taylor's study of central Mexican homicides from 1790 to 1810 provides a standard for comparison. In his study of 156 trials, Taylor documented a marked preference for utilitarian punishment—forced labor—and a disinclination to inflict either capital or corporal punishment. He found only four instances of each of the latter. He notes, by way of contrast, that the Acordada, a tribunal concerned mainly with the problem of highwaymen, "passed down most of the late colonial death sentences." In its most intense phase, the Acordada ordered fifty-five executions between December 1742 and January 1746, that is, about three every two months.[159] In June 1692, however, Mexico City witnessed nine executions and nearly thirty public floggings in the space of two and a half weeks—one of the most concentrated displays of judicial violence in the capital's history, surpassed only by the execution of black "conspirators" in 1612 and the great autos-da-fé of 1596 and 1646–1649.[160] The tumulto of 1692 verifies Taylor's contention that the courts could afford to be lenient "as long the lower classes . . . lacked group consciousness and were not mobilized in a class war or a struggle against Spanish rule."[161] But plebeian mobilization, even in the incipient, short-lived form of a corn riot, brought forth the more savage, vindictive side of Spanish justice.

Yet for all this, the prosecution of suspect rioters did not turn into a mere witch-hunt. As we have seen, the accused were allowed legal representation. The trials, although rushed, were recorded in detail. The courts employed torture—a considerable rarity—but kept the standard safeguards, including the presence of a defense attorney, limits to the number and duration of tortures inflicted, and the opportunity to retract a confession made under torture the following day.[162] The best evidence, of coure, is that 30 percent of those arrested were absolved. Many of these had been victims of group arrests; the courts supplied the discrimination lacking in constables and soldiers. The magistrates thus refused to abandon themselves to a crisis mentality; they bent the rules but did not break them.

If these proceedings preserved a modicum of fairness, if most of the people convicted did actually participate in one phase or another of the riot, then the trial records might furnish a roughly representative sample of the June 8 crowd. At any rate, this is our only hope for going beyond the impressionistic accounts of eyewitnesses. An analysis of these records provides three noteworthy suggestions about the crowd's composition. First, Indians predominated. We can see in table 7.2 that Indians outnumbered all other groups combined, by at least two-to-one, in every category of sentencing. The results may be biased by the Spaniards' belief that the riot

Table 7.2. Sentences for riot participants, by race

Race	Sentences: Capital Punishment	Corporal Punishment and/or Labor Service	Other	Absolved
Indians	11 (73.3%)	32 (76.2%)	2 (66.7%)	20 (76.7%)
Mestizo/castizo	2 (13.3%)	6 (14.3%)	0	4 (15.4%)
Mulatto	1 (6.7%)	2 (4.7%)	0	2 (7.7%)
Spanish	1 (6.7%)	2 (4.7%)	1 (33.3%)	0
Total	15	42	3	26

Source: AGI, Patronato, leg. 226, no. 1, rs. 3–15.

was a tumulto de indios; perhaps they concentrated on rounding up Indians and let castas and Spaniards slip through their net. However, a disproportionately large number of Indian participants is supported by evidence from two groups whose presence in the plaza is undeniable: the dead and the wounded. Of the eighteen wounded men treated in city hospitals after the riot, thirteen were Indian.[163] The plaza corpses, according to Saénz de Tagle, consisted of "nine Indians and mestizos, one mulatto, . . . and two Spaniards."[164] On this issue, the Spanish accounts of the riot, which tend to depict the crowd as multiracial but with an Indian majority, appear to be accurate.

Second, women played a relatively minor role. This is a surprising conclusion for a variety of reasons. 1.) "Women were regular and active participants in the riotous local rebellions" of rural Mexico; they "led a large minority of these rebellions and constituted a majority of participants in most of them."[165] 2.) We have argued above that the riot grew out of the politics (in the broad sense) of the grain crisis, or as a contemporary observer put it, "This rebellion did not come from any pulqueriá but from the alhóndiga."[166] Yet purchasing and preparing maize was a female task. Women constituted the granary's chief customers; and the mistreatment of women by alhóndiga officials helped trigger the riot (recall the incident of the "dead" woman). 3.) Several witnesses emphasized the presence of both men and women in the crowd.[167] Sigüenza y Góngora, in particular, heaped opprobrium on Indian women for instigation and exhortation of the rioters: "'Ah señoras,' the Indian women kept saying to each other in their own language, 'let us go joyfully into this strife. If God wills that the Spaniards be wiped out in it, it does not matter if we die without confession!'"[168]

Yet the courts convicted only seven women, all on the same grounds: possession of stolen property, which implied looting. All received an iden-

Table 7.3. Occupations of convicted defendants

Skilled Workers		Unskilled Workers	
Shoemakers	5	Porters	6
Hat makers	5	Peons	3
Tailors	4	Water carriers	2
Bricklayers	2	Other	2
Other artisans	8		
Apprentices	3		
Other	4		
Total	31		13

Source: AGI, Patronato, leg. 226, no. 1, rs. 3–15.

tical sentence: two hundred lashes. This was of course a humiliating and physically dangerous punishment, but it fell short of a capital sentence, which we may take to mean that the court did not believe that these women had taken part in the riot proper. Furthermore, women are absent among the plaza dead and wounded.[169] Participant accounts of the riot also treat them as a marginal element. A good example is the Indian woman who acted as Gonzales's accomplice. One must accord some leeway to the common male tendency to view women in a passive light. Still, the preponderance of evidence indicates that women indeed participated in the riot, especially in its early moments, but that they played a secondary role, urging on and supporting their men but perhaps hanging back from more direct and violent actions, such as assaulting the palace. One witness, the mulatto slave Francisco de Medina, illustrated this point by describing a sexual division of labor among the rioters: "The Indian women gathered rocks and gave them to the Indian men to throw."[170]

If this conclusion is correct, why were these women less aggressive than their rural sisters? John Tutino points to a possible answer when he suggests that peasant women were more independent minded and intransigent than their male counterparts because, unlike men, they were shielded from "regular reminders of their subordination within the colonial structure."[171] But this would not apply in an urban setting like Mexico City, where women lined up daily to receive maize at the alhóndiga.

Third, while the rioters were plebeian, they were far from the dregs of society. Artisans formed a clear majority of the condemned—in the case of castas and Spaniards, an overwhelming majority (see tables 7.3 and 7.4). These findings are in accord with studies of riots in ancien régime Europe, which have concluded that the *menu peuple*—artisans, peddlers, shopkeepers, and so on—rather than "slum dwellers and criminals" were "the main shock troops of preindustrial crowds."[172] But surely, we might

Table 7.4. Occupations of convicted Indian defendants

Skilled Workers		Unskilled Workers	
Shoemakers	3	Porters	6
Hat makers	3	Peons	3
Tailors	2	Water carriers	2
Bricklayers	2	Muleteer	1
Other artisans	6		
Apprentices	2		
Other	2		
Total	20		12

Source: AGI, Patronato, leg. 226, no. 1, rs. 3–15.

argue, the ethnic variety of Mexico City created special complications. Have we not just seen that this was an Indian riot? It would be unwise, however, to emulate elite Spaniards by treating the indigenous population as an undifferentiated mass. In fact, the Indians convicted of rioting and looting were rather atypical. For instance, two-thirds of them lived and worked in the traza, which contradicts the many observers who pinned the blame for the riot on the Indians of Santiago Tlatelolco. Furthermore, the occupational status of these Indians, while less favorable than that of their casta and Spanish counterparts, is still strikingly high. Let us pause to examine table 7.4 in light of our discussion, in chapter 5, of Indian occupational patterns. Table 5.2 presented a census that suggested that a surprisingly large number of traza Indians (over 40% of this sample) were skilled workers. The 1692 convicts have similar characteristics but in an exaggerated form. The same craft skills dominate—shoemakers, hat makers, bricklayers, and tailors represent over half of all artisians in both groups—but in table 7.4, skilled workers outnumber unskilled by a five-to-three ratio. Moreover, servants, who may have constituted 15 percent of the labor force in table 5.2, are completely absent from the 1692 sample.

If we can generalize from the trial records, then, Indian participation in the riot was skewed toward a particular subset of the indigenous population, one that was comparatively well integrated into the broader plebeian society; artisians, after all, formed the most ethnically diverse social sector. By plebeian standards, these people lived fairly comfortably and independently. They did not rely on direct patronage from Spaniards (note again the absence of servants in table 7.4). This independence, however, left them without a safety net in times of crisis, except for government paternalism. Yet at their most vulnerable moment, when they faced economic disaster, the government and its archpatron, the viceroy, had betrayed them, had quite literally closed the doors against them. For Indians, the special object of so much solicitous legislation, this betrayal may have been particularly galling. In any case, they took a leadership role, spearheading a short-lived, multiethnic uprising against such arrogant yet inadequate patrons.

The failure of dialogue that triggered the riot persisted in the post-mortem views of this event. The Spaniards, harshly reminded of their perch atop a human volcano, sought above all else for an explanation, for some way to make sense of the riot, to accommodate it to their world view. The most sophisticated analysts of the riot cannot be condemned as mono-causal theorists, since they invoked a wide variety of "deeper" causes for the riot: God's wrath against Spanish pride; an unfavorable planetary con-junction; the centuries-old Indian hatred for Spaniards: and, of course, the corn shortage.[173] But ultimately they turned toward a conspiracy model, for what obsessed them about the riot was the sheer insolence of the mob. A feeling of "how dare they!" colors all their accounts. Such boldness, they reasoned, was not happenstance but instead revealed a malevolent intelli-gence, a cunningly devised plot—hence the Spaniards' fruitless search for leaders of the riot.

Plebeian participants, in contrast, show little concern for the causes of the riot, which they viewed as largely inexplicable. For them, the riot was a liminal, almost festive event, a moment of sudden and sharp role reversal but one that could not last. Indeed, the spontaneous nature of the riot—the lack of a conspiracy—accounts for its evanescent impact on elite-plebeian relations. The riot began as a political message but degen-erated as it proceeded, its political content seeping away, until it ended as an "every man for himself" orgy of looting. These activities were de-structive and threatening in their own way, of course, but they neither posed a long-term challenge to Spanish authority nor offered permanent benefits for plebeians. The structure of Hispanic domination could not be dismantled in a day.

Conclusion

In 1763, Miguel Cabrera, Mexico's most renowned artist, executed an unusual series of paintings. At first sight, each painting seems a normal family portrait, with husband, wife, and child. On closer examination, a striking feature emerges: each family member belongs to a different race. Cabrera's entry into the genre of *pintura de castas*, which enjoyed an eighteenth-century vogue, is no mere curiosity or academic exercise but carries a definite social and political meaning. Such paintings attempted to confront and control the threat of mestizaje by presenting Mexico's racial divisions as objective, almost Linnaean categories. The subjects' skin color, dress, and activities—Spaniards are seen at indolent repose or striking a commanding attitude, while their inferiors perform manual labor, change diapers, argue vociferously, and so on—all are meant to show that Mexico's racial groups were well defined, natural, and inevitable.[1]

Cabrera's paintings portrayed the kind of society that elite Spaniards had always longed for: hierarchical, orderly, and controlled, a society in which racial difference marked and determined status. Such arrangements, however, are more easily obtained on canvas than in real life. As we have seen, castas and plebeians found ways to resist, even to manipulate, their social betters. Moreover, Spanish vecinos, as a corporate group, exercised limited disciplinary power. On occasion, as after the 1692 riot, the upholders of wealth and position would speak with a single voice, but in general, Mexico City's ruling class was hardly monolithic. How could it be, when the government daily engaged in a balancing act, playing off creole against peninsular and striking compromises between royal authority and colonial claims?[2] New Spain's racial code developed in the interstices of this system, relying heavily on improvisation and patchwork. The importance of maintaining a strict racial hierarchy may have seemed self-evident to local elites; the crown's commitment to this principle was more questionable. The institutional status of the sistema de castas left much to be desired. To function effectively, the sistema required a careful and systematic distribution of rights, privileges, and obligations, so that racial divisions would be clearly demarcated. Colonial legislation was far too inconsistent for this purpose. Some laws distinguished between different casta groups, but others lumped all mixed-bloods together. When the viceroy ordered the incorporation of mestizos and mulattoes into the post-

161

riot militias, he reinforced yet another (and older) model of society, the dichotomy between the Hispanic and Indian "republics." Moreover, legislation was unevenly enforced, frequently set aside in particular cases— recall the castas who received permission to bear arms—and in many instances, ignored altogether. Even slavery, an institution legally restricted to specific racial categories, did not provide an unambiguous assertion of racial hierarchy. Most blacks were slaves, but most mulattoes were not. When a mulatto could own other mulattoes, property rights prevailed over racial order.

What of the cultural realm? Mexico City did not lack symbolic demonstrations of Hispanic power and authority: the massive solidity of the churches, governmental buildings, and elite residences; the yearly round of rites, festivals, and processions sponsored by the church; the ritualized display of justice performed at the auto-da-fé and the public execution. Perhaps these succeeded in overawing the populace,[3] but what did they have to do with distinguishing castizos from mestizos, mulattoes from blacks? The "message" encoded in these structures and performances no doubt upheld the principle of hierarchy in a general sense, but it is difficult to see how this specifically reinforced the sistema de castas. The sistema was not ritually woven into the fabric of daily life. The casta paintings mentioned above and the greatly elaborated versions of the sistema developed during the eighteenth century circulated among the elite and may have given them some psychological comfort, but they had little or no effect on the castas themselves.

Finally, the city's socioeconomic structure actually militated against the development of a fully effective racial hierarchy. Imagine the sistema de castas as dual ladders, one for race and one for class, that parallel and reinforce each other, so that a specific racial label becomes naturally associated with a specific economic status. Now, how did capitalino conditions fail to meet these requirements? The problem was that the "economic" ladder lacked sufficient rungs, or put another way, that the socioeconomic structure of Mexico City more closely approximated a pyramid, with the vast majority of people languishing at the bottom.[4] In short, most castas were poor: many faced permanent or frequent unemployment; the fortunate ones worked as laborers, servants, or, at best, artisans. Any advantage that, for instance, a mestizo had over a mulatto in clambering on to the next level was so minor, I suggest, that few would allow their lives to be dominated by a desire for racial improvement, let alone thoughts of marrying "up" to improve their descendants' status. If we use Seed's figures (see chap. 5), in 1753 thirty-one mestizos—6.2 percent of mestizo males in the census—belonged to the "elite" or "shop owner" groups; the equivalent figure for mulattoes was thirty-eight, or 3.5 percent. Setting aside the likelihood that many of these elite castas achieved their positions through family connections, a mulatto who became a mestizo to improve his chances of entering these categories would still face odds of sixteen-to-one. Would this possibility weigh heavily on everyday behavior? Plebeians were more likely to spend their time finding their next meal.

Deprivation thus brought people of different races together and gave them similar life chances and similar positions vis-à-vis the elite. An inequitable society that rewarded the few and impoverished the many was fertile soil for the growth of a subculture based on the shared experience of the urban poor. This multiracial subculture was a source of collective strength, creating a certain space for ideological independence. I have attempted, by using a wide variety of sources and by paying careful attention to how the plebeians' themselves understood "race," to demonstrate that the castas did respond creatively to the elite's racial ideology. They rejected or modified the sistema de castas and even appropriated its racial categories for their own use.

One might take the argument a step further. However carefully we read them, these sources—all, to a greater or lesser extent, "official"—may still overstate the importance of racial hierarchy for the castas. One occasionally catches glimpses of a vaster indifference to racial labeling. While confessing his participation in the riot of 1692, Miguel Gonzales was asked why he had failed to identify the caste [*calidad*] of his friend José in previous testimony. He explained that he had not known it "for certain." José's mother was a mestiza, but Gonzales did not know his father, and José himself appeared to be a chino![5] This dissonance frustrated the authorities, but Gonzales (and, I would argue, most plebeians) did not share this need for certainty, this desire to assign each person a single, fixed place in the social hierarchy. Perhaps castas had a dual perspective on race, just as Mexico's indigenous peoples were "Indians" when they dealt with the colonial bureaucracy but still maintained a localized ethnic identity.[6]

The true burden of social control fell largely on the shoulders of individual Spaniards. Each Spanish patron was responsible for controlling "his" castas. Conversely, plebeians had certain expectations of their patrons. Furthermore, they extended the idiom of patronage into their relationship with government officials, whom they expected to dispense "justice"—a notion that included maintaining a minimal standard of social welfare. The economic component of patronage networks gave them a direct impact on plebeian life, a concrete reality that the sistema de castas lacked. Indeed, insofar as the elite racial ideology penetrated into the plebeian mentality, it probably did so most effectively along these networks, via the patrons' hiring practices, treatment of non-Spaniards, and general racial attitudes. The everyday, face-to-face nature of patron-client relations allowed for a degree of fine tuning impossible with a blunt weapon like royal cédulas. Yet here too exceptions flourished. Patronage was hardly dispensed according to exacting racial standards. Personal knowledge intervened; an employer would testify to the good character of his mestizo worker, or leave a substantial legacy to a black servant, precisely on the grounds that this particular casta was not "typical." In addition, patrons naturally took into account their own economic well-being. If a mulatto trader was a good credit risk, his putative racial inferiority ceased to be a significant issue.

The imperfect concordance between the racial hierarchy and the patronage system, however, did not prevent the latter from functioning as a system of social control. It was the act of discrimination, not its motive, that was important. By favoring some plebeians over others, by distributing rewards unevenly, by pitting clients against each other in a struggle to cut the best possible deal for themselves and their families, patronage networks divided the urban poor, opening fault lines in plebeian society. They also co-opted the more "successful" castas, integrating them into a system dominated, in the last analysis, by the elite.

The tumulto of 1692 showed that this system was not perfect. Traza Indians, who lived under the sway of Spanish householders, and artisans, who functioned as key middlemen in chains of clientage, both played central roles on June 8. But the riot and its aftermath also revealed that plebeians had neither the vision nor the mechanisms to construct an alternative to the colonial regime. The plebeian subculture, well adapted for daily resistance, could not easily be converted into the basis for effective political action. The riot began as a protest within the idiom of patron-client relations; denied their rightful dialogue with the viceroy, protesters became rioters, mounting an impressive but ultimately futile attack on their Hispanic overlords. Even at an early stage, the crowd began to fragment. Once the rioters' immediate moral rage cooled, they quickly—within a handful of hours—became vulnerable not simply to state-sponsored violence but to elite manipulation. The denouement featured scenes of plebeian accusation and counteraccusation, tale bearing, and betrayal.

Nevertheless, the elite did not have things all its own way. The castas' resistance to Hispanic ideology was part of a broader resilience that marked plebeian society. To improve their lives, plebeians begged, borrowed, and stole; they also worked hard, made shrewd business deals, joined cofradías, and badgered the legal authorities to enforce their rights. The patron-client system, as an individualistic method of social control, enacted a price. Elite-plebeian relations had to be constantly renegotiated, hammered out daily in thousands of implicit contracts with members of the plebe who were not passive, alienated, or crushed by feelings of racial inferiority and worthlessness. Plebeian society limited the Spaniards' racial domination.

Appendix
Notes
Selected Bibliography
Index

Appendix

List of Casta and Indian Wills

Mateo de Aguilar, mulatto. AN, vol. 60, José de Anaya y Bonillo (13), 12 July 1701, fols. 311r–313r.

Catalina de los Angeles, mulatta. AN, vol. 29, Antonio de Anaya (9), 8 April 1683, fols. 33r–34r.

Nicolasa de los Angeles, india. AGN, Bienes Nacionales, vol. 1,096, 3 June 1679.

Juana de los Angeles Canales, mestiza. AN, vol. 2,568, Felipe Muñoz de Castro (391), 14 May 1708, fols. 108r–111r.

Bernardina Angelina, india. AN, vol. 469, Domingo Barreda (63), 3 May 1675.

Madalena de Avila, mestiza. AN, vol. 4,685, Francisco Valdez (692), 31 July 1691, fols. 128v–129v.

Juan de Bohórquez, mestizo. AN, vol. 3,108, Juan Francisco Neri (453), 6 November 1692, fols. 22v–24v.

Gregoria de Bórges, mulatta. AN, vol. 1,459, Antonio Fernández de Guzmán (230), 7 July 1696.

Gregoria del Castillo, mulatta. AN, vol. 3,370, Marcos Pacheco de Figueroa (499), 4 May 1693, fols. 46r–47r.

María del Castillo, mulatta. AN, vol. 3,370, Marcos Pacheco de Figueroa (499), 28 January 1693, fols. 11r–12v.

José de Chavarría, mulatto. AN, vol. 27, Juan Azores (8), 14 August 1686.

María de la Concepción, mulatta. AN, vol. 2,200, Jiménez de Siles (326), 20 April 1678, fols. 14r–16v.

María de la Concepción, india. AJ, Civil, vol. 69, Registro de Juan Clemente Guerrero, 13 November 1698.

José de Correa, morisco. AN, vol. 1,459, Antonio Fernández de Guzmán (230), 7 July 1696.

Agustina de la Cruz, mestiza. AN, vol. 469, Domingo Barreda (63), 24 January 1673.

Hipólito de la Cruz, mestizo. AN, vol. 1,648, Francisco González Peñafiel (252), 4 April 1695, fols. 52v–53v.

Josefa de la Cruz, mulatta. AN, vol. 3,369, Marcos Pacheco de Figueroa (499), 12 December 1685, fols. 64r–65r.

Sebastiana de la Cruz y Mancia, india. AN, vol. 4,634, Nicolás de Vega (688), 4 February 1668.

Andrés Escobar, negro. AN, vol. 3,108, Juan Francisco Neri (453), 4 September 1688, fols. 19v–20v.

Nicolasa de Espinosa, mestiza. AN, vol. 3,370, Marcos Pacheco de Figueroa (499), 16 April 1692, fols. 18r–19r.

Pedro de Gobera, chino. AN, vol. 4,642, José Valdez (690), 25 October 1695, fols. 66v–68v.

Nicolás González, mulatto. AN, vol. 3,240, Miguel Ortiz (473), February 1698.

Lucas de Guevara, mulatto. AN, vol. 4,685, Francisco Valdez (692), 31 July 1691, fols. 128v–129v.

Nicolás Hernández, mestizo. AN, vol. 3,370, Marcos Pacheco de Figueroa (499), 29 April 1692, fols. 19v–23v.

Sebastiana Hernández, mestiza. AN, vol. 4,634, Nicolás de Vega (688), 16 November 1664.

Juan Jacinto, indio. AN, vol. 782, Diego de Castilleja Guzmán (121), 19 March 1692.

Doña Francisca Juana, india. AJ, Civil, vol. 62, exp. 3, fols. 2r–14r.

Antonio López del Castillo, mulatto. AN, vol. 1,648, Francisco González Peñafiel (252), 23 August 1695, fols. 170r–171v.

Teresa de Losado, mulatta. AN, vol. 776, José de Castro (119), 27 February 1690, fols. 37v–39v.

Pasquala María, mestiza. AN, vol. 460, Nicolás Bernal (61), 11 January 1677, fols. 3v–5r.

Marcos de Mesa, mulatto. AN, vol. 1,267, Diego Díaz de Rivera (198), 12 April 1697, fols. 96v–98r.

Pedro de Mora Esquivel, mulatto. AN, vol. 1,453, Tomás Fernández de Guevara (229), 6 September 1690, fols. 135r–137v.

Juan de Oliva y Olvera, mestizo. AN, vol. 750, Pedro del Castillo Grimaldo (114), 9 March 1686, fols. 38r–40r.

Juana de Ordaz, castiza. AN, vol. 469, Domingo Barreda (63), 21 January 1674.

Juan de la Plata, mestizo. AN, vol. 4,634, Nicolás de Vega (688), 9 February 1670, fol. 4.

Juan Ramírez, mulatto. AN, vol. 4,410, Sebastián Sánchez de las Fraguas (639), 21 October 1690.

Pasquala de los Reyes, india. AN, vol. 4,634, Nicolás de Vega (688), 7 August 1670, fol. 51.

Josefa de Salas, mulatta. AN, vol. 2,101, Matías Herrero Gutiérrez (306), 9 June 1704, fols. 40v–42v.

Francisco de Salazar, mulatto. AN, vol. 3,369, Marcos Pacheco de Figueroa (499), 22 April 1687, fol. 24r–26r.

Ana de Samudio, mestiza. AN, vol. 4,634, Nicolás de Vega (688), 5 September 1664.

Tomasa de San Juan, mestiza. AGN, Bienes Nacionales, vol. 678, exp. 32.

Pascuala de Santoyo, negra. AN, vol. 2,525, Cristóbal Muñoz (381), 21 March 1677, fols. 6r–9r.

José de Tovar, castizo. AN, vol. 1,420, Ramón de Espinosa (218), 29 July 1699, fols. 173r–175v.

José del Valle, mulatto. AN, vol. 1,315, Juan Díaz de Rivera (199), 10 January 1693, fols. 6r–7v.

Gerónima de Vega y Vique, mulatta. AN, vol. 4,395, Francisco Solís y Alcázar (636), 20 August 1702, fols. 292r–294v.

Notes

Introduction

1. For a superb study of early Spanish attempts to evaluate and categorize the Indians, see Anthony Pagden, *The Fall of Natural Man: The American Indian and the Origins of Comparative Ethnology* (Cambridge: Cambridge University Press, 1982).

2. Bernal Díaz del Castillo, *The Conquest of New Spain*, trans. and introd. J. M. Cohen (Baltimore: Penguin Books, 1963): 214.

3. The most thorough study of the "two republic" model is Magnus Mörner, *La Corona española y los foráneos en los pueblos de indios de América* (Stockholm: Almquist & Wiksell, 1970).

4. Patrick J. Carroll, *Blacks in Colonial Veracruz: Race, Ethnicity and Regional Development* (Austin: University of Texas Press, 1991): 32.

5. James Lockhart, *Nahuas and Spaniards: Postconquest Central Mexican History and Philology* (Stanford: Stanford University Press, 1991): 20.

6. For an excellent study of the mutual misunderstandings of Indians and friars, see Inga Clendinnen, *Ambiguous Conquests: Maya and Spaniard in Yucatan, 1517–1570* (Cambridge: Cambridge University Press, 1987).

7. For the indigenous response to Christianity, see J. Jorge Klor de Alva, "Spiritual Conflict and Accommodation in New Spain: Toward a Typology of Aztec Responses to Christianity," in George A. Collier et al., eds., *The Inca and Aztec States, 1400–1800: Anthropology and History* (New York: Academic Press, 1982).

8. Anya Peterson Royce, *Ethnic Identity: Strategies of Diversity* (Bloomington: Indiana University Press, 1982): 210.

9. Racial labeling is here viewed as a subset of ethnic adscription, one in which physical and moral qualities are directly linked to biological heritage. Since putative ancestry (often expressed in very physical terms, e.g., *limpieza de sangre* or *mala raza*) was central to social categorization in colonial Mexico, I will generally employ the term "race" rather than "ethnicity."

10. Lockhart, *Nahuas and Spaniards*, 54.

11. For the use of this term, see Royce, *Ethnic Identity*, 29.

12. Ibid., 26.

13. Robert Stephen Haskett, *Indigenous Rulers: An Ethnohistory of Town Government in Colonial Cuernavaca* (Albuquerque: University of New Mexico Press, 1991): 161.

14. Eric Wolf, *Sons of the Shaking Earth* (Chicago: University of Chicago Press, 1959): 238–244.

15. James Lockhart, "Introduction," in Ida Altman and James Lockhart, eds.,

Provinces of Early Mexico: Variants of Spanish American Regional Evolution (Los Angeles: UCLA Latin American Center Publications, University of California, 1976): 15. See also the critique of Wolf in John K. Chance, "On the Mexican Mestizo," *Latin American Research Review* 14, no. 3 (1979): 153–168.

16. Wolf, *Sons of the Shaking Earth*, 243–245, 247.

Chapter 1. Race and Class in Colonial Mexico City, 1521–1660

1. Archivo Histórico de la Ciudad de Mexico (hereafter cited as AHCM), Clausura de Callejones, vol. 443, exp. 3, fol. 1r.

2. This was, indeed, an important motive for rebuilding on the site of the Aztec capital; Cortés wrote to Charles V, "Considering that [the city] had once been so renowned and of such importance, we decided to settle in it and also to rebuild it." Hernán Cortés, *Letters from Mexico*, trans. and ed. Anthony Pagden, introd. J. H. Elliot (New Haven: Yale University Press, 1986): 270.

3. Ross Hassig, *Trade, Tribute and Transportation: The Sixteenth-Century Political Economy of the Valley of Mexico* (Norman: University of Oklahoma Press, 1985): 257.

4. Peter Boyd-Bowman, *Patterns of Spanish Emigration to the New World (1493–1590)* (Buffalo: Council on International Studies, State University of New York at Buffalo, 1973): 28.

5. Ibid., 76; Nicolás Sanchez-Albornoz, *The Population of Latin America: A History*, trans. W. A. R. Richardson (Berkeley: University of California Press, 1974): 79.

6. These figures are calculated from data presented in Charles Gibson, *The Aztecs under Spanish Rule: A History of the Indians of the Valley of Mexico, 1519–1810* (Stanford: Stanford University Press, 1964): 381; and Sánchez-Albornoz, *The Population of Latin America*, 69.

7. Francisco Morales, *Ethnic and Social Background of the Franciscan Friars in Seventeenth-Century Mexico* (Washington, D.C.: Academy of American Franciscan History, 1973): 117–118; *Epistolario de Nueva España, 1505–1818* (hereafter cited as ENE), ed. Francisco del Paso y Troncoso (Mexico: Antigua Libreria Robredo, 1939–1942), XV: 151–155.

8. Manuel Carrera Stampa, *Los gremios mexicanos: La organización gremial en Nueva España*, introd. Rafael Altamira (México: Edición y Distribución Ibero-Americana de Publicaciones, S.A., 1954): 260–263.

9. Quoted in James Lockhart and Enrique Otte, eds., *Letters and People of the Spanish Indies: Sixteenth Century* (Cambridge: Cambridge University Press, 1976): 145.

10. Dennis Nodin Valdés, "The Decline of the Sociedad de Castas in Mexico City" (Ph.D. dissertation, University of Michigan, 1978): 2.

11. Gibson, *The Aztecs under Spanish Rule*, 370–371.

12. Ibid., 370; Francisco Cervantes de Salazar, *Mexico en 1554*, trans. Joaquín García Icazbalceta, introd. Julio Jiménez Rueda (Mexico: Ediciones de la Universidad Nacional Autónoma, 1952): 95.

13. See *A Sor Juana Anthology*, trans. Alan S. Trueblood (Cambridge: Harvard University Press, 1988): 122–129.

14. Thomas Gage, *Thomas Gage's Travels in the New World*, ed. and introd. J. Eric S. Thompson. (Norman: University of Oklahoma Press, 1958): 68.

15. D. A. Brading, *The First America: The Spanish Monarchy, Creole Patriots, and the Liberal State, 1492–1867* (Cambridge: Cambridge University Press, 1991): 371.

16. Juan de Ortega y Montañez, *Instrucción reservada que el Obispo-Virrey Juan de Ortega y Montañez dio a su sucesor en el mando el Conde de Moctezuma*, ed. and introd. Norman F. Martin (Mexico: Editorial Jus., 1965): 64.

17. See Enrique Florescano, "La formación de los trabajadores en la época colonial, 1521–1750," in *La clase obrera en la historia de México: De la colonia al imperio* (Mexico: Siglo Veintiuno Editores, S.A., 1980): 9–124; Charles Gibson, *Spain in America* (New York: Harper & Row, 1966); and for a specific focus on the Valley of Mexico, Gibson, *The Aztecs under Spanish Rule*.

18. John Leddy Phelan, "The Problem of Conflicting Spanish Imperial Ideologies in the Sixteenth Century," in *Latin American History: Identity, Integration, and Nationhood*, ed. Frederick B. Pike (New York: Harcourt, Brace & World, 1969): 63.

19. Richard E. Greenleaf, *La Inquisición en Nueva España: Siglo xvi*, trans. Carlos Valdés (Mexico: Fondo de Cultura Económica, 1981): 16–54; Lesley Byrd Simpson, *The Encomienda in New Spain: The Beginnings of Spanish Mexico*, rev. and enlarged ed. (Berkeley: University of California Press, 1968): 133, 140; Gibson, *Spain in America*, 58–62, 143–144.

20. I am here following the estimates of William T. Sanders, "The Population of the Central Mexican Symbiotic Region, the Basin of Mexico, and the Teotihuacán Valley in the Sixteenth Century," in *The Native Population of the Americas in 1492*, ed. William M. Denevan (Madison: University of Wisconsin Press, 1967): 76–150.

21. *Documentos para la historia del México colonial* (hereafter cited as DHMC), ed. France V. Scholes and Eleanor B. Adams, 7 vols. (Mexico City: Jose Porrúa e Hijos, 1955–1961), II: 47; *Colección de documentos inéditos para la historia de España* (hereafter cited as CDE), ed. Martín Fernández Navarrete et al., 112 vols. (Madrid: Imprenta de la Viuda de Calero, 1842–1895), XXVI: 174.

22. In this context, "free" might be translated as unfettered by slavery or by encomienda and repartimiento obligations and hence able to enter into long-term contracts with Spanish employers. Once employed, these workers might be tied to a particular location by debt, or even physically imprisoned in bakeries or obrajes.

23. P. J. Bakewell, *Silver Mining and Society in Colonial Mexico: Zacatecas, 1546–1700* (Cambridge: Cambridge University Press, 1971): 225.

24. Gibson, *The Aztecs under Spanish Rule*, 232–233; *Actas de Cabildo de la Ciudad de México* (Mexico City: Imprenta de Aguilar e Hijos, 1889–1916), XXVII: 188.

25. William B. Taylor, *Drinking, Homicide, and Rebellion in Colonial Mexican Villages* (Stanford: Stanford University Press, 1979): 35–36.

26. Ibid., 170.

174   Notes to Pages 13–16

27. The vast majority of these slaves were Africans, but parish records reveal the existence of a few enslaved Filipinos (called chinos) and Chichimecs (Indians from northern New Spain captured in wars).

28. D. A. Brading, *Miners and Merchants in Bourbon Mexico, 1763–1810* (Cambridge: Cambridge University Press, 1971): 7–8.

29. Colin A. Palmer, *Slaves of the White God: Blacks in Mexico, 1570–1650* (Cambridge: Harvard University Press, 1976): 7, 28, 46; Bradley Benedict, "El estado en la época de los Hapsburgo," *Historia Mexicana* 23 (1973–74): 608–609.

30. Taylor, *Drinking, Homicide, and Rebellion,* 16.

31. Florescano, "La formación de los trabajadores," 70, 100–104; Gibson, *The Aztecs under Spanish Rule,* 247–248; J. I. Israel, *Race, Class and Politics in Colonial Mexico, 1610–1670* (London: Oxford University Press, 1975): 185–186.

32. *Fuentes para la historia del trabajo en Nueva España* (hereafter cited as FHT), ed. Silvio Zavala and Maria Castelo, 8 vols. (Mexico City: Fondo de Cultura Económica, 1939–1946), VIII: 124.

33. Richard Konetzke, "El mestizaje y su importancia en el desarrollo de la población hispanoamérica durante la época colonial," pt. 2, *Revista de Indias* 24 (1946): 218.

34. Israel, *Race, Class and Politics,* 62. See, e.g., a 1542 petition by the Mexico City cabildo requesting that the crown allow the illegitimate sons of encomenderos to inherit their fathers' encomiendas, in *Documentos inéditos del siglo xvi para la historia de México* (hereafter cited as DSM), ed. Mariano Cuevas (Mexico City: José Porrúa e Hijos, 1914): 110.

35. DSM, 152–153.

36. Richard M. Morse, "A Prolegomenon to Latin American Urban History," *Hispanic American Historical Review* 52 (1972): 367.

37. Quoted in John K. Chance, *Race and Class in Colonial Oaxaca* (Stanford: Stanford University Press, 1978): 97.

38. Antonio Vázquez de Espinosa, *Description of the Indies (c. 1620),* trans. Charles Upson Clark, Smithsonian Miscellaneous Collections, vol. 102 (Washington, D.C.: Smithsonian Institution Press, 1968): 156.

39. Archivo Histórico del Instituto Nacional de Antropología e Historia, Colección Antigua 253, "Itinerario de las provincias, obispados, ciudades, villas y lugares del distrito de la Inquisición de México, 1654," fol. 14.

40. DSM, 172.

41. *Colección de documentos para la historia de la formación social de Hispanoamérica* (hereafter cited as CFS), ed. Richard Konetzke, 3 vols. (Madrid: Consejo Superior de Investigaciones Científicas, 1953–1962), I: 513.

42. Mörner, *La Corona,* 17–18; Gonzálo Gómez de Cervantes, *La vida económica y social de Nueva España al finalizar el siglo xvi,* ed. and introd. Alberto María Carreño (Mexico: José Porrúa e Hijos, 1944): 88; *Actas de Cabildo,* VII: 344; Juan López de Velasco, *Geografía y descripción universal de las Indias,* ed. Marcos Jiménez de la Espada and introd. María del Carmen González Muñoz (Madrid: Ediciones Atlas, 1971): 22.

43. CDE, XXVI: 387.

44. Mörner, *La Corona,* 29–30.

45. CFS, I: 256; *Recopilación de leyes de los reynos de las Indias* (hereafter cited as RLI), 3 vols. (Madrid: La Viuda de D. Joaquín Ibarra, 1948), II: 212; DHMC, II: 52, III: 27.

46. Mörner, *La Corona*, 47–48; Gibson, *The Aztecs under Spanish Rule*, 372.

47. RLI, 153, 243, 288, 369; Archivo General de la Nación, Mexico City (hereafter cited as AGN), Reales Cédulas Duplicadas, vol. 103, fol. 194; AGN, Ordenanzas, vol. 2, fol. 270r.

48. Leslie B. Rout, Jr., *The African Experience in Spanish America: 1502 to the Present Day*, Cambridge Latin American Studies, no. 23 (Cambridge: Cambridge University Press, 1976): 21–22.

49. *Ordenanzas de gremios de la Nueva España*, ed. Francisco del Barrio Lorenzot, introd. Genaro Estrada, 2 vols. (Mexico City: Dirección de Talleres Graficos, 1920), I: 39, 124. For the relative proportions of the races in the 1570s, see Benedict, "El estado," 608–609.

50. David M. Davidson, "Negro Slave Control and Resistance in Colonial Mexico, 1519–1650," *Hispanic American Historical Review* 46 (1966): 243–244; Palmer, *Slaves of the White God*, 134.

51. Quoted in Palmer, *Slaves of the White God*, 135.

52. Ibid., 135–140.

53. AGN, Ordenanzas, vol. 1, fols. 149v–150r; AGN, Reales Cédulas Duplicadas, vol. 103, fol. 41r; CFS, I: 501.

54. Norman F. Martin, *Los vagabundos en la Nueva España: Siglo xvi* (Mexico City: Editorial Jus., 1957): 95.

55. DSM, 155.

56. CDE, XXVI: 289; Gibson, *The Aztecs under Spanish Rule*, 383. For an overview of Spanish attempts to educate mestizos, see Lino Gómez Canedo, *La educación de los marginados durante la época colonial: Escuelas y colegios para indios y mestizos en la Nueva España*, Biblioteca Porrúa, no. 78 (Mexico City: Editorial Porrúa, S.A., 1982).

57. Magnus Mörner, *Race Mixture in the History of Latin America* (Boston: Little, Brown, 1967): 27; Gonzalo Aguirre Beltrán, *La población negra de Mexico, 1519–1810: Estudio etnohistórico* (Mexico City: Fondo de Cultura Económica, 1946): 250; Mörner, *La Corona*, 105.

58. *Ordenanzas de gremios*, 250. For other examples, see 224, 230, 260; and *Legislación del trabajo en los siglos xvi, xvii y xviii*, ed. Genaro V. Vázquez, Historia del Movimiento Obrero en Mexico, vol. 1 (Mexico City: Departamento Autónomo de Prensa y Publicidad, 1935): 63.

59. This schematic presentation is adopted from Verena Martinez-Alier, *Marriage, Class and Colour in Nineteenth-Century Cuba: A Study of Racial Attitudes and Sexual Values in a Slave Society*, Cambridge Latin American Studies, no. 17 (Cambridge: Cambridge University Press, 1974): 131.

60. López de Velasco, *Geografía y descripción*, 22; CDE, XXVI: 387; Juan de Solórzano y Pereira, *Política Indiana*, ed. Francisco Ramiro de Valenzuela, 5 vols. (Madrid: Compañía Ibero-Americana de Publicaciones, 1647), I: 445, 447–448, II: 57.

61. CFS, II: 694; FHT, VII: 265.

62. Gregorio M. de Guijo, *Diario, 1648–1664*, ed. and introd. Manuel Romero de Terreros, 2 vols. (Mexico City: Editorial Porrúa, S.A., 1953), II: 10.

63. Gibson, *The Aztecs under Spanish Rule*, 142. The population estimates are based on the multipliers for 1570 and 1800, given in Gibson, pp. 499–500, n. 15, and p. 501, n. 26.

64. Ibid., 376. The English friar Thomas Gage, describing the city in the 1620s, wrote, "The Spaniards daily cozen them [the Indians] of the small plot of ground where their houses stand, and of three or four houses of Indians they build up one good and fair house after the Spanish fashion with gardens and orchards." Gage, *Thomas Gage's Travels*, 67. For an example of an elite Spanish residence (valued at 3,400 pesos) located in an Indian barrio, see AGN, Bienes Nacionales, vol. 71, exp. 2.

65. Gibson, *The Aztecs under Spanish Rule*, 376.

66. Ibid., 376–377.

67. For some examples of this, see AGN, Indios, vol. 10, exp. 39, fol. 19; vol. 12, exp. 215, fols. 135v–136r.

68. Quoted in Richard Everett Boyer, *La gran inundación: Vida y sociedad en México (1629–1638)*, trans. Antonieta Sánchez Mejorada (Mexico City: Sepsetentas, 1975): 43.

69. AGN, Reales Cédulas Duplicadas, vol. 3, exp. 7, fol. 4; CFS, II: 72.

70. Gómez de Cervantes, *La vida económica y social*, 100.

71. AGN, Indios, vol. 17, fol. 1; Reales Cédulas Duplicadas, vol. 67, fol. 17v; Ordenanzas, vol. 5, fol. 3.

72. Archivo de Notarías del Distrito Federal, Mexico City (hereafter cited as AN), vol. 3,857, Francisco de Rivera (559), 3 September 1660, fols. 16r–19v.

73. AGN, Tributos, vol. 33, exp. 13, fol. 108r.

74. AGN, Reales Cédulas Duplicadas, vol. 16, fols. 319r–323v.

75. *Ordenanzas del trabajo, siglos xvi y xvii*, ed. Silvio Zavala (Mexico City: Editorial "Elede," S.A., 1947): 229.

76. Gage, *Thomas Gage's Travels*, 68.

77. See the discussion of these terms in Chance, *Race and Class*, 127, and Brading, *Miners and Merchants*, 20–21. For the noble-commoner division in Spain, see John Lynch, *Spain and America: 1598–1700*, Vol. II of *Spain Under the Habsburgs* (Oxford: Basil Blackwell, 1969): 140–155.

78. Carlos de Sigüenza y Góngora, "Letter of Don Carlos de Sigüenza y Góngora to Admiral Pez Recounting the Incidents of the Corn Riot in Mexico City, June 8, 1692," in Irving A. Leonard, *Don Carlos de Sigüenza y Góngora, a Mexican Savant of the Seventeenth Century* (Berkeley: University of California Press, 1929): 240; *Instrucciones que los vireyes de Nueva España dejaron a sus sucesores, añadense algunas que los mismos trajeron de la Corte y otros documentos semejantes a las instrucciones* (Mexico City: Imprenta Imperial, 1867): 7.

79. *Actas de Cabildo*, XXV: 102; Rodrigo Pacheco y Ossorio, marqués de Cerralvo, "Relación del estado en que dejo el gobierno de la Nueva España el excelentisimo señor don Rodrigo Pacheco y Ossorio, Marqués de Cerralvo," in *Descripción de la Nueva España en el siglo xvii por el padre Fray Antonio Vázquez*

de Espinosa y otros documentos del siglo xvii, ed. Mariano Cuevas (Mexico City: Editorial Patria, S.A., 1944): 222.

80. For a brief account of the 1624 riot, see Rosa Feijoo, "El tumulto de 1624," *Historia Mexicana* 14 (1964–65): 42–70.

81. CDE, XXVI: 171; *Don Juan de Palafox y Mendoza: Su virreinato en la Nueva España, sus contenidas con los P. P. Jesuítas, sus apariciones, sus escritos escogidos, etc., etc.,* Vol. VII of *Documentos inéditos ó muy raros para la historia de México,* ed. Genaro García and Carlos Pereyra (Mexico City: Librería de la Viuda de Ch. Bouret, 1906): 28.

82. Sigüenza y Góngora, "Letter of Don Carlos de Sigüenza y Góngora," 240.

83. Fredrik Barth, "Introduction," in *Ethnic Groups and Boundaries: The Social Organization of Culture Difference,* ed. Fredrik Barth (Boston: Little, Brown, 1969): 14.

84. Mörner, *Race Mixture,* 53–56; Aguirre Beltrán, *La población negra de Mexico,* 163; Chance, *Race and Class,* 126, 193.

85. For the Santa Veracruz parish, see Edgar F. Love, "Marriage Patterns of Persons of African Descent in a Colonial Mexico City Parish," *Hispanic American Historical Review* 51 (1971): 80–81.

86. Aguirre Beltrán, *La población negra de Mexico,* 166–172.

87. Patricia Seed, "Social Dimensions of Race: Mexico City, 1753," *Hispanic American Historical Review* 62 (1982): 573–574.

88. Barth, "Introduction," 16.

89. My remarks on creole marriages have been heavily influenced by Martinez-Alier, *Marriage, Class and Colour,* passim.

90. As noted above, blacks and mulattoes were the most despised of the castas. They were also considered the most cohesive: see Ortega y Montañez, *Instrucción,* 62–63. Furthermore, while intermarriage with Spaniards could eventually "whiten" persons with some Indian blood, this was not (in theory) true for those of African ancestry. See Rout, *The African Experience,* 131.

91. *Instrucciones que los vireyes de Nueva España dejaron,* 259.

92. Ibid., as quoted in Israel, *Race, Class and Politics,* 64–65.

93. *Ordenanzas del trabajo, siglos xvi y xvii,* 211–212.

94. E.g., *Actas de Cabildo,* XXXV: 18–19; Sigüenza y Góngora, "Letter of Don Carlos de Sigüenza y Góngora," 259.

Chapter 2. Life among the Urban Poor: Material Culture and Plebeian Society

1. The best account of conditions in the city (though focused on the late eighteenth century) is Donald B. Cooper, *Las epidemias en la ciudad de México, 1761–1813,* trans. Roberto Gómez Ciriza (Mexico: Instituto Mexicano del Seguro Social, 1980).

2. AGN, Obras Públicas, vol. 27, exp. 1, fol. 9r.

3. AHCM, Policía: Salubridad, vol. 3,668, exp. 1, fol. 8r, exps. 7, 11.

4. The extent of Mexico City's population loss is discussed in Louisa Hoberman, "Bureaucracy and Disaster: Mexico City and the Flood of 1629," *Journal of Latin American Studies* 6 (1974): 214–215.

5. Gibson, *The Aztecs under Spanish Rule*, 237–239; Cooper, *Las epidemias*, 22.

6. AHCM, Ríos y Acequias, vol. 3,871, exp. 15, fol. 1r.

7. Gibson, *The Aztecs under Spanish Rule*, 385.

8. AHCM, Puentes, vol. 3,716, exps. 2, 6, 9.

9. Cooper, *Las epidemias*, 34.

10. Gibson, *The Aztecs under Spanish Rule*, 385–387; Gabriel James Haslip, "Crime and the Administration of Justice in Colonial Mexico City, 1696–1810," (Ph.D. dissertation, Columbia University, 1980): 23, 67–68.

11. AHCM, Policía: Salubriadad, vol. 3,668, exp. 1, fols. 1r–2r, 17r.

12. Ibid., fol. 13; AHCM, Calzadas y Caminos, vol. 440, exp. 3, fols. 7r–8r; Cooper, *Las epidemias*, 33–35.

13. AHCM, Calzadas y Caminos, vol. 440, exp. 3, fol. 2r; AHCM, Ríos y Acequias, vol. 3,871, exp. 15, fols. 1v–2r.

14. This concept of a "housing hierarchy" was first developed (to my knowledge) in Valdés, "The Decline of the Sociedad de Castas in Mexico City," 114–138.

15. AGN, Bienes Nacionales, vol. 45, exp. 26, fol. 2.

16. AN, vol. 3,370, Marcos Pacheco de Figueroa (499), 16 April 1692, fol. 18v.

17. AN, vol. 750, Pedro del Castillo Grimaldo (114), 9 March 1686, fol. 39r; vol. 461, Nicolás Bernal (61), 23 July 1680, fol. 96; and Archivo del Tribunal Superior de Justicia del Distrito Federal (hereafter cited as AJ), Civil, vol. 62, exp. 3, fol. 2r.

18. AN, vol. 4,634, Nicolás de Vega (688), 9 September 1665, fol. 53v; vol. 469, Domingo Barreda (63), 3 May 1675; vol. 1,421, Manuel de Esquivel (219), 26 August 1701, fol. 36v.

19. AN, vol. 4,634, Nicolás de Vega (688), 15 December 1665, fol. 64v; 9 February 1670, fol. 4v.

20. AN, vol. 3,370, Marcos Pacheco de Figueroa (499), 16 April 1692, fol. 18v; vol. 2,568, Felipe Muñoz de Castro (391), 14 May 1708, fols. 109v–110r; vol. 4,634, Nicolás de Vega (688), 16 November 1664.

21. Giovanni Francesco Gemelli Carreri, *Viaje a la Nueva España*, ed. and trans. Francisca Perujo (Mexico City: UNAM, Dir. Gral. de Publicaciones, 1976): 22; AGN, Bienes Nacionales, vol. 237, exp. 4.

22. Haslip, "Crime and the Administration of Justice," 19.

23. AGN, Bienes Nacionales, vol. 457, exp. 18, fol. 21r; AN, vol. 3,240, Miguel Ortiz (473), 29 August 1704; AGN, Bienes Nacionales, vol. 237, exp. 4. fol. 123v.

24. AGN, Bienes Nacionales, vol. 457, exp. 18, fols. 7r, 12r.

25. AGN, Templos y Conventos, vol. 103, exp. 1, fols. 49r, 53r.

26. AGN, Bienes Nacionales, vol. 237, exp. 3, fol. 53r; vol. 457, exp. 18, fol. 21r.

27. Ibid., vol. 457, exp. 18, fols. 61r, 80r.

28. Ibid., vol. 1,213, exp. 10, fols. 194v–195r, 198v.

29. Ibid., vol. 237, exp. 3, fol. 39v; vol. 262, exp. 71, fols. 1r–3r; vol. 457,

exps. 1, 18, fols. 56v, 64v–65r, 72r; vol. 823, exp. 2; Templos y Conventos, vol. 160, exp. 9, fols. 315v, 324r.

30. AJ, Penal, vol. 1, exp. 73.

31. For examples, see ibid., exps. 8, 68, 74.

32. E.g., see the case of Nicolás de Paniagua in AGN, Inquisición, vol. 571, exp. 1.

33. AGN, Inquisición, vol. 562, exp. 7.

34. Ibid., vol. 442, exp. 7, fol. 192v.

35. Ibid., exp. 7, fol. 201r, passim.

36. *Instrucciones que los vireyes de la Nueva España dejaron*, 307.

37. Ibid., 306–307.

38. For a concrete example of the gobernadores being held responsible for the regulation of the city's Indians, see AHCM, Policía: Salubridad, vol. 3668, exp. 1, fol. 9.

39. José Jesús Hernández Palomo, *La renta del pulque en Nueva España, 1665–1810* (Seville: Escuela de Estudios Hispano-Americanos, 1979): 79.

40. Ibid., 58; AJ, Penal, vol. 1, exp. 58, fol. 2r, exp. 12.

41. AJ, Penal, vol. 1, exp. 58, fol. 4r.

42. Michael C. Scardaville, "Alcohol Abuse and Tavern Reform in Late Colonial Mexico City," *Hispanic American Historical Review* 60 (1980): 647. For pulquería ordinances, see Hernández Palomo, *La renta del pulque*, 59, 62. Scardaville's comments refer to the late eighteenth century, but Taylor and Hernández Palomo indicate that the same conditions prevailed in seventeenth-century pulquerías. See, e.g., Taylor, *Drinking, Homicide, and Rebellion*, 66–67.

43. AGN, Inquisición, vol. 520, exp. 124.

44. AHCM, Cédulas y Reales Ordenes, vol. 2,977, exp. 7, fol. 11r.

45. Taylor, *Drinking, Homicide, and Rebellion*, 66.

46. Ibid., 66–67; AJ, Penal, vol. 2, exp. 65; Hernández Palomo, *La renta del pulque*, 76.

47. AGN, Inquisición, vol. 722, exp. 5.

48. AGN, Edictos de la Santa y General Inquisición, vol. 1, exp. 13, fol. 16, and exp. 20, fol. 23.

49. AHCM, Cédulas Reales, vol. 426A, II, fol. 251v. For a brief description of Mexico City's markets, see Gibson, *The Aztecs under Spanish Rule*, 395.

50. AHCM, Alcaicería, vol. 343, exp. 1, fols. 140vff., 194r–198v; Plaza Mayor, vol. 3618, exp. 5, fol. 6r.

51. AHCM, Ordenanzas, vol. 2,982, exp. 7, fol. 35v.

52. AHCM, Plaza Mayor, vol. 3,618, exp. 5, fol. 6r.

53. AHCM, Cédulas Reales, vol. 426A, II, fol. 251. For a modern view of the market's utility, see Haslip, "Crime and the Administration of Justice," 82.

54. Ortega y Montañez, *Instrucción*, 172–174; AJ, Penal, vol. 1, exp. 65; Haslip, "Crime and the Administration of Justice," 82–83.

55. AGN, Bienes Nacionales, vol. 546, exp. 3.

56. A classic example of this process occurred in the aftermath of the 1692 riot.

The viceroy ordered all Indians living in the traza (except for those employed in the bakeries) to return to their barrios. Yet just a year later, the city's governadores unanimously reported that the Indians had obeyed the edict for only a few months, and were now moving back to the traza. AHCM, Historia en General, vol. 2,254, exp. 2.

57. We will return to this point below.

58. Gibson, *The Aztecs under Spanish Rule*, 396; *Boletín del Archivo general de la Nación*, 1st ser., IX: 1–34, passim; CFS, II: 567–568, 586; RLI, II: 364.

59. E. P. Thompson, "Patrician Society, Plebeian Culture," *Journal of Social History* 7 (1974): 387.

60. Irving A. Leonard, *Baroque Times in Old Mexico: Seventeenth-Century Persons, Places, and Practices* (Ann Arbor: University of Michigan Press, 1959): 33.

61. Thompson, "Patrician Society," 389.

62. *Instrucciones que los vireyes de la Nueva España dejaron*, 258.

63. Ortega y Montañez, *Instrucciones*, 61.

64. *Actas de Cabildo*, XIII: 115.

65. AN, vol. 4,638, José de Valdez (690), 10 November 1672, fols. 36r–37r.

66. Haslip, "Crime and the Administration of Justice," 94.

67. Taylor, *Drinking, Homicide, and Rebellion*, 97–106; Colin M. MacLachlan, *Criminal Justice in Eighteenth-Century Mexico: A Study of the Tribunal of the Acordada* (Berkeley: University of California Press, 1974): 79–82.

68. Antonio de Robles, *Diario de sucesos notables (1665–1703)*, ed. and introd. Antonio Castro Leal, 3 vols. (Mexico City: Editorial Porrúa, S.A., 1946), I: 113–114.

69. AGN, Inquisición, vol. 673, exp. 4.

70. Ibid., fol. 103r.

71. AGN, Inquisición, vol. 571, exp. 1, fol. 31r.

72. AHCM, Cédulas y Reales Ordenes, vol. 2,977, exp. 19, fol. 1.

73. John Leddy Phelan, *The Kingdom of Quito in the Seventeenth Century: Bureaucratic Politics in the Spanish Empire* (Madison: University of Wisconsin Press, 1967): 163. AN, vol. 3,240, Miguel Ortiz (473), 6 June 1694.

74. AHCM, Cédulas y Reales Ordenes, vol. 2,977, exp. 19, fol. 1.

75. Hernández Palomo, *La renta del pulque*, 75.

76. AJ, Penal, vol. 1, exp. 63, fols. 2v–3v.

77. Ibid., exp. 74; see also, exp. 8.

78. Israel, *Race, Class and Politics;* Taylor, *Drinking, Homicide and Rebellion*, 113–151. Among important works dealing with European crowds are E. J. Hobsbawm, *Primitive Rebels: Studies in Archaic Forms of Social Movement in the Nineteenth and Twentieth Centuries* (New York: W.W. Norton, 1959); George Rudé, *The Crowd in History: A Study of Popular Disturbances in France and England, 1730–1848* (New York: John Wiley & Sons, 1964); E. P. Thompson, "The Moral Economy of the English Crowd in the Eighteenth Century," *Past and Present* 50 (1971): 76–136; Robert L. Woods, Jr., "Individuals in the Rioting Crowd: A New Approach," *Journal of Interdisciplinary History* 14 (Summer 1983): 1–24.

79. Hobsbawm, *Primitive Rebels*, 115–116.

80. Sigüenza y Góngora, "Letter of Don Carlos de Sigüenza y Góngora," 245.

81. AJ, Penal, vol. 1, exp. 53, fols. 2v–4v.

82. AJ, Penal, vol. 2, exp. 3.

83. Ortega y Montañez, *Instrucciones*, 25, 172.

84. The broader context of patron-client relationships will be discussed in chaps. 5 and 6.

85. E.g., see AJ, Civil, vol. 60, Registro de Juan Clemente Guerrero, 3 June 1698.

86. John Leddy Phelan, "Authority and Flexibility in the Spanish Imperial Bureaucracy," *Administrative Science Quarterly* 5 (1960): 47–65.

87. AHCM, Artesanos-Gremios, vol. 381, exp. 3, fol. 36r.

88. AGN, Indios, vol. 13, exp. 375, fols. 310v–311r.

89. AHCM, Plaza Mayor, vol. 3,613, exp. 5, fol. 6r.

90. AGN, Obras Públicas, vol. 21, exp. 1, fol. 33.

91. AGN, Indios, vol. 13, fols. 200r–202r.

92. For an example of such manipulation in Peru, see Steve J. Stern, *Peru's Indian Peoples and the Challenge of Spanish Conquest: Huamanga to 1640* (Madison: University of Wisconsin Press, 1982): 114–137.

93. AGN, Inquisición, vol. 539, exp. 2, fols. 10r–11r.

94. AGN, Templos y Conventos, vol. 158A, exp. 46.

95. AGN, Matrimonios, vol. 70, exp. 2.

96. AHCM, Ordenanzas, vol. 2,981, "Diputados de Elecciones, y Pobres," nos. 1–2.

97. Sigüenza y Górgora, "Letter of Don Carlos de Sigüenza y Góngora," 250.

98. Israel, *Race, Class and Politics*, 264.

99. Guijo, II: 211–212.

100. Robles, I: 29.

101. Israel, *Race, Class and Politics*, 265.

102. Ibid., 266.

103. Compare the comments in Hobsbawm, *Primitive Rebels*, 119–120.

104. AGN, Edictos de la Santa y General Inquisición, vol. 1, exp. 12, fol. 15r.

Chapter 3. The Significance and Ambiguities of "Race"

1. This term is used by Fredrik Barth: "One might thus . . . say that it [ethnic status] is *imperative*, in that it cannot be disregarded and temporarily set aside by other definitions of the situation." Barth, "Introduction," 17.

2. Stephen Jay Gould, "Why We Should Not Name Human Races—A Biological View," in *Ever Since Darwin: Reflections in Natural History* (New York: W.W. Norton, 1977): 232.

3. Ibid., 233.

4. Ibid., 234–236.

5. Marvin Harris, *Patterns of Race in the Americas* (New York: Walker and Company, 1964): 54.

6. Ibid., 56.

7. H. Hoetink, *The Two Variants in Caribbean Race Relations: A Contribution to the Sociology of Segmented Societies*, trans. Eva M. Hooykaas (London: Oxford University Press, 1967): 120.

8. Ibid., 134–135.

9. Aguirre Beltrán, *La población negra de Mexico*, 163, 168–169.

10. Valdés, "The Decline of the Sociedad de Castas in Mexico City," 188.

11. Ibid., 181, 188.

12. AGN, Inquisición, vol. 520, exp. 139, fols. 220v–221r.

13. Ibid., vol. 722, exp. 5, fols. 194v–195r, 197r.

14. AGN, Civil, vol. 1,558, exp. 20, fols. 1v, 3r, 5r.

15. AJ, Penal, vol. 2, exp. 3.

16. See, e.g., AGN, Inquisición, vol. 667, exp. 4, fol. 114v.

17. Ibid., vol. 680, exp. 34, fols. 242r, 244r passim.

18. Ibid., vol. 571, exp. 1.

19. Ibid., vol. 677, exp. 4, fol. 104r.

20. Ibid., vol. 677, exp. 4, fol. 114v.

21. Ibid., vol. 677, exp. 4, fols. 111–126.

22. Ibid., vol. 677, exp. 4, fol. 127. I was unable to find the actual record of this marriage.

23. Ibid., vol. 667, exp. 2, fol. 89r.

24. No resolution of this case is recorded. I have taken the liberty of assuming that Felipe had, as he claimed, been born of Indian parents, for three reasons: (1) Felipe gave detailed information on his parents, which should have been fairly easy to check; (2) Felipe claimed that his father had been an "indio de capa," that is, an elite and probably a Hispanicized Indian; this would have facilitated passing; and (3) the Inquisitor handling the case showed an unusual reluctance to delve into Felipe's ancestry and seemed to be disgusted at the mere possibility that Felipe might escape prosecution. Felipe's claim to Indian status was "undoubtedly a lie," said the Inquisitor. "He admits at the same time that he has been taken . . . as a mestizo, and if he had been an Indian it would not have been easy for him to become a mestizo" (ibid., vol. 667, exp. 2, fol. 99r). This last view was not held by many other observers of the period. The Inquisitor concluded with a legal quibble, saying that Felipe should be judged under the principle "como te hallo, te jusgo."

25. AGN, Inquisición, vol. 667, exp. 2, fols. 89–90.

26. Ibid., vol. 667, exp. 3, fol. 154.

27. Ibid., vol. 667, exp. 4, fol. 100v; vol. 677, exp. 3, fol. 154.

28. Valdés, "The Decline of the Sociedad de Castas in Mexico City," 24.

29. Most plebeians entered the work force through informal arrangements. But parents apprenticing their sons might well sign formal contracts, and apprenticeship agreements nearly always recorded the apprentice's race.

30. Richard Konetzke, "Documentos para la historia y crítica de los registros parroquiales en las Indias," *Revista de Indias* 25 (1946): 585–586, as quoted in Chance, *Race and Class*, 129.

31. Typically, this information included the name, race, marital status (single or

widowed), and birthplace of each of the partners; the name of the officiating priest; and the name of the couple's compadres.

32. See, e.g., the entries for Teresa Rosa (1 September 1692), Tomás de los Reyes (2 October 1692), and Angela de la Rosa (28 June 1693), in the Archivo de Genealogía y Heráldica, Sagrario Metropolitano, Libro de matrimonios de castas, roll 520, vol. 7, fols. 85r, 86v, 107r.

33. The problematic nature of parish records will be discussed further in chap. 4.

34. AGN, Inquisición, vol. 571, exp. 1, fol. 9.

35. Ibid., vol. 677, exp. 2, fol. 89v.

36. *Informes* provided by candidates for the Franciscan order amply support this assertion. A candidate usually called on four to six witnesses (*testigos*) to affirm his good character, economic standing, and freedom from "tainted" blood. Typically, witnesses could provide fairly detailed information—including full name, race, place of birth, and occupation—on the candidate, his parents, and his grandparents. But great-grandparents are very rarely mentioned. Moreover, a single witness would frequently not be acquainted with both sets of grandparents. Archivo Histórico del Instituto Nacional de Antropología e Historia, Fondo Franciscano, vol. 2, passim. For a broader discussion of these candidates and their informes, see Morales, *Ethnic and Social Background*.

37. AGN, Inquisición, vol. 677, exp. 3, fol. 154.

38. AN, vol. 3,240, Miguel Ortiz (473), 24 November 1694.

39. AGN, Inquisición, vol. 571, exp. 1, fols. 9v–10r.

40. AGN, Bienes Nacionales, vol. 782, exp. 22.

41. Ibid., vol. 406, exp. 87.

42. See Herbert G. Gutman, *The Black Family in Slavery and Freedom, 1750–1925* (New York: Random House, 1976): 185–256.

43. AN, vol. 4,634, Nicolás de Vega (688), 5 September 1664.

44. Ibid., 16 November 1664.

45. AN, vol. 1,648, Francisco González Peñafiel (252), 23 August 1695, fol. 170.

46. AGN, Inquisición, vol. 673, exp. 4; vol. 518, fols. 352r, 359r.

47. AN, vol. 2,525, Cristóbal Muñoz (381), 21 March 1677, fol. 6r; AJ, Civil, vol. 60, Registro de Juan Clemente Guerrero, 13 November 1698. In fairness to María, it should be pointed out that her parents had died when she was a small child.

48. AGN, Matrimonios, vol. 70, exp. 2, fols. 34r, 62r.

49. AGN, Inquisición, vol. 287, exp. 7, fol. 9.

50. This sample of casta wills, referred to throughout the text, is listed in the Appendix.

51. One should also bear in mind that castas who made wills were a privileged group and therefore probably more likely to adopt Hispanic naming practices than their poorer counterparts.

52. AN, vol. 3,108, Juan Francisco Neri (453), 4 September 1688, fol. 19v.

53. The "casta" side of tables 3.1 and 3.2 is based on Sagrario Metropolitano's casta marriage registers for the years 1670–1672 and 1680–1682. (It includes data on Indians who married in the parish cathedral and were listed in these registers.)

There were no significant differences in surname frequencies between these two periods. Since Spanish marriages in Sagrario Metropolitano outnumbered casta marriages by approximately two to one, the "Spanish" side of the tables uses data from the years 1680–1682 only.

54. For surname frequencies (and nickname use) in modern Spanish pueblos, see Julian A. Pitt-Rivers, *The People of the Sierra*, 2d ed. (Chicago: University of Chicago Press, 1971): 160–169.

55. The argument is somewhat weakened by the fact that traza Indians were regarded as largely outside the control of the parish priests (see the discussion in chap. 5). In fact, Indian legitimacy rates in Sagrario Metropolitano Parish during the eighteenth century were slightly lower than those for mestizos, suggesting that priestly authority over these Indians was limited. See Valdés, "The Decline of the Sociedad de Castas in Mexico City," 33.

56. This figure includes forty-two professional soldiers.

57. See the statistical summary in "Gente de España en la cuidad de México, año de 1689," *Boletín del Archivo general de la nación*, 2d ser., 7, nos. 1–2 (1966): 349–365.

58. Rodney Anderson found significant socioeconomic differences between dons and non-dons in late colonial Guadalajara; for instance, "creole commoners [i.e., non-dons] were overrepresented as both laborers and servants." See Rodney D. Anderson, "Race and Social Stratification: A Comparison of Working-Class Spaniards, Indians, and Castas in Guadalajara, Mexico, in 1821," *Hispanic American Historical Review* 68 (1988): 209–243. The quotation is from p. 237.

59. The difference was already apparent in sixteenth-century Spanish America: see James Lockhart, *Spanish Peru: A Colonial Society* (Madison: University of Wisconsin Press, 1968): 35–36.

60. AGN, Tributos, vol. 11, exp. 10, fol. 145v passim.

Chapter 4. Plebeian Race Relations

1. AGN, Bienes Nacionales, vol. 702, exp. 166, fols. 1r–3r.

2. None of Domingo's witnesses were men of high status: in addition to Cárdenas, he presented a shoemaker and a tailor, and all three men were illiterate. This suggests that Velásquez came from a rather humble family, which may explain why his baptismal partida is misfiled in the first place.

3. For a more detailed discussion of the sex ratios in specific racial groups, see below.

4. This is based on baptismal records for 1661, 1665, and 1670 in Archivo de Genealogía y Heráldica, Sagrario Metropolitano, Libro de bautismos de castas, roll 647, vol. 15, fols. 45r–147r; vol. 16, fols. 1r–97r; roll 648, vol. 18, fols. 121r–206r. For the continued high illegitimacy rates in eighteenth-century Mexico City, see Valdés, "The Decline of the Sociedad de Castas in Mexico City," 33.

5. Thomas Calvo, *La Nueva Galicia en los siglos xvi y xvii* (Guadalajara: El Colegio de Jalisco, 1989), argues that this was the case in seventeenth-century

Guadalajara: "el entrecruzamineto de razas prosigue a través del concubinato" (74).

6. See, e.g., AN, vol. 2,525, Cristóbal Muñoz (381),\21 March 1677; AGN, Bienes Nacionales, vol. 1096, 3 June 1679; AN, vol. 4,686, Francisco de Valdez (692), 21 November 1692, fol. 184v.

7. For plebeian ambivalence toward the Inquisition (especially among women), see Ruth Behar, "Sex and Sin, Witchcraft and the Devil in Late-Colonial Mexico," *American Ethnologist* 14 (1987): 34–54.

8. Calvo, *La Nueva Galicia*, 81.

9. AGN, Tributos, vol. 11, exp. 10, fol. 146r.

10. Another group that is underrepresented—in comparison to its citywide distribution—is Indians. Each of Sagrario Metropolitano's registers was divided in two: one section for Spaniards, another for castas. The latter also accommodated Indians, who did not have a separate register of their own. Indians were not supposed to live in the central city, the traza, although thousands did so. But it is not clear how frequently these Indians had their baptisms, marriages, and burials recorded in Sagrario Metropolitano rather than in their "home" parishes. Record-keeping practices apparently varied from register to register: Indians were far more likely to appear in Sagrario Metropolitano's marriage records than in its libro de defunciones. However, many of the Indians married in Sagrario Metropolitano were designated *indios extravagantes*. It seems that numerous Indians, including the nobility of nearby pueblos, made a special point of coming to Mexico City's cathedral to be married.

11. Valdes, "The Decline of the Sociedad de Castas in Mexico City," 153–158.

12. This figure is calculated on the basis of the marriages in which both partners' race is identified—about 78% of total marriages.

13. Patricia Seed, "Social Dimensions of Race: Mexico City, 1753," *Hispanic American Historical Review* 62 (1982): 600.

14. D. A. Brading and Celia Wu, "Population Growth and Crisis: León, 1720–1866," *Journal of Latin American Studies* 5 (1973): 22.

15. Ibid., 31.

16. Under this criterion, the year 1696 should be included. Unfortunately, only 55% of the burials that year contained racial identifications, rendering it useless for our purposes.

17. For instance, see Brading and Wu, "Population Growth and Crisis," 30, and Claude Morin, "Population et épidemies dans une paroisse mexicaine: Santa Inés Zacatelco, XVIIe–XIXe siécles," *Cahiers des Amériques Latines, series sciences de l'homme* 6 (1972): 42–73. Similar increases have been found for rural parishes in Europe. See E. A. Wrigley, *Population and History* (New York: McGraw-Hill, 1969): 64–65.

18. For a brief history and description of the pósito/alhóndiga system, see Enrique Florescano, *Precios del maíz y crises agrícolas en México (1708–1810)* (Mexico: El Colegio de México, 1969): 43–50.

19. In contrast, it tended to widen the gap between the wealthy, particularly hacendados, and plebeians who had no access to cropland. Ibid., 105–110.

20. Indians are a special case. If the term "critical years" is restricted to those

years in which burials were at least 50% higher than normal—1678, 1692, and 1693—then this group does exhibit unusually heightened mortality. In these three years, Indian burials rose by 110%, as opposed to 71.2% for mestizos and 68.5% for mulattoes. So perhaps Indians were more vulnerable to famine and disease. However, the small size of the Indian sample (fewer than twenty burials per year over the 1672–1700 period) and the difficult problem of whether the Indians involved were native to the parish renders this assertion questionable. An answer would depend on the examination of a specifically Indian parish in Mexico City. Conclusions about castizo mortality are also vitiated by the small sample size. However, the argument in the text really rests on the comparison of the major racial groups— blacks, mulattoes, and mestizos—and here the results do not change regardless of the definition of "critical years."

21. Valdés, "The Decline of the Sociedad de Castas in Mexico City," 19.

22. Seed, "Social Dimensions of Race," 591.

23. The overall trace rate between these two registers was approximately 16%, somewhat lower than the 25% location rate achieved in other historical studies employing nominal record linkage (ibid., 592). The most probable reasons for not obtaining more linkages are (1) inconsistent naming practices (as discussed above); (2) movement of the couples in question to other parishes; and (3) incomplete racial identifications in the marriage records.

24. The other nine cases all involve mestizos, and they include six instances of mestizo-Indian passing—underlining the close links between these two groups. This matter will be discussed in more detail below.

25. This includes one case in which a "castizo" and "mestiza" became a "mestizo" and an "india."

26. A third possible influence on the racial variability in table 4.6—elapsed time between marriage and burial—is a red herring. It could be argued that a longer period of time would give castas a better chance to pass. But this was not the case. For those who changed their racial status, the average length of time between marriage and burial was seven years, two and one-half months; for the others, it was nine years, six months. This information does, however, provide a sad commentary on the brief life expectancy of residents in colonial Mexico City.

27. Barth, "Introduction," 15–16.

28. The literature on this subject is immense. For a classic study that uses intermarriage rates to measure social assimilation, see Milton Gordon, *Assimilation in American Life* (New York: Oxford University Press, 1964). Racial endogamy has also been at the heart of the continuing debate over whether colonial Latin American cities had a "class" or "estate" structure. For various sides of this debate, see John D. Chance and William B. Taylor, "Estate and Class in a Colonial City: Oaxaca 1972," *Comparative Studies in Society and History* 19 (1977): 454–487; Robert McCaa, Stuart B. Schwartz, and Arturo Grubessich, "Race and Class in Colonial Latin America: A Critique," *Comparative Studies in Society and History* 21 (1979): 421–433; Patricia Seed and Philip F. Rust, "Estate and Class in Colonial Oaxaca Revisted," *Comparative Studies in Society and History* 25 (1983): 703–710.

29. Philip F. Rust and Patricia Seed, "Equality of Endogamy: Statistical Approaches," *Social Science Research* 14 (1985): 74.

30. Ibid., 64–74. The use of Cohen's kappa to measure endogamy was first suggested in David J. Strauss, "Measuring Endogamy," *Social Science Research* 6 (1977): 244–245.

31. For the log-linear method, see Robert McCaa, "Modeling Social Interaction: Marital Miscegenation in Colonial Spanish America," *Historical Methods* 15 (Spring 1982): 45–66.

32. Archivo de Genealogía y Heráldica, Sagrario Metropolitano, Libro de matrimonios de castas, roll 519, vol. 3, fol. 133v–roll 520, vol. 8, fol. 167r.

33. Valdés, "The Decline of the Sociedad de Castas in Mexico City," 57–62, documents these patterns for the eighteenth century.

34. Ibid., 37, 41, presents marriage data for the years 1665–1670, 1723–1725, 1752–1754, 1781–1783, and 1810–1812 showing that Spanish-mestizo and Spanish-mulatto marriages remained rare throughout this entire period.

35. Ibid., 28–29.

36. AGN, Inquisición, vol. 677, exp. 3, fol. 143r.

37. AN, vol. 4,634, Nicolás de Vega (688), 16 November 1664.

Chapter 5. Patrons and Plebeians: Labor as a System of Social Control

1. Seed, "Social Dimensions of Race."

2. Ibid., 577.

3. Ibid., 581.

4. Ibid., 582.

5. AN, vol. 1,648, Francisco González Peñafiel (252), 4 April 1695, fol. 53v; AJ, Civil, vol. 62, exp. 62, fol. 4.

6. AN, vol. 29, Antonio de Anaya (9), 8 April 1683, fols. 33v–34r.

7. Valdés, "The Decline of the Sociedad de Castas in Mexico City," 161.

8. Laborers on public work projects, for instance, typically received three reales a day; but the projects themselves usually lasted just three to six weeks. See the labor accounts in AHCM, Puentes, vol. 3,716, exps. 4, 8; Cárceles en General, vol. 495, exp. 2; AGN, Caminos y Calzadas, vol. 2, exp. 1.

9. Seed, "Social Dimensions of Race," 576.

10. The Indians in the census are grouped by families, and (except in the case of widowed or single women) only the husband's occupation is listed.

11. AHCM, Fincas y Edificios Ruinosos, vol. 1,092, exp. 4.

12. See, for instance, Felipe de la Cruz, Pascual de los Angeles, and Lorenzo Melchor in AGN, Historia, vol. 413, exp. 1, fols. 32v, 52r.

13. Ibid., fol. 53v; Jorge González Angulo Aguirre, *Artesanado y ciudad a finales del siglo xviii* (Mexico: Fondo de Cultura Económica, 1983): 78. For other examples, see AGN, Historia, vol. 413, exp. 1, fols. 33v, 35v, 36v, 56v.

14. Archivo de Genealogía y Heráldica, Sagrario Metropolitano, Libro de defunciones de castas, roll 559, vol. 3, fol. 60v.

15. "Sobre los inconvenientes de vivir los indios en el centro de la cuidad," in *Boletín del Archivo general de la nación* 9 (1938): 12.

16. AGN, Historia, vol. 413, exp. 1, fols. 37v, 38r, 41v, 54v. The landlords' occupations were not given in the censuses but have been discovered through other documents. See n. 20 below.

17. AN, vol. 4,634, Nicolás de Vega (688), 16 November 1664; vol. 1,420, Ramón de Espinosa (218), 29 July 1698, fol. 174; vol. 1,453, Tomás Fernández de Guevara (229), 6 September 1690, fol. 137r.

18. AN, vol. 4,634, Nicolás de Vega (688), 12 June 1663, fol. 24.

19. See table 5.1 and the preceding comments on Indian artisans. By 1753, of course, blacks had ceased to be a "major" racial group.

20. AN, vol. 3,857, Francisco de Rivera (559), 3 January 1661, fol. 1; vol. 4,634, Nicolás de Vega (688), 12 June 1663, fol. 25r; AGN, Matrimonios, vol. 90, fol. 286v.

21. See table 4.9. For specific examples of traza Indians with casta spouses, see AGN, Historia, vol. 413, exp. 1, fols. 32v, 37r, 39; Bienes Nacionales, vol. 546, exp. 3, fol. 12v.

22. "Sobre los inconvenientes," p. 13.

23. *Actas de Cabildo,* XXXV: 18–19.

24. AGN, Indios, vol. 12, no. 215, fols. 135v–136r. This example dates from earlier in the century, 1631, but the problem persisted throughout the colonial period. See Gibson, *The Aztecs under Spanish Rule,* 391–393.

25. Chester L. Guthrie, "Colonial Economy: Trade, Industry, and Labor in Seventeenth-Century Mexico City," *Revista de Historia de America* 7 (1939): 132–133, fn. 88.

26. "Sobre los inconvenientes," 24.

27. Ibid., 13.

28. Ibid., 14; AGN, Bienes Nacionales, vol. 45, exp. 30, fol. 38; Inquisición, vol. 518, fol. 352r.

29. AN, vol. 29, Antonio de Anaya (9), 8 April 1683, fol. 33v; vol. 809, José del Castillo (124), 18 May 1699, fol. 241r.

30. AN, vol. 809, José del Castillo (124), 28 October 1699, fols. 536v–537r.

31. AN, vol. 4,634, Nicolás de Vega (688), 25 August 1662, fols. 3v–4r.

32. AGN, Bienes Nacionales, vol. 1,161, exp. 7, fols. 3r, 5.

33. AN, vol. 3,108, Juan Francisco Neri (453), 4 September 1688, fols. 19v–20v.

34. AJ, Civil, vol. 44, exp. 8; Richard J. Salvucci, *Textiles and Capitalism in Mexico: An Economic History of the Obrajes, 1539–1840* (Princeton: Princeton University Press, 1987): 101. This was a mean average, with a standard deviation of twenty-eight.

35. AJ, Penal, vol. 2, exp. 3, fol. 9v.

36. See, e.g., the apprenticeship agreement in AN, vol. 29, Antonio de Anaya (9), 27 February 1684, fol. 37r.

37. Franklin W. Knight, *Slave Society in Cuba During the Nineteenth Century* (Madison: University of Wisconsin Press): 82–84. For a discussion of slave mor-

tality on Brazilian sugar plantations, see Stuart B. Schwartz, *Sugar Plantations in the Formation of Brazilian Society: Bahia, 1550–1835* (Cambridge: Cambridge University Press, 1985): 338–378.

38. AGN, Reales Cédulas Duplicadas, vol. 103, fol. 194.

39. See Valdés, "The Decline of the Sociedad de Castas in Mexico City," 155–156: "By the end of the seventeenth century, the slave trade practically ceased. During the entire eighteenth century, only 20,000 African slaves are estimated to have been imported into the country."

40. AGN, Matrimonios, vol. 70, exp. 2.

41. One master, José de Villalta Enríquez, made a point of stipulating that the artisan could not sell his slave. This suggests that the slave truly did pass into the artisan's control during the apprenticeship. See AN, vol. 4,692, Francisco de Valdez (692), 27 January 1700, fol. 119.

42. AN, vol. 3,857, Francisco de Rivera (559), 10 November 1660, fols. 25v–26r.

43. AN, vol. 469, Domingo Barreda (63), 27 August 1676.

44. AN, vol. 3,878, Martín del Río (563), 26 March 1681, fol. 201.

45. AGN, Inquisición, vol. 722, exp. 5, fol. 194.

46. AN, vol. 4,692, Francisco de Valdez (692), 27 January 1700, fol. 116.

47. AN, vol. 3,878, Martín del Río (563), 21 July 1681, fol. 587r.

48. Her full name was Gregoria del Castillo. The fact that she used her mistress's surname may itself be evidence of an emotional link between the two.

49. AN, vol. 3,878, Martín del Río (563), 21 July 1681, fol. 587r.

50. Ibid., 21 October 1681, fol. 779.

51. AN, vol. 469, Domingo Barreda (63), 21 May 1676.

52. AN, vol. 3,878, Martín del Río (563), 31 July 1681, fol. 608.

53. AN, vol. 3,877, Martín del Río (563), 3 March 1680, fol. 155.

54. AN, vol. 38, Andrés de Almogueras (11) 13 January 1683, fol. 7r.

55. AN, vol. 809, José del Castillo (124), 16 June 1698, fol. 162.

56. Ibid., 5 March 1699, fol. 357.

57. Gibson, *The Aztecs under Spanish Rule*, 243.

58. For a discussion of "free labor" in the context of the obraje, as well as an examination of apprentices, convicts, and slaves as obraje workers, see Salvucci, *Textiles and Capitalism in Mexico*, 105–134.

59. AJ, Penal, vol. 1, exp. 44, fol. 2r.

60. Ibid., exp. 19, fol. 1r.

61. Ibid., fols. 2v–3r.

62. See the calculations in Gibson, *The Aztecs under Spanish Rule*, 311–312.

63. For information on Mexico's maize price cycle, see Ibid., Appendix V, 452–459; Florescano, *Precios del maíz*, 111–139.

64. AJ, Penal, vol. 1, exp. 19, fol. 15r.

65. Ibid., fols. 7–8.

66. Antonio de la Peña presented several witnesses who testified to the prevalence of this rate; and a concurrent criminal investigation of another panadería (AJ, Penal, vol. 1, exp. 44) revealed the same wage scale there. AN, vol. 782, Diego de Castilleja Guzmán (121), 9 February 1692, provides an example of a free black

190 Notes to Pages 100–106

entering a panadería under the same terms. This was apparently still the standard rate in Mexico City in 1765; see Salvucci, *Textiles and Capitalism in Mexico*, 125, 215, n. 153.

67. AJ, Penal, vol. 1, exp. 19, fols. 13v–14r.

68. Ibid., fol. 15r.

69. Richard E. Greenleaf, "Viceregal Power and the Obrajes of the Cortés Estate," *Hispanic American Historical Review* 48 (1968): 365–379.

70. AJ, Penal, vol. 1, exp. 44, fol. 27v.

71. AJ, Civil, vol. 56, 1692–93.

72. Samuel Kagan, "Penal Servitude in New Spain: The Colonial Textile Industry" (Ph.D. dissertation, City University of New York, 1977): 120–127.

73. AN, vol. 782, Diego de Castilleja Guzmán (121), 9 February 1692.

74. AJ, Civil, vol. 61, 14 October 1698, fol. 76. Cf. ibid., vol. 44, 4 March 1672.

75. Taylor, *Drinking, Homicide, and Rebellion*, 97–106.

76. AGN, Criminal, vol. 224, fol. 369v.

77. Taylor, *Drinking, Homicide, and Rebellion*, 101.

78. AGN, Criminal, vol. 75, exp. 2, fol. 5, passim.

79. AJ, Civil, vol. 62, exp. 22, fol. 2.

80. Ibid.

81. AN, vol. 3,240, Miguel Ortiz (473), 4 December 1694, 29 January 1699, 10 February 1699; vol. 1,421, Manuel de Esquivel (219), 24 May 1701, fol. 15r; vol. 1,422, Manuel de Esquivel (219), 28 April 1703, fol. 86.

82. AJ, Civil, vol. 60, Registro de Juan Clemente Guerrero, 12 July 1698. In his study of obrajes, Salvucci presents a less than sanguine view of the life led by apprentices, whom he sees as a source of cheap labor. However, he admits that "for some, life in an obraje, whatever its hardships, was better than starving." Salvucci, *Textiles and Capitalism in Mexico*, 106.

83. Quoted in Taylor, *Drinking, Homicide, and Rebellion*, 103.

84. AN, vol. 809, José del Castíllo (124), 21 October 1698, fol. 250.

85. AN, vol. 1,422, Manuel dé Esquivel (219), 28 April 1703, fol. 86.

86. AN, vol. 809, José del Castillo (124), 26 August 1697, inserted between fols. 326 and 327.

87. Seed, "Social Dimensions of Race," 585–590.

88. AGN, Bienes Nacionales, vol. 45, exp. 30; vol. 181, exp. 2.

89. Ibid., vol. 45, exp. 30, fol. 47.

90. Ibid., fol. 82.

91. Ibid., fol. 138; vol. 181, exp. 2, fol. 43.

Chapter 6. The Fragility of "Success": Upwardly Mobile Castas in Mexico City

1. AJ, Civil, vol. 61, exp. 3, fols. 40r–52, 61r.

2. AGN, Bienes Nacionales, vol. 1,393, exp. 23, fol. 3r.

3. AJ, Civil, vol. 61, exp. 3, fol. 23.

4. AGN, Bienes Nacionales, vol. 1,393, exp. 23, fols. 2v–3r.

5. Ibid., fol. 3v.

6. AN, vol. 776, José de Castro (119), 27 February 1690, fol. 38; vol. 3,370, Marcos Pacheco de Figueroa (499), 20 and 28 June 1692, fols. 26v–34v; vol. 469, Domingo Barreda (63), 24 January 1673. Some studies of sixteenth-century Andean cities have suggested that at least among Indians, women may have more readily adapted to the urban commercial setting than their male counterparts. See Elinor C. Burkett, "Indian Women and White Society: The Case of Sixteenth-Century Peru," in *Latin American Women: Historical Perspectives,* ed. Asunción Lavrin (Westport, Conn.: Greenwood Press, 1978): 117–121; Frank Salomon, "Indian Women of Early Colonial Quito as Seen through Their Testaments," *The Americas* 44, no. 3 (1988): 325–341. Ann Zulawski, however, argues that by the seventeenth century, large numbers of both Indian men and women had begun to participate in the urban market economy and that "the economic partnership of men and women was always desirable and in many cases became indispensable for negotiating the colonial system." Ann Zulawski, "Social Differentiation, Gender, and Ethnicity: Urban Indian Women in Colonial Bolivia, 1640–1725," *Latin American Research Review* 25 (1990): 93–119. The quotation is from p. 109.

7. For examples of financial loss, see AN, vol. 733, Gabriel de la Cruz (112), 10 January 1633, fol. 3; vol. 4,692, Francisco de Valdez (692), 10 February 1700, fol. 166r; vol. 29, Antonio de Anaya (9), 29 April 1683, fol. 55r; vol. 765, Juan de Castro Peñalosa (116), 14 May 1692, fols. 174r–175v.

8. Manuel Carrera Stampa, *Los gremios mexicanos,* 38–40.

9. AGN, Archivo Histórico de Hacienda, vol. 270, exp. 4, fols. 6r–9v.

10. "Literate" persons are here defined as those able to write their names. Several types of documents (such as notarial contracts and transcriptions of testimony before the Inquisition and judicial tribunals) required the signature of the person involved. If he was unable to write his name, this fact was noted: "No lo firmó porque dijo no saber escribir."

11. AN, vol. 733, Gabriel de la Cruz (112), 9 December 1660. See also, ibid., 15 July 1663, fol. 46r; vol. 3,857, Francisco de Rivera (559), 8 September 1661, fol. 43r; AJ, Civil, vol. 60, Registro de Juan Clemente Guerrero, 13 February 1698.

12. See, e.g., the sale of two sets of carpentry tools for 142 pesos and 185 pesos, respectively, in AN, vol. 809, José de Castillo (124), 13 October 1698, fols. 229v–230r, and vol. 29, Antonio de Anaya (9), 25 September 1693, fol. 157.

13. There is little information on the daily or weekly wages earned by oficiales who worked in artisanal shops. Those who participated in public works projects typically earned 6 reales a day, but these projects were sporadic and of short duration. In addition to the sources listed in chapter 5, n. 8, see AHCM, Puentes, vol. 3,716, exp. 3; AGN, Hospitales, vol. 67, exp. 1; Bienes Nacionales, vol. 356, exp. 10; Templos y Conventos, vol. 103, exp. 2.

14. AGN, Inquisición, vol. 571, exp. 1, fols. 10v–11r.

15. AN, vol. 3,720, Francisco de Quiñones (571), 28 January 1692, fols. 40v–41r.

16. For an example, see AN, vol. 3,109, Juan Francisco Neri (453), 10 October 1697, fol. 34r.

17. According to John Coatsworth, "Roughly half of all Colonial revenues were exported as net fiscal revenues throughout the colonial era." John H. Coatsworth, "The Limits of Colonial Absolutism: The State in Eighteenth-Century Mexico," in *Essays in the Political, Economic and Social History of Colonial Latin America,* ed. Karen Spalding (Newark: University of Delaware, 1979): 27. See also Murdo MacLeod, "Aspects of the Internal Economy of Colonial Spanish America: Labour; Taxation; Distribution and Exchange," in Leslie Bethell, ed., *Colonial Latin America,* vol. 2 of *The Cambridge History of Latin America* (Cambridge: Cambridge University Press, 1984): 263–264; Geoffrey Walker, *Spanish Politics and Imperial Trade, 1700–1789* (Bloomington: Indiana University Press, 1979): 117–128; John E. Kicza, *Colonial Entrepreneurs: Families and Business in Bourbon Mexico City* (Albuquerque: University of New Mexico Press, 1983): 231–233.

18. For instance, some testators direct their executors to consult private memoranda that list their debtors and creditors; others, rather than enumerate their possessions, refer to "the goods that can be found . . . in my house." AN, vol. 4,685, Francisco Valdez (692), 21 November 1692, fol. 184v.

19. AJ, Civil, vol. 61, 1698–99, fol. 6.

20. AN, vol. 3,370, Marcos Pacheco de Figueroa (499), 29 April 1692, fols. 19v–21v.

21. AN, vol. 1,648, Francisco González Peñafiel (252), 23 August 1695, fols. 170r–171r.

22. AN, vol. 4,634, Nicolás de Vega (688), 16 November 1664.

23. AJ, Civil, vol. 61, exp. 3; AN, vol. 4,634, Nicolás de Vega (688), 1 September 1665, fol. 52.

24. AN, vol. 1,453, Tomás Fernández de Guevara (229), 6 September 1690, fols. 135r–137v.

25. AN, vol. 2,101, Matías Herrero Gutiérrez (306), 9 June 1704, fols. 40v–42r.

26. AN, vol. 776, José de Castro (119), 27 February 1690, fol. 38v; vol. 798, Juan de Condarco y Cáceres (122), 19 July 1701, fols. 180v–181r.

27. AN, vol. 1,453, Tomás Fernández de Guevara (229), 6 September 1690, fols. 135r–137v.

28. AN, vol. 2,101, Matías Herrero Gutiérrez (306), 9 June 1704, fols. 40v–42r.

29. AN, vol. 60, José de Anaya y Bonilla (13), 12 July 1701, fols. 311v–312v.

30. AJ, Civil, vol. 60, Registro de Juan Clemente Guerrero, 13 November 1698.

31. AN, vol. 27, Juan Azores (8), 14 August 1686.

32. AN, vol. 4,634, Nicolás de Vega (688), 1 September 1665, fol. 52.

33. AN, vol. 2,200, Jiménez de Siles (326), 20 April 1678, fol. 14.

34. AN, vol.798, Juan de Condarco y Cáceres (122), 19 July 1701, fols. 181v–182r; vol. 469, Domingo Barreda (63), 24 January 1673.

35. AN, vol. 60, José de Anaya y Bonilla (13), 12 July 1701, fols. 311r–313r.

36. AN, vol. 1,420, Ramón de Espinosa (218), 28 July 1699, fols. 173r–175v.

37. AN, vol. 750, Pedro del Castillo Grimaldo (114), 9 March 1686, fols. 38r–40r.

38. AN, vol. 1,267, Diego Díaz de Rivera (198), 19 April 1697, fol. 97v; vol. 3,370, Marcos Pacheco de Figueroa (499), fols. 46r–47r.

39. AN, vol. 4395, Francisco Solís y Alcázar (636), 20 August 1702, fol. 293.

40. In thirty-three of the fifty-eight marriages, the partners' race is not recorded.

I suggest that either these were marriages that did not enhance the testators' status—i.e., marriages to other castas or Indians—or that even these upwardly mobile castas, who had perhaps begun to assimilate elite notions of race, still did not fully accept the sistema de castas and were not thinking in terms of marrying up or down.

41. AGN, Ordenanzas, vol. 5, fols. 13–14, 73–74, 88–90; vol. 6, fols. 3–8, 17–18, 44, 53r, 59r, 61r, 70–73, 77, 103r; vol. 7, fols. 11v–12r; vol. 8, fols. 3v–4v.

42. AN, vol. 4,395, Francisco Solís y Alcázar (636), 20 August 1702, fols. 292r–294r.

43. AN, vol. 1,315, Juan Díaz de Rivera (199), 10 January 1693, fols. 6r–7v; vol. 4,634, Nicolás de Vega (688), 5 September 1664.

44. AN, vol. 3,370, Marcos Pacheco de Figueroa (499), 20 June 1692, fol. 28r.

45. AGN, Ordenanzas. vol. 5, fol. 13r.

46. For instance, compare the entries in the Archivo de Genealogía y Heráldica, Sagrario Metropolitano, Libro de defunciones de castas, roll 559, vol. 3, fol. 72r, and vol. 4, fol. 77v, with respectively, AN, vol. 1,453, Tomás Fernández de Guevara (229), 6 September 1690, fol. 135r (will of Pedro de Mora Esquivel); vol. 1,648, Francisco González Peñafiel (259), 28 August 1695, fol. 160r (will of Antonio López del Castillo). It may also be significant that four testators called themselves "pardos," a less pejorative term for Afro-Mexicans than "mulatto" and one that very rarely appeared in the parish records of the period.

47. AN, vol. 3,108, Juan Francisco Neri (453), 16 July 1688, fols. 15–16r.

48. AN, vol. 3,877, Martín del Río (563), 7 April 1680, fol. 251r; vol. 3,369, Marcos Pacheco de Figueroa (499), 6 October 1685, fols. 46v–47r; AJ, Civil, vol. 60, 18 June 1698.

49. AN, vol. 469, Domingo Barreda (63), 24 January 1673.

50. AN, vol. 460, Nicolás Bernal (61) 30 August 1677, fols. 75v–76r.

51. For the role of real estate in the investment strategies of the elite, see John Tutino, *From Insurrection to Revolution in Mexico: Social Bases of Agrarian Violence, 1750–1940* (Princeton: Princeton University Press, 1986): 101–102.

52. These were almost surely "substitute" children. Of the twenty orphans mentioned in these wills, fifteen were adopted by childless men or women; none were adopted by testators with four or more children.

53. Elizabeth Kuznesof (personal communication) has suggested that the sample may be biased because of Hispanic inheritance practices. Childless couples were more likely to leave wills to ensure the proper distribution of their estates, since provisions for automatic inheritance by children would not be in effect. Salomon (328) remarks on the same possibility in his study of Indian women in sixteenth-century Quito. However, even if the sample is biased, it would not affect the argument for these particular testators. Small family size, then, did prove economically beneficial for at least some castas.

54. For some examples of the wealth of the Mexico City elite in the mid-seventeenth century, see Brading, *Miners and Merchants*, 13.

55. For a similar argument about "successful" Indians in seventeenth-century Peru, see Stern, *Peru's Indian Peoples*, 158–183.

194   Notes to Pages 125–131

Chapter 7. The Riot of 1692

1. Compare the treatments of seventeenth-century Mexico in Leonard, *Baroque Times* (originally published in 1959) and Israel, *Race, Class and Politics* (1975).
2. Israel, *Race, Class, and Politics*, 135–160.
3. Guthrie, "Colonial Economy," 114; Florescano, *Precios del maíz*, 97.
4. Sigüenza y Góngora, "Letter of Don Carlos de Sigüenza y Góngora," 231.
5. Thompson, "Moral Economy," 76–77.
6. AGI, Patronato, leg. 226, no. 1, r. 8, fol. 3r.
7. Ibid., fol. 9.
8. AGI, Patronato, leg. 226, no. 1, r. 2, fols. 8r, 15v.
9. AGI, Patronato, leg. 226, no. 1, r. 12, fols. 13v–14v.
10. AGI, Patronato, leg. 226, no. 1, r. 1, fols. 1–2r.
11. Sigüenza y Góngora, "Letter of Don Carlos de Sigüenza y Góngora," 244–245.
12. AGI, Patronato, leg. 226, no. 1, r. 25, carta 4, fol. 1.
13. AGI, Patronato, leg. 226, no. 1, r. 18, fol. 29. See Hassig, *Trade, Tribute, and Transportation*, 211–219, for a discussion of the comparative costs of water and land transportation in central Mexico.
14. AGI, Patronato, leg. 226, no. 1, r. 18, fols. 3v–6r.
15. AGI, Patronato, leg. 226, no. 1, r. 21. A fanega is equal to 46 kilograms.
16. AGI, Patronato, leg. 226, no. 1, r. 20, fols. 14v–15v. See Gibson, *The Aztecs under Spanish Rule*, 329, for Chalco harvests in other years.
17. AGI, Patronato, leg. 226, no. 1, r. 20, fols. 3v–4v.
18. Ibid., fols. 14v–15v.
19. Florescano, *Precios del maíz*, 59.
20. Sigüenza y Góngora, "Letter of Don Carlos de Sigüenza y Góngora," 234; John Tutino, *From Insurrection to Revolution in Mexico*, 61–65; Gibson, *The Aztecs under Spanish Rule*, 322–329.
21. According to Sigüenza y Góngora's figures (234), the price approximately doubled; the archbishop estimated the increase at 367%. AGI, Patronato, leg. 226, no. 1, r. 22, fol. 2r.
22. Ibid.
23. Sigüenza y Góngora, "Letter of Don Carlos de Sigüenza y Góngora," 236.
24. AGI, Patronato, leg. 226, no. 1, r. 18, fol. 8v.
25. Florescano, *Precios del maíz*, 36, 52, n. 26.
26. Sigüenza y Góngora, "Letter of Don Carlos de Sigüenza y Góngora," 239.
27. AGI, Patronato, leg. 226, no. 1, r. 18, fols. 9v–13r.
28. Ibid., fols. 13v–16v.
29. Ibid., fol. 18v.
30. Ibid., fols. 18v–19r.
31. AGI, Patronato, leg. 226, no. 1, r. 20, fols. 4v–6v.
32. This was the price at which tribute in kind could be converted to tribute in cash. The actual purchase price of maize varied throughout the agricultural year, but in good years, the average price was not far from 9 reales.

33. Migration, unless one had an assured job on a hacienda, was not an inviting alternative, since the countryside was being drained of maize precisely to supply Mexico City.

34. Sigüenza y Góngora, "Letter of Don Carlos de Sigüenza y Góngora," 238; AGI, Patronato, leg. 226, no. 1, r. 20, fol. 16r.

35. Sigüenza y Góngora, "Letter of Don Carlos de Sigüenza y Góngora," 245, 252; AGI, Patronato, leg. 226, no. 1, r. 25, carta 2, fol. 1; r. 19, fol. 32r.

36. Ibid.

37. Barrington Moore, Jr., *Injustice: The Social Bases of Obedience and Revolt* (White Plains: M. E. Sharpe, 1978): 459.

38. They may have been peninsular bureaucrats. I infer this from their obvious knowledge of government functions and their disdainful attitudes toward the creole elite, whom they called "little gentlemen . . . who are cape-snatchers, gamecock breeders, and cockfighters," clearly unfit for a serious military task ["cabos militares de agua dulce"]. AGI, Patronato, leg. 226, no. 1, r. 25, carta 1.

39. Ibid., fols. 3r–4r.; Robles, II: 257.

40. Sigüenza y Góngora, "Letter of Don Carlos de Sigüenza y Góngora," 243, 251–252.

41. Ibid.

42. AGI, Patronato, leg. 226, no. 1, r. 25, carta 2, fol. 2r.

43. Ibid., fol. 2.

44. AGI, Patronato, leg. 226, no. 1, r. 9, fol. 12r.

45. Sigüenza y Góngora, "Letter of Don Carlos de Sigüenza y Góngora," 253.

46. Ibid.

47. AGI, Patronato, leg. 226, no. 1, r. 2, fol. 14r.

48. Ibid., fol. 16r.

49. AGI, Patronato, leg. 226, no. 1, r. 9, fol. 11v.

50. For the archibishop's reputation, see Sigüenza y Góngora, "Letter of Don Carlos de Sigüenza y Góngora," 224–225; Leonard, *Baroque Times*, 160–161. For the structural antagonism between viceroys and archbishops, see Lockhart and Otte, *Letters and People of the Spanish Indies*, 203; Israel, *Race, Class, and Politics*, esp. 267–273.

51. Palmer, *Slaves of the White God*, 138.

52. AGI, Patronato, leg. 226, no. 1, r. 25, carta 2, fol. 2.

53. Sigüenza y Góngora, "Letter of Don Carlos de Sigüenza y Góngora," 252.

54. The archbishop's account of the riot (AGI, Patronato, leg. 226, no. 1, r. 22) discreetly omits any reference to the scene at his residence, but Escalante y Mendoza suggests that the archbishop was put off by the noise and uproar of the crowd: r. 25, carta 2, fol. 2.

55. AGI, Patronato, leg. 226, no. 1, r. 25, carta 7, fol. 2.

56. AGI, Patronato, leg. 226, no. 1, r. 2, fol. 13v.

57. Ibid., fol. 15v.

58. AGI, Patronato, leg. 226, no. 1, r. 1, fols. 3v–4r; r. 2, fol. 17r; Sigüenza y Góngora, "Letter of Don Carlos de Sigüenza y Góngora," 216.

59. AGI, Patronato, leg. 226, no. 1, r. 2, fols. 14v, 17.

60. AGI, Patronato, leg. 226, no. 1, r. 1.
61. Taylor, *Drinking, Homicide and Rebellion*, 117.
62. This point is discussed more fully below.
63. AGI, Patronato, leg. 226, no. 1, r. 15, fol. 6.
64. Ibid., fol. 8v; r. 12, fol. 14v.
65. AGI, Patronato, leg. 226, no. 1, r. 9, fols. 41v–43r.
66. Ibid., fol. 44.
67. Ibid., fols. 46r, 48r.
68. AGI, Patronato, leg. 226, no. 1, r. 2, fol. 6r.
69. AGI, Patronato, leg. 226, no. 1, r. 4, fol. 2.
70. Ibid., fols. 11, 13.
71. Ibid., fol. 18v.
72. Ibid., fols. 5r, 13v. He added an additional incriminating detail—that Santos was known for throwing stones.
73. Cf. Nicolas Calderón's claim that an "indio achinado en cuerpo" set fire to the jail: AGI, Patronato, leg. 226, no. 1, r. 2, fol. 8v.
74. AGI, Patronato, leg. 226, no. 1, r. 4, fol. 24v.
75. AGI, Patronato, leg. 226, no. 1, r. 9, fol. 13r. Of course, this may merely have been a malicious act on Gonzales's part, an attempt to gain the sympathy of the magistrates.
76. AGI, Patronato, leg. 226, no. 1, rs. 8–9, passim.
77. Sigüenza y Góngora, "Letter of Don Carlos de Sigüenza y Góngora," 259–263; AGI, Patronato, leg. 226, no. 1, r. 19, fols. 2, 7v, 12v, 21v; r. 25, carta 2, fol. 2v.
78. AGI, Patronato, leg. 226, no. 1, r. 19, fols. 18v, 20r.
79. Sigüenza y Góngora, "Letter of Don Carlos de Sigüenza y Góngora," 257; AGI, Patronato, leg. 226, no. 1, r. 4, fol. 3r; r. 2, fol. 12v.
80. AGI, Patronato, leg. 226, no. 1, r. 9, fol. 12; r. 12, fol. 17r; Sigüenza y Góngora, "Letter of Don Carlos de Sigüenza y Góngora," 257.
81. AGI, Patronato, leg. 226, no. 1, r. 2, fol. 10v.
82. AGI, Patronato, leg. 226, no. 1, r. 19, fol. 32v; Sigüenza y Góngora, "Letter of Don Carlos de Sigüenza y Góngora," 262.
83. AGI, Patronato, leg. 226, no. 1, r. 6, fol. 19r; see also r. 2, fol. 8r; r. 8, fol. 11v.
84. AGI, Patronato, leg. 226, no. 1, r. 3, fol. 7v; r. 4, fol. 24v; r. 9, fol. 20r.
85. AGI, Patronato, leg. 226, no. 1, r. 2, fols. 4v, 14v; Sigüenza y Góngora, "Letter of Don Carlos de Sigüenza y Góngora," 257, 262.
86. AGI, Patronato, leg. 226, no. 1, r. 2, fols. 7v–8r.
87. AGI, Patronato, leg. 226, no. 1, r. 19, fol. 20v.
88. Sigüenza y Góngora, "Letter of Don Carlos de Sigüenza y Góngora," 260–263; AGI, Patronato, leg. 226, no. 1, r. 19, fol. 2v; r. 26, carta 2, fol. 3r.
89. AGI, Patronato, leg. 226, no. 1, r. 19, fol. 20v; r. 15, fols. 2r–3r; r. 25, carta 6, fol. 1v.
90. Sigüenza y Góngora, "Letter of Don Carlos de Sigüenza y Góngora," 261–262.

91. I do not mean to suggest that they use this word or image. Most Spaniards were probably unaware that such a creature existed.

92. AGI, Patronato, leg. 226, no. 1, r. 2, fol. 10r.

93. For example, Pedro Román, a sergeant of the guard, identified *two* Indians whom he said had shouted, "Long live the king and death to this cuckold viceroy!" AGI, Patronato, leg. 226, no. 1, r. 15, fol. 8r.

94. AGI, Patronato, leg. 226, no. 1, r. 19, fols. 2r, 24.

95. For instance, AGI, Patronato, leg. 226, no. 1, r. 2, fols. 12v–13r. In physical terms, the immense Mexico City plaza, even cluttered with over two hundred shops and stalls, could accommodate a crowd of 10,000 with considerable room to spare. In 1982, an estimated crowd of 500,000 jammed the plaza in support of Pres. López Portillo's bank nationalization. The author took forty-five minutes to jostle his way from one end of the plaza to the other. Accounts of the 1692 riot suggest a very different, much lower person/space ratio.

96. AGI, Patronato, leg. 226, no. 1, r. 2, fols. 4r, 11v, 13r, 21.

97. AGI, Patronato, leg. 226, no. 1, r. 25, carta 2, fol. 3r.

98. AGI, Patronato, leg. 226, no. 1, r. 9, fol. 12v.

99. AGI, Patronato, leg. 226, no. 1, r. 9, fol. 13.

100. Ibid., fols. 13r–14v.

101. AGI, Patronato, leg. 226, no. 1, r. 4, fol. 25r.

102. AGI, Patronato, leg. 226, no. 1, r. 4, fols. 24v–25r.

103. AGI, Patronato, leg. 226, no. 1, r. 8, fol. 3v.

104. AGI, Patronato, leg. 226, no. 1, r. 2, fol. 15v.

105. AGI, Patronato, leg. 226, no. 1, r. 9, fol. 23v.

106. AGI, Patronato, leg. 226, no. 1, r. 14, fol. 19r; Sigüenza y Góngora, "Letter of Don Carlos de Sigüenza y Góngora," 265–266.

107. AGI, Patronato, leg. 226, no. 1, r. 2, fol. 13v; Sigüenza y Góngora, "Letter of Don Carlos de Sigüenza y Góngora," 265.

108. AGI, Patronato, leg. 226, no. 1, r. 5, fol. 7v; rs. 8–9, passim.

109. AGI, Patronato, leg. 226, no. 1, r. 5, fols. 4v, 9v, 12v, 16r, 18r; r. 4, fol. 25; r. 6, fol. 2v; r. 12, fol. 17; Sigüenza y Góngora, "Letter of Don Carlos de Sigüenza y Góngora," 266–267.

110. Cf. Don Benito Naboa Salgado: "acabado el robo se acabó el tumulto." AGI, Patronato, leg. 226, no. 1, r. 25, carta 6, fol. 1v.

111. AGI, Patronato, leg. 226, no. 1, r. 9, fol. 14r.

112. AGI, Patronato, leg. 226, no. 1, r. 6, fol. 2v; r. 12, fol. 17v; r. 14, fols. 19, 23.

113. AGI, Patronato, leg. 226, no. 1, r. 2, fol. 11r; r. 19, fol. 10r.

114. AGI, Patronato, leg. 226, no. 1, r. 2, fol. 11r; r. 5, passim; r. 7, fol. 3r.

115. AGI, Patronato, leg. 226, no. 1, r. 19, fol. 13; r. 2, fol. 11v.

116. The provisor "directly oversaw the administration of the diocese and acted as an intermediary between the bishop and the clergy in general." John Frederick Schwaller, *The Church and Clergy in Sixteenth-Century Mexico* (Albuquerque: University of New Mexico Press, 1987): 19.

117. AGI, Patronato, leg. 226, no. 1, r. 1, r. 2, fol. 17v.

118. AGI, Patronato, leg. 226, no. 1, r. 19, fol. 13v.

119. AGI, Patronato, leg. 226, no. 1, r. 14, fol. 17r.

120. AGI, Patronato, leg. 226, no. 1, r. 19, fol. 35r; r. 25, carta 6, fol. 1v; r. 2, fol. 17v.

121. The most complete description of the destruction wrought by the riot is in AGI, Patronato, leg. 226, no. 1, r. 1, fols. 4r–5r. Saénz de Tagle estimated "el perjuicio que el comercio ha reconocido" at more than 400,000 pesos: r. 24, fol. 1.

122. AGI, Patronato, leg. 225, no. 1, r. 19, fols. 29v–31r.

123. Ibid., fol. 3. Bakery workers are, in fact, conspicuous by their absence in accounts of the riot, perhaps because they were locked up in their panaderías.

124. AGI, Patronato, leg. 226, no. 1, r. 2, fol. 11v; r. 14, fol. 3r; r. 19, fols. 3r, 10v, 29v, 38v.

125. Bakewell, *Silver Mining and Society in Colonial Mexico*, 213.

126. AGI, Patronato, leg. 226, no. 1, r. 19, fol. 39r.

127. Ibid., fol. 40v.

128. Ibid., fol. 11; r. 1, fol. 4r; r. 17, fols. 16r–17v. Those enlisted in the new militia companies also received a onetime lump sum payment of 8 and 6 pesos, respectively; the professional soldiers of the guard were given a 3-peso bonus.

129. AGI, Patronato, leg. 226, no. 1, r. 11, fols. 2v–3r.

130. AGI, Patronato, leg. 226, no. 1, r. 19, fol. 4v.

131. AGI, Patronato, leg. 226, no. 1, r. 7, fol. 2v.

132. Ibid., fols. 1, 5v–6r.

133. AGI, Patronato, leg. 226, no. 1, r. 9, fols. 1r, 11r.

134. AGI, Patronato, leg. 226, no. 1, r. 7, fol. 5v; r. 14; fols. 4r–5r.

135. AGI, Patronato, leg. 226, no. 1, r. 6, fols. 1r–2r.

136. AGI, Patronato, leg. 226, no. 1, r. 9, fols. 7v–8r.

137. AGI, Patronato, leg. 226, no. 1, r. 12, fols. 15v–16r.

138. AGI, Patronato, leg. 226, no. 1, r. 2, fol. 11v; r. 15, fol. 3.

139. AGI, Patronato, leg. 226, no. 1, r. 3, fols. 1v–2v.

140. AGI, Patronato, leg. 226, no. 1, r. 1, fol. 4v.

141. For example, the fiscal, commenting on an Indian's claim that he had been intimidated into shouting, "Long live the king and death to bad government!" stated that this excuse "could only be allowed in another type of person who was not an Indian." AGI, Patronato, leg. 226, no. 1, r. 3, fol. 7r. See also the discussion of sentencing patterns, below.

142. AGI, Patronato, leg. 226, no. 1, r. 13, fol. 21r.

143. AGI, Patronato, leg. 226, no. 1, r. 14, fols. 21v–22r.

144. AGI, Patronato, leg. 226, no. 1, r. 12, fol. 4. For another example of this "just visiting" defense, see r. 13, fols. 4v–5r. For a mirror image claim—a landlady blaming her tenants—see r. 14, fols. 5v–6r, 20–21r.

145. AGI, Patronato, leg. 226, no. 1, r. 12, fols. 4r, 6, 7r, 17.

146. Ibid., fol. 5.

147. Ibid., fol. 16v. Cf. r. 14, fol. 25r.

148. AGI, Patronato, leg. 226, no. 1, r. 17, fols. 17v–18v. In subsequent de-

crees throughout June and July, Galve closed the baratillo, banned pulque, forced Indians living in the traza to return to their barrios, and ordered that they wear traditional Indian garb: fols. 3v–13r.

149. AGI, Patronato, leg. 226, no. 1, r. 9, fols. 5v–6r, 15.

150. AGI, Patronato, leg. 225, no. 1, r. 5, fols. 8v, 12v; r. 15, fols. 4r, 5r. In Spanish courts, intoxication was grounds for reduced responsibility: see Taylor, *Drinking, Homicide, and Rebellion*, 63–65.

151. AGI, Patronato, leg. 226, no. 1, r. 9, fols. 11v–18v.

152. AGI, Audiencia de México, leg. 333, no. 13, 5 July 1692.

153. For a discussion of "contested space," see Mary Ryan, "The American Parade: Representations of Nineteenth-Century Social Order," in *The New Cultural History*, ed. Lynn Hunt (Berkeley: University of California Press, 1989): 131–153.

154. AGI, Patronato, leg. 226, no. 1, r. 15, fol. 9r.

155. Ibid., fol. 9v; Robles, II: 258.

156. The length of the trial may result partly from its late start, on June 30. By this time, the perceived need for urgent and exemplary punishment had ebbed. In addition, as noted above, the evidence against Santos was unusually detailed, with numerous eyewitness accounts.

157. AGI, Patronato, leg. 226, no. 1, r. 14.

158. AGI, Patronato, leg. 226, no. 1, r. 7.

159. Taylor, *Drinking, Homicide, and Rebellion*, 98.

160. In 1612, thirty-five blacks and mulattoes were executed in a single day: Palmer, *Slaves of the White God*, 140. For the auto-da-fé of 1596, see Martin A. Cohen, *The Martyr: The Story of a Secret Jew and the Mexican Inquisition in the Sixteenth Century* (Philadelphia: Jewish Publication Society of America, 1973): 253–259. For its seventeenth-century counterparts, see *Documentos inéditos ó muy raros para la historia de México*, 133–259.

161. Taylor, *Drinking, Homicide and Rebellion*, 112.

162. For instance, AGI, Patronato, leg. 226, no. 1, r. 9, fols. 41v–43r. Contrast the much less controlled use of torture by friars in sixteenth-century Yucatán, as discussed in Inga Clendinnen, *Ambivalent Conquests*, 72–92.

163. AGI, Patronato, leg. 226, no. 1, r. 5.

164. AGI, Patronato, leg. 226, no. 1, r. 19, fol. 39r.

165. John Tutino, "Power, Class, and Family: Men and Women in the Mexican Elite, 1750–1810," *The Americas* 39, no. 3 (January 1983): 380.

166. AGI, Patronato, leg. 226, no. 1, r. 25, carta 6, fol. 1v.

167. In Spanish, a masculine noun encompasses both genders, so these witnesses had to say explicitly "indios y indias, mulatos y mulatas," etc.

168. Sigüenza y Góngora, 252–257; the quotation is from p. 257.

169. AGI, Patronato, leg. 226, no. 1, r. 5; Archivo de Genealogía y Heráldica, Sagrario Metropolitano, Libro de defunciones de castas, roll 544, vol. 3, fol. 110v.

170. AGI, Patronato, leg. 226, no. 1, r. 2, fol. 15v.

171. Tutino, "Power, Class, and Family," 380.

172. George Rudé, *The Crowd in History*, 204.

173. Robles, II: 258; AGI, Audiencia de México, leg. 333, no. 14; Sigüenza y Góngora, "Letter of Don Carlos de Sigüenza y Góngora," 246.

Conclusion

1. See the articles in "La pintura de castas," *Artes de México*, no. 8 (Summer 1990): 17–88; *Mexico: Splendors of Thirty Centuries*, introd. Octavio Paz (New York: Metropolitan Museum of Art, 1990): 432–433.

2. For the colonial bureaucracy as mediator, see John Leddy Phelan, "Authority and Flexibility in the Spanish Imperial Bureaucracy," *Administrative Science Quarterly* 5 (1960): 47–65.

3. For instance, colonial architecture does seem to have shaped the plebeians' conception of urban space. Many Inquisition and court witnesses, when asked where they lived, located themselves in reference to ecclesiastical buildings. Marcos de la Cruz, a mulatto slave, stated that he lived "next to the great monastery of San Francisco." AGN, Inquisición, vol. 677, exp. 3, fol. 140r. Also see, among numerous other examples, ibid., vol. 667, exp. 4, fol. 100r; vol. 673, exp. 4, fol. 85r; vol. 722, exp. 5, fol. 196v; vol. 731, exp. 4, fol. 105r.

4. The analogy of the pyramid is not original, of course, but has been used several times previously; for example, Octavio Paz, *The Other Mexico: Critique of the Pyramid*, trans. Lysander Kemp (New York: Grove Press, 1972): 80–112.

5. AGI, Patronato, leg. 226, no. 1, r. 9, fol. 17v.

6. For the utilization of ethnic "duality" among modern Mexican Indians, see Royce, *Ethnic Identity*.

Selected Bibliography

Archival Sources

Archivo de Genealogía y Héraldica
  Sagrario Metropolitano
    Libro de defunciones de castas
    Libro de matrimonios de castas
    Libro de matrimonios de españoles
    Padrones
Archivo General de la Nación, Mexico City [AGN]
  Archivo Histórico de Hacienda
  Bienes Nacionales
  Caminos y Calzadas
  Civil
  Criminal
  Edictos de la Santa y General Inquisición
  Historia
  Hospitales
  Indios
  Inquisición
  Matrimonios
  Obras Públicas
  Ordenanzas
  Reales Cédulas Duplicadas
  Templos y Conventos
  Tributos
Archivo Histórico de la Ciudad de México [AHCM]
  Alcaicería
  Artesanos—Gremios
  Calzadas y Caminos
  Cárceles en General
  Cédulas y Reales Ordenes
  Clausura de Callejones
  Fincas y Edificios Ruinosos
  Historia en General
  Ordenanzas
  Plaza Mayor
  Policia: Salubridad

Puentes
Ríos y Acequias
Archivo Histórico del Instituto Nacional de Antropología e Historia, Mexico City
Colección Antigua
Fondo Franciscano
Archivo de Notarías del Distrito Federal, Mexico City [AN]
Archivo del Tribunal Superior de Justicia del Distrito Federal, Mexico City [AJ]
Civil
Penal
Archivo General de las Indias, Seville, Spain [AGI]
Audiencia de México
Patronato

Published Primary Sources

Actas de Cabildo de la Ciudad de México. Title varies. 54 vols. Mexico: Imprenta de Aguilar e Hijos, 1889–1916.

Cerralvo, Rodrigo Pacheco y Ossorio, Marqués de. "Relación del estado en que dejó el gobierno de la Nueva España el excelentísimo señor don Rodrigo Pacheco y Ossorio, Marqués de Cerralvo." In *Descripción de la Nueva España en el siglo xvii por el padre Fray Antonio Vázquez de Espinosa y otros documentos del siglo xvii.* Ed. Mariano Cuevas. Mexico: Editorial Patria, S.A., 1944.

Cervantes de Salazar, Francisco. *Mexico en 1554.* Trans. Joaquín García Icazbalceta. Introd. Julio Jiménez Rueda. Mexico: Ediciones de la Universidad Nacional Autónoma, 1952.

Colección de documentos inéditos para la historia de España. Ed. Martín Fernández Navarrete and others. 112 vols. Madrid: Imprenta de la Viuda de Calero, 1842–1895.

Colección de documentos inéditos relativos al descubrimiento, conquista y organización de las antiguas posesiones españoles de América y Oceanía, sacados de los archivos del Reino y muy especialmente del de Indias. 42 vols. Madrid: Imprenta Española, 1864–1884.

Colección de documentos para la historia de la formación social de Hispanoamérica. Ed. Richard Konetzke. 3 vols. Madrid: Consejo Superior de Investigaciones Científicas, 1953–1962.

Díaz del Castillo, Bernal. *The Conquest of New Spain.* Trans. and introd. J. M. Cohen. Baltimore: Penguin Books, 1963.

Documentos inéditos del siglo xvi para la historia de México. Ed. Mariano Cuevas. Mexico: Jose Porrúa e Hijos, 1914.

Documentos para la historia del México colonial. Ed. France V. Scholes and Eleanor B. Adams. 7 vols. Mexico: Jose Porrúa e Hijos, 1955–1961.

Don Juan de Palafox y Mendoza: Su virreinato en la Nueva España, sus contenidas con los P. P. Jesuítas, sus apariciones, sus escritos escogidas, etc., etc. Vol. VII of *Documentos inéditos ó muy raros para la historia de México*. Ed. Genaro García and Carlos Pereyra. Mexico: Librería de la Viuda de Ch. Bouret, 1906.

Epistolario de Nueva España, 1505–1818. Ed. Francisco del Paso y Troncoso. 16 vols. Biblioteca Historia Mexicana de Obras Inéditas, Segunda Serie. Mexico: Antigua Librería Robredo, 1939–1942.

Fuentes para la historia del trabajo en Nueva España. Ed. Silvio Zavala and María Castelo. 8 vols. Mexico: Fondo de Cultura Económica, 1939–1946.

Gage, Thomas. *Thomas Gage's Travels in the New World*. Ed. and introd. J. Eric. S. Thompson. Norman: University of Oklahoma Press, 1958.

Gemelli Carreri, Giovanni Francesco. *Viaje a la Nueva España*. Ed. and trans. Francisco Perujo. Mexico: Universidad Nacional Autónoma de México, Dirección General de Publicaciones, 1967.

"Gente de España en la ciudad de México, año de 1689." Ed. Ignacio Rubio Mañe. *Boletín del Archivo general de la nación*. 2d ser., 7 (1966): 5–405.

Gómez de Cervantes, Gonzalo. *La vida económica y social de Nueva España al finalizar el siglo xvi*. Ed. and introd. Alberto María Carreño. Mexico: José Porrúa e Hijos, 1944.

Guijo, Gregorio M. de. *Diario, 1648–1664*. Ed. and introd. Manuel Romero de Terreros. 2 vols. Mexico: Editorial Porrúa, S.A., 1953.

Instrucciones que los vireyes de Nueva España dejaron a sus sucesores, añadense algunas que los mismos trajeron de la Corte y otros documentos semejantes a las instrucciones. Mexico: Imprenta Imperial, 1867.

Legislación del trabajo en los siglos xvi, xvii y xviii. Ed. Genaro V. Vázquez. Historia del Movimiento Obrero en Mexico. Mexico: Departamento Autónomo de Prensa y Publicidad, 1935.

López de Velasco, Juan. *Geografía y descripción universal de las Indias*. Ed. Marcos Jiménez de la Espada. Introd. María del Carmen González Muñoz. Madrid: Ediciones Atlas, 1971.

Ordenanzas de gremios de la Nueva España. Ed. Francisco del Barrio Lorenzot. Introd. Genaro Estrada. 2 vols. Mexico: Dirección de Talleres Gráficos, 1920.

Ortega y Montañez, Juan de. *Instrucción reservada que el Obispo-Virrey Juan de Ortega y Montañez dio a su sucesor en el mando el Conde de Moctezuma*. Ed. and introd. Norman F. Martin. Mexico: Editorial Jus., 1965.

Recopilación de leyes de los reynos de las Indias. 3 vols. Madrid: La Viuda de D. Joaquín Ibarra, 1943.

Robles, Antonio de. *Diario de sucesos notables (1665–1703)*. Ed. and introd. Antonío Castro Leal. 3 vols. Mexico: Editorial Porrúa, S.A., 1946.

Sigüenza y Góngora, Carlos de. "Letter of Don Carlos de Sigüenza y Góngora to Admiral Pez Recounting the Incidents of the Corn Riot in Mexico City, June 8, 1692." In Irving A. Leonard, *Don Carlos de Sigüenza y Góngora, a Mexican Savant of the Seventeenth Century*. Berkeley: University of California Press, 1929. Pp. 210–277.

"Sobre los inconvenientes de vivir los indios en el centro de la cuidad." *Boletín del Archivo general de la nación* 9 (1938): 1–34.

Solórzano y Pereira, Juan de. *Política Indiana*. Ed. Francisco Ramiro de Valenzuela. 5 vols. Madrid: Compañía Ibero-Americana de Publicaciones, 1647.
"Tumulto acaecido en la ciudad de México el año de 1692." In *Tumultos y rebeliones acaecidos en México*. Vol. X of *Documentos inéditos ó muy raros para la historia de México*. Ed. Genaro García and Carlos Pereyra. Mexico: Editorial Porrúa, S.A., 1982. Pp. 369–380.
Vázquez de Espinosa, Antonio. *Description of the Indies (c. 1620)*. Trans. Charles Upson Clark. Smithsonian Miscellaneous Collections, vol. 102. Washington, D.C.: Smithsonian Institution Press, 1968.
Zurita, Alonso de. "Breve y sumaria relación de los señores de la Nueva España." In *Colección de documentos inéditos relativos al descubrimiento, conquista y organizacion de las antiguas posesiones españoles de América y Oceanía, sacados de los archivos del Reino y muy especialmente del de Indias*. Vol. II. Madrid: Imprenta Española, 1864.

Secondary Sources

Aguirre Beltrán, Gonzalo. *Medicina y magia*. Mexico: Instituto Nacional Indigenista, 1963.
Aguirre Beltrán, Gonzalo. *La población negra de México, 1519–1810: Estudio etnohistórico*. Mexico: Fondo de Cultura Económica, 1946.
Anderson, Rodney D. "Race and Social Stratification: A Comparison of Working-Class Spaniards, Indians, and Castas in Guadalajara, Mexico in 1821." *Hispanic American Historical Review* 68 (1988): 209–243.
Bakewell, P. J. *Silver Mining and Society in Colonial Mexico: Zacatecas, 1546–1700*. Cambridge: Cambridge University Press, 1971.
Barth, Fredrik. "Introduction." In *Ethnic Groups and Boundaries: The Social Organization of Culture Difference*. Ed. Fredrik Barth. Boston: Little, Brown, 1969.
Behar, Ruth. "Sex and Sin, Witchcraft and the Devil in Late-Colonial Mexico." *American Ethnologist* 14 (1987): 34–54.
Benedict, Bradley. "El estado en la época de los Hapsburgo." *Historia mexicana* 23 (1973–74): 551–610.
Borah, Woodrow. *New Spain's Century of Depression*. Berkeley: University of California Press, 1951.
Boyd-Bowman, Peter. *Indice geobiográfico de cuarenta mil pobladores españoles de América en el siglo xvi*. 2 vols. Mexico: Editorial Jus., 1968.
Boyd-Bowman, Peter. *Patterns of Spanish Emigration to the New World (1493–1590)*. Buffalo: Council on International Studies, State University of New York at Buffalo, 1973.
Boyer, Richard Everett. *La gran inundación: Vida y sociedad en México (1629–1638)*. Trans. Antonieta Sánchez Mejorada. Mexico: Sepsetentas, 1975.
Boyer, Richard Everett. "Mexico in the Seventeenth Century: Transition of a Colonial Society." *Hispanic American Historical Review* 57 (1977): 455–478.

Brading, D. A. *The First America: The Spanish Monarchy, Creole Patriots, and the Liberal State, 1492–1867*. Cambridge: Cambridge University Press, 1991.

Brading, D. A. "Government and Elite in Late Colonial Mexico." *Hispanic American Historical Review* 53 (1973): 389–414.

Brading, D. A. *Miners and Merchants in Bourbon Mexico, 1763–1810*. Cambridge: Cambridge University Press, 1971.

Brading, D. A., and Celia Wu. "Population Growth and Crisis: León, 1720–1866." *Journal of Latin American Studies* 5 (1973): 1–36.

Burkett, Elinor C. "Indian Women and White Society: The Case of Sixteenth-Century Peru." In *Latin American Women: Historical Perspectives*. Ed. Asunción Lavrin. Westport, Conn.: Greenwood Press, 1978.

Calvo, Thomas. *La Nueva Galicia en los siglos xvi y xvii*. Guadalajara: El Colegio de Jalisco, 1989.

Carrera Stampa, Manuel. *Los gremios mexicanos: La organización gremial en Nueva España*. Introd. Rafael Altamira. Mexico: Edición y Distribución Ibero-Americana de Publicaciones, S.A., 1954.

Carroll, Patrick J. *Blacks in Colonial Veracruz: Race, Ethnicity, and Regional Development*. Austin: University of Texas Press, 1991.

Chance, John K. "On the Mexican Mestizo." *Latin American Research Review* 14, no. 3 (1979): 153–168.

Chance, John K. *Race and Class in Colonial Oaxaca*. Stanford: Stanford University Press, 1978.

Chance, John K., and William B. Taylor. "Estate and Class in a Colonial City: Oaxaca in 1792." *Comparative Studies in Society and History* 19 (1977): 454–487.

Clendinnen, Inga. *Ambivalent Conquests: Maya and Spaniard in Yucatán, 1517–1570*. Cambridge: Cambridge University Press, 1987.

Coatsworth, John H. "The Limits of Colonial Absolutism: The State in Eighteenth-Century Mexico." In *Essays in the Political, Economic and Social History of Colonial Latin America*. Ed. Karen Spalding. Newark: University of Delaware, 1979.

Cook, Sherburne F., and Woodrow Borah. *The Indian Population of Central Mexico, 1531–1610*. Berkeley: University of California Press, 1960.

Cooper, Donald B. *Las epidemias en la ciudad de México, 1761–1813*. Trans. Roberto Gómez Ciriza. Mexico: Instituto Mexicano del Seguro Social, 1980.

Cortés, Hernán. *Letters from Mexico*. Trans. and ed. Anthony Pagden. Introd. J. H. Elliot. New Haven: Yale University Press, 1986.

Crosby, Alfred W., Jr. *The Columbian Exchange: Biological and Cultural Consequences of 1492*. With a foreword by Otto von Mering. Contributions in American Studies, no. 2. Westport, Conn.: Greenwood Press, 1972.

Cruz, Juana Inés de la. *A Sor Juana Anthology*. Ed. Alan S. Trueblood. Cambridge: Harvard University Press, 1988.

Davidson, David M. "Negro Slave Control and Resistance in Colonial Mexico, 1519–1650." *Hispanic American Historical Review* 46 (1966): 235–253.

Feijoo, Rosa. "El tumulto de 1692." *Historia mexicana* 14 (1964–65): 656–679.

Feijoo, Rosa. "El tumulto de 1624." *Historia mexicana* 14 (1964–65): 42–70.

Florescano, Enrique. "El abasto y la legislación de granos en el siglo xvi." *Historia mexicana* 14 (1964–65): 567–630.

Florescano, Enrique. "La formación de los trabajadores en la época colonial, 1521–1750." In *La clase obrera en la historia de México: De la colonia al imperio.* Mexico: Siglo Veintiuno Editores, S.A., 1980. Pp. 9–124.

Florescano, Enrique. *Precios del maíz y crisis agrícolas en México (1708–1810).* Mexico: El Colegio de Mexico, 1969.

Gibson, Charles. "The Aztec Aristocracy in Colonial Mexico." *Comparative Studies in Society and History* 2 (1959–60): 169–196.

Gibson, Charles. *The Aztecs under Spanish Rule: A History of the Indians of the Valley of Mexico, 1519–1810.* Stanford: Stanford University Press, 1964.

Gibson, Charles. *Spain in America.* New York: Harper & Row, 1966.

Gibson, Charles. "The Transformation of the Indian Community in New Spain, 1500–1810." *Cahiers d'Histoire Mondiale* 2 (1955): 581–607.

Gómez Canedo, Lino. *La educación de los marginados durante la época colonial: Escuelas y colegios para indios y mestizos en la Nueva España.* Biblioteca Porrúa, no. 78. Mexico: Editorial Porrúa, S.A., 1982.

González Angulo Aguirre, Jorge. *Artesanado y ciudad a finales del siglo xviii.* Mexico: Fondo de Cultura Económica, 1983.

Gordon, Milton M. *Assimilation in American Life.* New York: Oxford University Press, 1964.

Gould, Stephen Jay. "Why We Should Not Name Human Races—A Biological View." In *Ever Since Darwin: Reflection in Natural History.* New York: W. W. Norton & Company, 1977.

Greenleaf, Richard E. *La Inquisición en Nueva España: Siglo xvi.* Trans. Carlos Valdés. Mexico: Fondo de Cultura Económica, 1981.

Greenleaf, Richard E. "Viceregal Power and the Obrajes of the Cortés Estate." *Hispanic American Historical Review* 48 (1968): 365–379.

Guthrie, Chester L. "Colonial Economy: Trade, Industry, and Labor in Seventeenth-Century Mexico City." *Revista de Historia de América* 7 (1939): 103–134.

Guthrie, Chester L. "Riots in Seventeenth-Century Mexico City: A Study of Social and Economic Conditions." In *Greater America: Essays in Honor of Herbert Eugene Bolton.* Berkeley: University of California Press, 1945. Pp. 243–258.

Gutman, Herbert G. *The Black Family in Slavery and Freedom, 1750–1925.* New York: Random House, 1976.

Harris, Marvin. *Patterns of Race in the Americas.* New York: Walker and Company, 1964.

Haskett, Robert Stephen. *Indigenous Rulers: An Ethnohistory of Town Government in Colonial Cuernavaca.* Albuquerque: University of New Mexico Press, 1991.

Haslip, Gabriel James. "Crime and the Administration of Justice in Colonial Mexico City, 1696–1810." Ph.D. dissertation, Columbia University, 1980.

Hassig, Ross. *Trade, Tribute and Transportation: The Sixteenth-Century Political Economy of the Valley of Mexico*. Norman: University of Oklahoma Press, 1985.

Hernández Palomo, José Jesús. *La renta del pulque en Nueva España, 1665–1810*. Seville: Escuela de Estudios Hispano-Americanos, 1979.

Hoberman, Louisa. "Bureaucracy and Disaster: Mexico City and the Flood of 1629." *Journal of Latin American Studies* 6 (1974): 211–230.

Hobsbawm, E. J. *Primitive Rebels: Studies in Archaic Forms of Social Movement in the Nineteenth and Twentieth Centuries*. New York: W. W. Norton & Company, 1959.

Hoetink, H. *The Two Variants in Caribbean Race Relations: A Contribution to the Sociology of Segmented Societies*. Trans. Eva M. Hooykaas. London: Oxford University Press, 1975.

Israel, J. I. *Race, Class and Politics in Colonial Mexico, 1610–1670*. London: Oxford University Press, 1975.

Kagan, Samuel. "Penal Servitude in New Spain: The Colonial Textile Industry." Ph.D. dissertation, City University of New York, 1977.

Kicza, John E. *Colonial Entrepreneurs: Families and Business in Bourbon Mexico City*. Albuquerque: University of New Mexico Press, 1983.

Klor de Alva, J. Jorge. "Spiritual Conflict and Accommodation in New Spain: Toward a Typology of Aztec Responses to Christianity." In *The Inca and Aztec States, 1400–1800: Anthropology and History*. Ed. George A. Collier et al. New York: Academic Press, 1982.

Knight, Franklin W. *Slave Society in Cuba During the Nineteenth Century*. Madison: University of Wisconsin Press, 1970.

Konetzke, Richard. "Documentos para la historia y crítica de los registros parroquiales en las Indias." *Revista de Indias* 25 (1946): 581–586.

Konetzke, Richard. "El mestizaje y su importancia en el desarrollo de la población de Hispanoamérica durante la época colonial." pt. 2. *Revista de Indias* 24 (1946): 215–237.

"La pintura de castas." *Artes de México*, no. 8 (Summer 1990): 17–88.

Leonard, Irving A. *Baroque Times in Old Mexico: Seventeenth-Century Persons, Places, and Practices*. Ann Arbor: University of Michigan Press, 1966.

León-Portilla, Miguel. *Aztec Thought and Culture: A Study of the Ancient Nahuatl Mind*. Trans. Jack Emory Davis. Norman: University of Oklahoma Press, 1963.

Lockhart, James. "Encomienda and Hacienda: The Evolution of the Great Estate in the Spanish Indies." *Hispanic American Historical Review* 49 (1969): 411–429.

Lockhart, James. "Introduction." In *Provinces of Early Mexico: Variants of Spanish American Regional Development*. Ed. Ida Altman and James Lockhart. Los Angeles: UCLA Latin American Center Publications, University of California Press, 1976.

Lockhart, James. *Nahuas and Spaniards: Postconquest Central Mexican History and Philology*. Stanford: Stanford University Press, 1991.

Lockhart, James. *Spanish Peru, 1532–1560: A Colonial Society*. Madison: University of Wisconsin Press, 1968.

Lockhart, James, and Enrique Otte, ed. *Letters and People of the Spanish Indies: The Sixteenth Century.* Cambridge: Cambridge University Press, 1976.

Lockhart, James, and Stuart B. Schwartz. *Early Latin America: A History of Colonial Spanish America and Brazil.* Cambridge: Cambridge University Press, 1983.

Love, Edgar F. "Marrige Patterns of Persons of African Descent in a Colonial Mexico City Parish." *Hispanic American Historical Review* 51 (1971): 79–91.

Lynch, John. *Spain Under the Habsburgs.* 2 vols. Oxford: Oxford University Press, 1964–1969.

McCaa, Robert. "Modeling Social Interaction: Marital Miscegenation in Colonial Spanish America." *Historical Methods* 15 (Spring 1982): 45–66.

McCaa, Robert, Stuart B. Schwartz, and Arturo Grubessich. "Race and Class in Colonial Latin America: A Critique." *Comparative Studies in Society and History* 21 (1979): 421–433.

MacLachlan, Colin M. *Criminal Justice in Eighteenth-Century Mexico: A Study of the Tribunal of the Acordada.* Berkeley: University of California Press, 1974.

MacLeod, Murdo J. "Aspects of the Internal Economy of Colonial Spanish America: Labour; Taxation; Distribution and Exchange." In *Colonial Latin America.* Vol. II of the *Cambridge History of Latin America.* Ed. Leslie Bethell. Cambridge: Cambridge University Press, 1984.

Martin, Norman F. *Los vagabundos en la Nueva España: Siglo xvi.* Mexico: Editorial Jus., 1957.

Martinez-Alier, Verena. *Marriage, Class and Colour in Nineteenth-Century Cuba: A Study of Racial Attitudes and Sexual Values in a Slave Society.* Cambridge: Cambridge University Press, 1974.

Mexico: Splendors of Thirty Centuries. Introd. Octavio Paz. New York: Metropolitan Museum of Art, 1990.

Miranda, José. *La función económica del encomendero en los orígenes del regimen colonial (Nueva España, 1525–1531).* Instituto de Investigaciones Históricas, Serie Histórica, no. 12. Mexico: Universidad Nacional Autónoma de México, 1965.

Moore, Barington, Jr. *Injustice: The Social Bases of Obedience and Revolt.* White Plains, N.Y.: M. E. Sharpe, 1978.

Morales, Francisco. *Ethnic and Social Background of the Franciscan Friars in Seventeenth-Century Mexico.* Washington, D.C.: Academy of American Franciscan History, 1973.

Morin, Claude. "Population et épidemies dans une pariosse mexicaine: Santa Inés Zacatelco, XVIIᵉ–XIXᵉ siecles." *Cahiers des Amériques Latines.* Serie sciences de l'homme 6 (1972): 42–73.

Mörner, Magnus. *La Corona española y los foráneos en los pueblos de indios de América.* Institute of Ibero-American Studies, Stockholm, Publication Series A, no. 1. Stockholm: Almquist & Wiksell, 1970.

Mörner, Magnus. *Race Mixture in the History of Latin America.* Boston: Little, Brown, 1967.

Morse, Richard M. "A Prolegomenon to Latin American Urban History." *Hispanic American Historical Review* 52 (1972): 359–394.

Pagden, Anthony. *The Fall of Natural Man: The American Indian and the Origins of Comparative Ethnology.* Cambridge: Cambridge University Press, 1982.

Palmer, Colin A. *Slaves of the White God: Blacks in Mexico, 1570–1650.* Cambridge: Harvard University Press, 1976.

Paz, Octavio. *The Other Mexico: Critique of the Pyramid.* Trans. Lysander Kemp. New York: Grove Press, 1972.

Peña, José F. de la. *Oligarquía y propiedad en Nueva España, 1550–1624.* Mexico: Fondo de Cultura Económica, 1983.

Phelan, John Leddy. "Authority and Flexibility in the Spanish Imperial Bureaucracy." *Administrative Science Quarterly* 5 (1960): 47–65.

Phelan, John Leddy. *The Kingdom of Quito in the Seventeenth Century: Bureaucratic Politics in the Spanish Empire.* Madison: University of Wisconsin Press, 1967.

Phelan, John Leddy. "The Problem of Conflicting Spanish Imperial Ideologies in the Sixteenth Century." In *Latin American History: Identity, Integration, and Nationhood.* Ed. Fredrick B. Pike. New York: Harcourt, Brace & World, 1969. Pp. 39–64.

Pitt-Rivers, Julian A. *The People of the Sierra.* 2d ed. Chicago: University of Chicago Press, 1971.

Ricard, Robert. *The Spiritual Conquest of Mexico: An Essay on the Apostolate and the Evangelizing Methods of the Mendicant Orders in New Spain: 1523–1572.* Trans. Lesley Byrd Simpson. Berkeley: University of California Press, 1966.

Rout, Leslie B., Jr. *The African Experience in Spanish America: 1502 to the Present Day.* Cambridge: Cambridge University Press, 1976.

Royce, Anya Peterson. *Ethnic Identity: Strategies of Diversity.* Bloomington: Indiana University Press, 1982.

Rudé, George. *The Crowd in History: A Study of Popular Disturbances in France and England, 1730–1848.* New York: John Wiley & Sons, 1964.

Rust, Philip F., and Patricia Seed. "Equality of Endogamy: Statistical Approaches." *Social Science Research* 14 (1985): 57–79.

Ryan, Mary. "The American Parade: Representations of Nineteenth-Century Social Order." In *The New Cultural History.* Ed. Lynn Hunt. Berkeley: University of California Press, 1989.

Saloman, Frank. "Indian Women of Early Colonial Quito as Seen through Their Testaments." *The Americas* 44, no. 3 (1988): 325–341.

Salvucci, Richard J. *Textiles and Capitalism in Mexico: An Economic History of the Obrajes, 1539–1840.* Princeton: Princeton University Press, 1987.

Sánchez-Albornoz, Nicolás. *The Population of Latin America: A History.* Trans. W. A. R. Richardson. Berkeley: University of California Press, 1974.

Sanders, William T. "The Population of the Central Mexican Symbiotic Region, the Basin of Mexico, and the Teotihuacán Valley in the Sixteenth Century." In *The Native Population of the Americas in 1492.* Ed. William M. Denevan. Madison: University of Wisconsin Press, 1976.

Scardaville, Michael C. "Alcohol Abuse and Tavern Reform in Late Colonial Mexico City." *Hispanic American Historical Review* 60 (1980): 643–671.

Scholes, France V. "The Spanish Conqueror as a Business Man: A Chapter in the History of Fernando Cortés." *New Mexico Quarterly* 28 (1957): 15–29.

Scholes, Walter V. *The Diego Ramírez Visita.* University of Missouri Studies, vol. 20, no. 4. Columbia: University of Missouri Press, 1946.

Schwaller, John Frederick. *The Church and the Clergy in Sixteenth-Century Mexico.* Albuquerque: University of New Mexico Press, 1987.

Schwartz, Stuart B. *Sugar Plantations in the Formation of Brazilian Society: Bahia, 1550–1835.* Cambridge: Cambridge University Press, 1985.

Seed, Patricia. "Social Dimensions of Race: Mexico City, 1753." *Hispanic American Historical Review* 62 (1982): 559–606.

Seed, Patricia, and Philip F. Rust. "Estate and Class in Colonial Oaxaca Revisited." *Comparative Studies in Society and History* 25 (1983): 703–710.

Simpson, Lesley Byrd. *The Encomienda in New Spain: The Beginnings of Spanish Mexico.* Rev. and enl. ed. Berkeley: University of California Press, 1950; reprint ed., 1968.

Stern, Steve J. *Peru's Indian Peoples and the Challenge of Spanish Conquest: Huamanga to 1640.* Madison: University of Wisconsin Press, 1982.

Stowe, Noel J. "The Tumulto of 1624: Turmoil at Mexico City." Ph. D. dissertation, University of Southern California, 1970.

Taylor, William B. *Drinking, Homicide and Rebellion in Colonial Mexican Villages.* Stanford: Stanford University Press, 1979.

Thompson, E. P. "The Moral Economy of the English Crowd in the Eighteenth Century." *Past and Present* 50 (1971): 76–136.

Thompson, E. P. "Patrician Society, Plebeian Culture." *Journal of Social History* 7 (1974): 382–405.

Valdés, Dennis Nodin. "The Decline of the Sociedad de Castas in Mexico City." Ph. D. dissertation, University of Michigan, 1978.

Walker, Geoffrey J. *Spanish Politics and Imperial Trade, 1707–1789.* Bloomington: Indiana University Press, 1979.

Wolf, Eric. *Sons of the Shaking Earth.* Chicago: University of Chicago Press, 1959.

Wrigley, E. A. *Population and History.* New York: McGraw-Hill, 1969.

Zulawski, Ann. "Social Differentiation, Gender, and Ethnicity: Urban Indian Women in Colonial Bolivia, 1640–1725." *Latin American Research Review* 25 (1990): 93–119.

Index

Aguardiente, 36
Aguilar, Agustín de, 21
Aguilar, José de, 117
Aguilar, Mateo de, 118–19
Aguirre, Juan de, 98
Alcaicería, 36
Alcoholic beverages. *See* Aguardiente; Pulque
Alhóndiga: government officials at, 46, 133–34; burning of, in 1692, 146; mentioned, 157, 158
Alhóndiga/pósito system: impact of, on Mexico City mortality rates, 75; and riot of 1692, 128–34 *passim*
Almaceneros, 110
Alonso, Martín, 30
Álvarez, Teresa, 103–4
Angeles, Catalina de los, 88
Angeles, Martín de los, 126
Angeles, Pascuala de los, 152–53
Angeles Canales, Juana de los, 30
Angelina, Bernarda, 29
Antonio, Juan, 99–100
Antonio, Pedro, 104
Aposentos, 30–32 *passim*
Apprentices: disciplining of, 94–95; slaves as, 96–97; in obrajes, 102–4 *passim*, 190*n*82; runaway, 103
Apprenticeship: used to rehabilitate juvenile offenders, 103–4
Arellano, Nicolás, 116
Arenas, Juan de: use of oral contracts by, 103–4; financial success of, 118
Arriaga Agüero, Alonso de, 130–31
Arroyo, María de, 119
Artiaga, Antonio de, 116
Artisan guilds. *See* Gremios
Artisans: and variety of crafts in Mexico City, 10; ethnic diversity of, 88, 91, 159; authority of, over apprentices, 94–95; literacy among, 108; social mobility among, 108–9, 119; credit networks of, 114–16; in

riot of 1692, 141, 158–59; in militia units, 149; mentioned, 89, 162
Asencio, Diego de, 116
Audiencia, view of 1692 riot, 138
Autos-da-fé, 156, 162, 199*n160*
Avila, Josefa de, 34–35
Aviles, Francisco de, 117
Ayuntamiento. *See* Cabildo
Aztecs, 3

Baesa, Juan Luis, 106
Bajío, 129
Bakeries: size of labor force in, 94; use of corporal punishment in, 99; labor relations in, 99–102; wage rates in, 100, 189*n66*
Bakers: responses to imprisonment, 100–101; absence in riot of 1692, 149, 198*n23*
Balvanera, Convent of, 30, 31
Baratillo, 37, 41, 141
Barrientos, Martín de, 116
Barrios, Juan de, 57–58
Bástida, Pedro de la, 128
Benítez, Andrés, 43–44, 53
Bernal, Nicolás, 91
Bigamy: among Indians and castas, 53–54 *passim;* mentioned, 45
Blacks: Spanish perception of, 17; and conspiracies against Spanish rule, 18; economic activities of, 20–21, 22; in sistema de castas, 24; changing endogamy rates among, 80–81; and mulattoes, 83; demographic decline of, in Mexico City, 83; social protests by, 136; in riot of 1692, 151; mentioned, 4, 5, 15, 16, 19, 20, 29, 38, 39, 41, 45, 50, 67, 72, 101, 102, 133, 156, 164. *See also* Castas; Slavery, African; Slaves
Bocanegra, Pascual, 121
Bread, 37, 42–43, 111, 117. *See also* Bakeries

211

Burial records: problem of interpreting, 71. *See also* Parish registers

Cabecillas, 144–45
Cabeza de Vaca, Fernando, 97
Cabildo: on conditions of Mexico City's infrastructure, 29; offices burned in riot of 1692, 138, 143–44
Cabrera, Miguel, 161
Caciques, 3, 119
Cajones: burned and looted in riot of 1692, 138, 143–47 *passim;* mentioned, 36
Calderón, Pedro, 93
Canals, 10
Cañas, Salvador de, 114–15
Canoes, 10, 28
Cano Moctezuma, Francisco, 53
Capital Punishment: meted out to blacks and mulattoes, 18, 39, 156, 199n160; meted out to rioters in 1692, 155–56
Cárdenas, Bartolomé de, 68
Cárdenas, Lorenzo de, 97
Casas de vecindad: definition of, 30; lack of privacy in, 32–33; criminal investigations in, 32–33, 151–53 *passim;* illegal consumption of pulque in, 34; multiracial character of, 91, 151–53 *passim*
Casta elite: mestizos among, 19–20; possessions of, 110, 116, 119, 120; as both creditors and debtors, 110–12 *passim,* 116–17; religious orthodoxy of, 111, 120; financial insecurity of, 112; and kinship ties with Spaniards, 118–19; upward mobility of, 118–20; hypergamy among, 119–20; family size, 122–23; reinforcing social structure, 123; naming practices of, 183n51; racial attitudes of, 193n40
Castas: definition of, 4; compared to Indians, 5–6; lack of institutional structure of, 6, 51; economic activities of, 14, 20–21, 22, 29–30, 110, 151; with Spanish parents, 14–15, 118–19; Spaniards' view of, 15–16, 38, 51, 161; legal restrictions on, 16–17, 18, 21; perceived influence of, on Indians, 16, 92, 127, 141; access to arms, 21, 38, 120; attitude toward Catholicism, 33, 36, 40, 120; as consumers of pulque, 34; naming practices of, compared with those of Spaniards, 62–63; illegitimacy rates among, 68; mortality rates among, 69, 75; resistance

of, to elite racial ideology, 78, 162–63; sex ratios among, 81; social networks of, 83, 87; as apprentices, 103–4; social mobility of, 105, 120; intermarriage with Spaniards, 121; in riot of 1692, 135–47 *passim,* 151–53, 157–58. *See also* Blacks; Castizos; Mestizos; Mulattoes; Plebeians
Castilla, Mariscal de, 143
Castillo, Barbara del, 97–98
Castillo, Cristóbal del, 117
Castillo, José del (friend of Bernabé de la Cruz), 54
Castillo, José del (tailor), 32
Castizos: economic activities of, 21, 88, 105; in sistema de castas, 24; as minor racial category, 73, 77; marriages to mestizos, 82, 83; feelings of racial superiority of, 121; mentioned, 52, 56, 66, 72, 162. *See also* Castas
Castro, Tomasa de, 103
Cayetano de Valdés, Juan, 117
Celaya: maize shipments from, 128, 131; mentioned, 149
Cerralvo, Rodrigo Pacheco y Ossorio, marqués de, 22–23
Chalco: as source of maize, 128, 149; as wheat producer, 129; mentioned, 117
Charles V, 16
Chavarría, José de, 117
Chávez, Juan de, 93–94
Children: and inheritance of parents' names, 57–61; and transmission of racial identity, 57, 84; tendency to adopt parents' occupations, 87; of master artisans, 108; and downward social mobility, 122; adopted by plebeians, 123, 193n51,52
Chinos: as barber-surgeons, 21; racial variability among, 77; as slaves, 118, 174n27; mentioned, 15, 57, 93, 102, 163
Chirini, Jacome, 45–46
Chirinos, Juan Antonio, 103
Church, Catholic. *See* Clergy, Catholic
Clergy, Catholic: attempt of, to Christianize Indians, 5; as opponents of encomenderos, 11–12; friars *vs.* seculars within, 16; attempts at popular mobilization, 46–47; in riot of 1692, 133–36 *passim,* 143, 148; and social control, 162
Clientage: in labor relations, 91–102 *passim. See also* Patron-client relations
Coca, Baltasar de, 151–53

Cofradías, 6, 119, 120, 164
Cohen's kappa, 79–80
Colegio de San Juan de Letrán, 18
Colón, Ignacio de, 151–52
Compadrazgo, 6, 88, 92, 95, 106
Concepción, María de la (fruit vendor), 59, 117
Concepción, María de la (wife of Miguel de Silva), 118, 122
Concepción, Tomasa de la, 148, 153–54
Concubinage, 68–69
Congregaciones, 12
Contreras, Juan de, 91
Correa, Felipa, 117
Corregidor, 37, 132–33, 144, 146. See also Government officials
Corres, Juana, 121
Cortés, Gaspar, 59
Credit: as key to social mobility, 109; as essential to economic system, 112–13; flow of, 112, 114–16. See also Loans
Crédito: dual meaning of, 113
Creoles. See Spaniards
Criminal activity: in casas de vecindad, 32–33; in plaza mayor, 37; among plebeians, 37; perceived as increasing in late seventeenth century, 39. See also Judicial system
Criminals: able to hide from authorities, 34; rehabilitation of, 103–4
Crowd: gathering at arrests, 43–44; in riot of 1624, 47; at alhóndiga, 132; in riot of 1692, 135–36, 137, 141–47 passim; multiracial nature of, 157; fragmentation of, 164. See also Riot of 1692
Crown, Spanish: and encomenderos, 11–12; attempts to segregate Indians, 16; use of racial terminology, 19, 23; opposition to debt peonage, 101–2; and sistema de castas, 161. See also Judicial system
Cruz, Agustina de la, 118, 122
Cruz, Antonio de la, 126, 147
Cruz, Bentura de la, 113
Cruz, Bernabé de la, 53–54, 55
Cruz, Diego de la, 43
Cruz, Felipe de la, 139, 154
Cruz, Francisco de la, 91
Cruz, Gerónimo de la, 33
Cruz, Gracia de la, 45–46, 59, 96
Cruz, Hipólito de la, 88
Cruz, José de la, 101–2

Cruz, Josefa de la, 110, 112
Cruz, Juan de la, 45–46
Cruz, Juana Inés de la, 11
Cruz, Marcos de la, 103
Cruz, María de la, 112
Cruz, Miguel de la, 113
Cruz, Nicolás de la, 154
Cruz, Pedro de la, 142
Cruz, Sebastián de la, 102
Cruz, Tomás de la, 99
Cuartos, 30–31
Cuckold: as term of abuse, 140, 142
Cueva, Francisco de la, 150

Dávalos, Andrés, 150–51
Debtors' Prison, 101
Debt peonage: compared to slavery, 98–99; in obrajes and bakeries, 98–102 passim; royal opposition to, 99, 101–2
Desagüe, 21, 27
Deza Y Ulloa, Antonio de, 148
Dios, Juan de, 151, 153
Dominga, María, 29
Doñas: as tenants, 30–31; surnames among, 65–66; mentioned, 117
Dowries: and slaves, 98, 118; as sign of social status, 108; among casta women, 118, 122; for Spanish orphans, 121
Dueñas, Antonia de, 40, 59

Encarnación, Micaela de, 121
Encomienda, 11–12
Enríquez, Martín, 19
Ensinas, Alonso de, 91, 120, 153
Escalante y Mendoza, Juan de: urges vengeance on rioters, 126–27; suggestions for dealing with maize shortage, 130; at alhóndiga, 132–34 passim; on riot of 1692, 143, 145
Escobar, Andrés, 93–94
Espíritu Santo, María del, 98
Esteban, Juan, 152
Estrada, Juan de, 93

Fanega: definition of, 194n15
Filipinos. See Chinos
Fiscal, 126
Francisca, Micaela, 54–55
Francisca, Sebastiana, 152–53
Francisco, Miguel, 109
Francisco, Nicolás, 100

Gachupines, 110, 140. *See also* Peninsulares; Spaniards

Gage, Thomas, 11, 22, 38

Galve, Gaspar de Sandoval Silva y Mendoza, conde de: as failed patron, 48; takes measures to alleviate 1692 grain shortage, 127–30 *passim;* blamed for grain shortage, 132–33; in monastery of San Francisco during riot of 1692, 136, 137, 143; responds to riot of 1692, 149–50, 198–99*n148*

Gambling, 41, 91, 122

Garay, Luis de, 103

García, Andrés, 10

García, Felipe, 54–56 *passim*

Garfias, Tomás, 39–40

Gelves, Diego Carrillo de Mendoza y Pimentel, marqués de: ordinances on castas by, 21–22; and riot of 1624, 47

Gente decente, 22, 24

Gerónimo, Tomasina, 45

Gómez, Alonso, 33

Gonzales, Miguel: on beginning of riot of 1692, 134, 136; participation in riot by, 145–46; disposal of stolen goods by, 148, 153–54; confession of, 154; indifference of, to racial classification, 163; mentioned, 147, 158

González de Castro, Francisco, 44

González de Noriega, Juan, 98

González Ledo, José, 98

Government officials: search for non-Indian sources of labor, 20–21; and racial stereotypes, 21; clashing with plebeians, 42–44; as patrons, 44–45, 48, 163; and racial classification, 70; opposition to debt peonage from, 102; and explanations for riot of 1692, 127; role of, in riot, 128, 130–34 *passim,* 149; mentioned, 37, 66, 144, 146, 154. *See also* Judicial system

Gregorio, Francisco, 154

Gremios: establishment of, 10; exclusion of blacks and mulattoes, 17; discriminatory practices in, 45; elections in, 46; journeymen and masters in, 108–9. *See also* Artisans

Guadalajara, 129

Guadalupe, Nicolás de, 103, 104

Guadalupe, Sanctuary de Nuestra Señora de, 120

Guerrero, Francisco de, 93

Guevara, Catalina de, 106

Guridí, Antonio, 92

Gutiérrez Cabiedes, Lucas, 135

Hacendos, 13, 128

Haciendas, 12–13, 14, 20, 128

Hernández, Francisco, 59

Hernández, Nicolás, 111

Hernández, Sebastiana: disposes of her house in testament, 30; credit network of, 58–59, 112; links of, to Indians, 83–84; small scale of financial dealings, 117

Housing: as status symbol, 29; and hierarchy in Mexico City, 30–32

Ignacia, Lorenza, 32

Illegitimacy: effect on racial identification, 57; among castas, 68, 119; rates in Mexico City, 184*n55*

Indians: ascription of identity to, 3, 5, 163; resistance to Hispanic culture, 4–6, 13; response to Catholicism, 5; population decline, 12, 20; economic activities of, 11–13, 14, 30; Hispanicization of, 14, 54–55, 91–93; living in traza, 20, 31, 89–93, 185*n10;* as clients of Spaniards, 20, 90–93 *passim;* evasion of tribute and labor drafts, 20, 92; in sistema de castas, 24; urban *vs.* rural, 45; use of religious surnames, 63; endogamy among, 78–80 *passim;* marriages with castas, 78–82 *passim,* 91; as artisans, 90–91, 159; protest grain shortage, 132; in riot of 1692, 134–47 *passim,* 153, 156–60 *passim;* subject to indiscriminate arrests after riot, 152; flight from traza, 153; mentioned, 34, 35, 37, 43, 51, 53, 56, 57, 89, 103, 126, 154, 164

Indio amestizado, 53

Inquisition: and encomenderos, 12; reliance on informers, 33; trials cited, 33–34, 36, 39–40, 52–57 *passim;* complains about popular religious celebrations, 36; view of castas, 40; condemns veneration of Juan de Palafox y Mendoza, 47; and racial identification, 52; and bigamy, 53, 54; mentioned, 109

Jacales, 31, 32, 89, 150

Jalapa, 117
Jiménez, José, 42–43
Jiménez, Miguel, 152–53
Jiménez, Nicolás, 152–53
Journeymen: difficulty in reaching master status, 108–9; literacy among, 109; as recipients of loans, 109, 114, 116; in militia units, 152; wages of, 191n13. *See also* Artisans
Judicial system: reliance on informers, 33, 150–51; used by plebeians, 37, 45, 101; weakness of police powers, 39; preference for utilitarian sentences, 39, 102, 106; use of theatrical punishments, 39, 154–55, 162; leniency toward juvenile offenders, 104; response to riot of 1692, 138–39, 150–51. *See also* Crown, Spanish; Government officials
Justice: plebeian understanding of, 44, 159–60, 163
Juzgado de la Diputación, 42

Kinship: and naming practices among plebeians, 58–61; impact on employment opportunities, 87–88; impact on financial success, 118–19

Labor systems: evolution of, in Valley of Mexico, 11–14; unanswered historical questions regarding, 86; informal contracts in, 86, 182n29; coercion and paternalism in, 94–95. *See also* Patron-client relations; Slavery, African
Landlords: ecclesiastical, 30–32; Spanish vecinos, 91, 92; castas, 110, 116; mentioned, 141, 152, 191n144
León, Diego de, 109
León, Francisco de, 117
León, José de, 33
León, Melchor de, 154
Lezcano, Nicolás de, 40
Limpieza de sangre, 33, 183n36
Linares, Fernando de Alencastre Noroña y Silva, duque de, 34
Literacy: definition of, 191n10
Loans: to compadres, 88; as form of patronage, 91, 116–17, 123; to slaves for purchasing freedom, 97; types of, 100, 109, 116, 117; secured by oral agreements, 113–14; to muleteers, 117; mentioned,

84, 111, 146. *See also* Credit; Patron-client relations
López del Castillo, Antonio, 59, 112
López de Velasco, Juan, 19
López Godines, Juan, 45
Losada, Teresa, 110, 111, 113

Maize: as food of urban poor, 10; commercialization of, 13; and alhóndiga/pósito system, 75, 128–30; cost of week's supply, 99; price increases in 1692, 126, 131–32; shortage as cause of riot of 1692, 126, 157; proposed price ceiling on, 130–31
Mancera, Antonio Sebastián de Toledo, marqués de: on racial divisions among plebeians, 25, 26; advocates paternalism toward blacks and mulattoes, 39
Mancio, Gregorio, 29
Manzo, Tomás, 20
María, Rosa, 57–58, 61
Markets, in Mexico City, 36–37
Márquez, Miguel, 97
Marriage: as mechanism for maintaining ethnic boundaries, 25, 78; plebeian attitudes toward, 68–69; between Indians and castas, 78–82 *passim*, 91; between slaves and free castas, 81–82; mentioned, 67. *See also* Miscegenation
Martínez, José, 147, 151
Martínez de Peralta, Alonso, 66–67, 70, 71, 84
Mateo, Juan, 97
Medina, Francisco, 158
Medina, Lucía de, 32
Melena, 53, 54
Mendoza, Antonio de, 12, 18
Merchants: mulattoes as, 106, 112; as patrons, 109; and credit, 111–17 *passim*; ability of, to amass capital, 118
Mesa, Marcos de, 98, 119
Mesillas, 36, 37
Mestizaje, 66. *See also* Miscegenation
Mestizo achinado, 140, 141
Mestizo prieto, 54
Mestizos: as vagabonds, 6; and miscegenation, 14, 83; anomalous position of, 14–15; seen as illegitimate, 18; favored over blacks and mulattoes, 18, 26; as mediators between Spaniards and Indians,

Mestizos (*continued*)
20; in artisan crafts, 21–22, 87; in sistema de castas, 24; in plaza mayor, 36–37; differentiation of from Indians, 51–55 *passim;* endogamy among, 78–80, *passim;* marriages with mulattoes, 79, 81–82, 84; links to Indians, 83–84, 87; in riot of 1692, 134, 136, 140–47 *passim;* in militia units, 152, 161–62; mentioned, 5, 16, 17, 19, 32, 33, 38, 39, 41, 45, 56, 57, 66, 67, 72, 73, 89, 97, 110, 153, 158, 163, 164. *See also* Castas
Mexico City: as center of Hispanic society, 4, 6, 9–10; racial diversity in, 7, 159; immigration to, 10; infrastructure of, 10, 28; and economic organization of colony, 11, 13; Indian parishes in, 16; changing residential patterns in, 20, 176n64; flooding in, 27–28; pollution in, 27–29; housing hierarchy of, 29–32; ecclesiastical property in, 30–32; criminal activity in, 39; gambling in, 41; political intrigue in, 46–47, 125, 161; peninsulares in, 64–65; cash shortage in, 109–10; socioeconomic structure of, 162
Miguel, Juan, 53
Mines, 11, 12
Militia, 149–50, 152, 162
Miranda, Antonia de, 121
Miscegenation: between Spaniards and Indians, 14; between Spaniards and castas, 23–24, 68; and the sistema de castas, 70–71. *See also* Castas; Marriage
Moloteros, 35. *See also* Pulque
Montero, Alonso, 113
Montesclaros, Juan de Mendoza y Luna, marqués de, 23
Mora Esquivel, Pedro de, 60, 116
Morales, Andrés de, 41
Morales, Francisco de, 97
Moriscos, 24, 73, 107
Mulattoes: in Mexico City economy, 17, 21–22; as tribute payers, 21, 66; in sistema de castas, 24; endogamy among, 78–80 *passim;* marriages with mestizos, 79, 81–82, 84; marriages with slaves, 81–82; links to blacks, 83; as servants, 87, 110; as merchants, 106, 112; as slave owners, 119, 162; in riot of 1692, 136, 141–47 *passim;* in militia units, 152, 161–62;

mentioned, 4, 14, 15, 16, 18, 19, 32, 33, 37, 38, 41, 45, 51, 55, 57, 67, 72, 73, 89, 97, 110, 153, 158, 163. *See also* Castas; Slaves

Najarros, Juan, 109
Names: as element in racial classification, 53; changing of, by bigamists, 54
Naming practices: value of, for studying social history, 58; of Spaniards contrasted with those of castas, 62–63
Navarijo, Diego de, 140–41, 143
New Laws of 1542, 12
Nicknames: examples of, 32, 97, 114; significance among plebeians, 58–59
Nolasco, Pedro, 61

Obrajeros, 12
Obrajes: in economic evolution of Mexico, 12; imprisonment of workers in, 43, 45, 91; size of labor force in, 94; used for rehabilitation of criminals, 102–3; apprentices in, 103–4, 190n82
Obras pías, 121
Oficiales. *See* Journeymen
Oliva y Olvera, Juan de, 110, 119
Ortega, Andrés de, 108
Ortega y Montañez, Juan de, 37, 39
Ortiz, Diego, 33
Ossorio de Escobar, Diego, 46–47

Pacheco, Marcos, 103–4
Padilla, Francisca de, 97
Palace of the marqués del Valle: saved from burning in riot of 1692, 138, 148; as post-riot headquarters of viceroy, 150
Palace, Royal: burned in riot of 1692, 126, 137, 138, 143–46 *passim;* guard's actions during riot, 137–38, 145; women evacuated from, 145
Palafox y Mendoza, Juan de: view of plebeian Spaniards, 23; as object of popular veneration, 47
Panaderías. *See* Bakeries
Paniagua, Nicolás de: on gambling, 41; confused racial status of, 53, 56; and knowledge of his relatives, 56–57; as journeyman, 109
Parish registers: value of, for studying social history, 7, 69, 74; and racial classification,

54–56, 68–70; and surnames, 59, 61–67
passim; reliability of, 68; lacunas in, 70–
74 *passim,* 185*n10,16;* nominal record
linkage between, 76, 186*n23*
Passing. *See* Racial Variability
Patron-client relations: between Spaniards
and Indians, 91–93; two-sided nature of,
95; and plebeians, 105, 116, 117; as form
of social cooptation, 123, 164; and riot
of 1692, 136, 164; and elite racial ideol-
ogy, 163–64; mentioned, 7, 44. *See also*
Credit; Labor systems; Loans
Pawning, 110–12 *passim*
Peña, Antonio de la, 99, 101
Peninsulares: attitudes of, toward creoles,
24; naming patterns among, 65; occupa-
tions of, 65, 184*n56. See also* Spaniards
Pérez, Domingo, 118
Pérez, Toribio, 117
Pérez de Villareal, Agustín, 93
Pérez Merino, Juan de, 148
Pintura de castas, 161
Plata, Juan de la, 30
Platero, Francisco, 117
Plaza del volador, 37, 39, 106
Plaza mayor: symbolic meaning of, 9, 154;
variety of market activity in, 36, 109; as
gathering place for castas, 36–37; criminal activity in, 37; burning and looting
of shops in, 138, 143–47 *passim;* deaths
during riot of 1692 in, 157, 158. *See also*
Riot of 1692
Plebeians: Spanish attitudes toward, 22–23;
26; divisions among, 25, 151–54 *passim,*
164; poor living conditions of, 27; lack
of decent housing, 29–32; lack of privacy among, 32–33; criminal behavior
among, 32–33, 34, 37, 39; resistance to
being informers, 33–34; violence toward
Spaniards, 39–40; access to arms, 43;
conflicts with minor government officials,
43–44; had knowledge of their rights, 45;
venerated Palafox y Mendoza, 47; criteria
for racial classification among, 56–57, 67;
illiteracy among, 57; and surnames, 58–
63; attitude of, toward marriage, 68–69;
resistance of, to Spanish racial ideology,
70–71, 76, 78; roadblocks to social mobility of, 108–10 *passim,* 163; range of
possessions among, 110–12; view of riot

of 1692, 145–47 *passim;* and expectations of justice, 159–60, 163; and urban
space, concept of, 200*n3. See also* Castas;
Sistema de Castas
Plebeian society: racially mixed nature of,
22–23, 32, 49; and Spanish elite, 38–39;
lack of institutional basis of, 94; recruitment of female workers in, 104–5; stress
caused in, by maize price increases,
131–32; mentioned, 159, 165
Plebeian subculture: as oppositional culture, 6, 161, 163; recognized by Duke
of Linares, 34; and Catholic church, 36,
68–69
Ponce, Ana, 117
Pósito. *See* Alhóndiga/pósito system
Pozo y Alarcón, Carlos Tristán de, 103
Prendas, 111
Provisor, 148, 197*n116*
Puebla, 47, 103, 109
Pulque: commercialization of, 13; unsuccessful attempts to regulate, 34–35;
disinhibiting effect of, 35; elite investments in, 38; banned after riot of 1692,
127; mentioned, 34, 118, 122
Pulquerías: as meeting place for plebeians,
35; violence in, 35; constables forbidden
to enter in, 43; multiracial clientele of,
91; and conspiracy theory of the riot of
1692, 139, 157; mentioned, 34, 88

Race: and ethnicity, 5, 7, 171*n9;* and marriage, 25; as substitute for economic
categories, 26; used as guide to moral
qualities, 26, 40–41; as a social construct,
49–50, 83; in personal identifications,
58–59; defined at family level, 67, 70–
71, 84; and class, 73–74, 89, 162–63; and
social mobility, 75–76, 162–63; plebeian
attitudes toward, 76, 78, 163; role of, in
the division of labor, 87
Racial classification: based on phenotype,
24–25; conflicting criteria in, 51–57, 67,
69–70; stability of categories used in, 73,
78
Racial ideology: Spanish, 4, 17–25 *passim;*
impact of, on casta elite, 120–21. *See also*
Plebeians; Sistema de Castas; Spaniards
Racial variability: between Indians and
mestizos, 54–55, 77, 182*n24;* rates among

Racial variability (*continued*)
castas and Indians, 76–77; direction of,
77–78; among husbands and wives, 78;
limited material advantages offered by,
78, 84, 162–63; and casta marriage patterns, 82; significance of, for casta elite,
121
Ramírez, Antonio, 31
Ramírez, Juan, 30
Ramos, Antonio, 153
Ramos, José, 139–40
Real estate: urban, owned by casta elite,
29, 110; as secure investment, 122
Rendón, Antonia, 97
Rents: for housing in traza, 30–31; evasion
of, 32; in plaza mayor, 36
Repartimiento: 12, 45
República de los españoles: recognized by
crown, 3; Spanish-casta division within,
19; mentioned, 50. See also Spaniards
República de los indios: recognized by
crown, 3; incompatibility with Spanish
república, 12; mentioned, 50. See also
Indians
Rettes, José de, 116
Revolts, urban: as means of political protest,
42; infrequency of, 42, 125. See also
Rioters; Riot of 1692
Reyes, Diego de los, 104
Reyes, Lázaro de los, 31
Reyes, Lorenzo de los, 150
Reyes, Melchor de los, 122
Reyes, Pascuala de los, 98
Rioters: shouts and slogans of, 42, 142, 145–
47 *passim*, 157; sense of brotherhood
among, 147; opportunism among, 147;
disposal of stolen goods by, 148, 150–54
passim; arrests of, 150–53 *passim*; confessions by, 154; sentences given to, 155–56;
Indians among, 156–60 *passim*; artisans
among, 158–59. See also Crowd; Riot of
1692
Riot of 1624, 23, 47, 125
Riot of 1692: maize shortage as cause of,
46, 125–26, 143; and Indian segregation policy, 89, 127, 198–99n48; seen
as tumulto de indios, 125, 152, 156,
157; witness vs. participant accounts of,
125, 134–35, 138, 144–47 *passim*, 160;
blamed on Indians' perfidy, 126–27;

beginning of, 134–38; failure of communication as trigger of, 135–37; multiracial
composition of rioting crowd, 135–36,
137, 141, 146–47, 157, 160; and patron-
client relations, 136, 164; noise and
confusion in, 141–43; changing nature
of, over time, 143–44; fragmentation of
crowd in, 144–47; as seen by plebeians,
145–47 *passim*; destruction caused by,
146, 198n121; conclusion of, 147–49;
Spanish backlash against, 148; multi-
causal explanations of, 160; mentioned,
36, 37, 41, 156, 161. See also Crowd;
Rioters
Riot of 1696, 42, 44
Riot of 1715, 42
Rivera, Ana de, 98
Robles, Antonio de, 47
Rodríguez, Juan Antonio, 41
Rojas, Juan de, 117
Romero, Benito: and creditors, 106, 113,
118; suicide of, 106–7; as example of
upwardly-mobile casta, 107
Romero, Juan, 57
Rosa, Juan de la, 41
Rosa, María de la, 61
Ruido: as term used to describe riot of
1692, 142

Saénz de Tagle, Luis, 149, 157
Sagrario Metropolitano: as traza church,
16; parish registers of, 24, 56, 61, 69–82
passim; black and mulatto parishioners
in, 83; underrepresentation of Indians in,
185n10
Sala de Crimen, 33, 102
Salas, Josefa, 116–17
Salazar, Felipe, 53
Salazar, María de, 32
Saldívar, Josefa de, 31
Samudio, Ana de, 58, 120–21
San Agustín, monastery of, 120
San Bernardo, church of, 91
Sánchez, Ana, 88
Sánchez, Juan, 114
San Francisco, monastery of, 136, 137, 143,
145
San José, parish of, census, 89–90
San Juan, Antonio de, 101
San Juan, barrio of, 148

San Pablo, parish of, 92
San Sebastián, barrio of, 57
Santa Catalina Martír, church of, 52
Santander, Mariana de, 93
Santiago, conde de, 147, 148, 150
Santiago, condesa de, 90
Santiago, Sebastián de, 57
Santiago Tlatelolco: parish of, 82; Indian residents of, participating in riot of 1692, 126, 139, 159
Santos, José de los: accused of being riot leader, 140–41; testimony of, on riot, 146–47; as looter, 147; trial of, 155, 199n156; mentioned, 144
Santoyo, Pascuala, 59
Saramullos, 23, 36
Sebastián, Andrés, 52
Segregation: of Indians, 10–11, 16, 179–80n56; in parish registers, 24, 68, 185n10; in housing hierarchy, 32; of taverns by gender, 35
Serafín, Antonio, 103
Serecedo, Juan de, 143, 145
Servants, domestic: Indians as, 91; receiving bequests from employers, 93; converted into clients, 93–94; in convents, 104–5; mentioned, 159, 162
Sex ratios: impact on endogamy, 79–80; among castas, 81
Siete Partidas, 104
Sigüenza, Francisco, 149
Sigüenza y Góngora, Carlos de: attitude of, toward Mexican populace, 11; view of plebeian Spaniards, 23; and conspiracy theory of riot of 1692, 127; on riot of 1692, 134–48 passim, 157
Silva, Miguel de, 122
Sistema de castas: as divide-and-conquer mechanism, 4, 25–26; development of, 24; limited applicability of, 25; plebeian attitudes toward, 70–71; as flawed model of society, 83; lack of institutional basis of, 161–62; mentioned, 7. See also Castas; Race; Racial ideology
Slavery, African: impact of, on black and mulatto marriage patterns, 81–82; rural vs. urban, 95–96; supported by state's police power, 96. See also Blacks; Mulattoes; Slaves
Slavery, Indian, 12, 174n27

Slaves: role in colonial economy, 3, 13–14; possession of, as status symbols, 13–14, 96; disproportionate numbers of, in Mexico City, 14; revolts and protests by, 17, 136; conspiracies of, against Spanish rule, 18; use of masters' surnames among, 60–61, 189n48; demographic decline of, 72, 83; price differentials among, 88; varieties of resistance employed by, 96; as apprentices, 96–97; importance of personal relationship with master, 96–98 passim; personal mobility of, 97; retention of earnings, 97–98; manumitted, 97–98; social mobility of, 98; in riot of 1692, 151–52. See also Blacks; Mulattoes; Slavery, African
Slave trade: in sixteenth century, 16; curtailed after 1650, 96, 189n39
Soberón, Pedro de, 113
Solórzano y Pereira, Juan de, 19–20
Somatic norm image, 51–52, 78
Sorilla, Juan Cayetano, 102
Spaniards: view of Indians, 3; and commercialization of Mexican agriculture, 13; attitudes toward castas, 15, 17, 19–20, 25–26; fear of slave revolts, 17; as members of urban poor, 21, 22–24; divisions among, 24, 161, 195n38; creoles vs. peninsulares, 24, 64–65; as consumers of pulque, 34; as vendors in plaza mayor, 37; as patrons, 38, 90–93 passim, 104–5, 123, 163–64; naming practices of, contrasted with those of castas, 62–63; endogamy among, 78–80 passim; racial beliefs of, effect on labor market, 88–89; as compadres of Indians, 92; and casta servants, 93; and benefits to, apprenticing slaves, 96–97; and safety net, 121; as participants in riot of 1692, 136, 137, 147, 158; search of, for leaders of riot, 138–41, 144; in pinturas de castas, 161; knowledge of own ancestry, 183n36; mentioned, 32, 56, 57, 58, 67, 154
Sumptuary legislation, 22

Tapia, Diego de, 117
Taverns. See Pulquerias
Tenants, in traza, 30–32
Tenochtitlán: fall of, 3; and Mexico City, 9, 10, 172n2; mentioned, 14

Tenochtitlán, San Juan, 10
Tianguillo, 37
Theft, 41. *See also* Criminal Activity
Tlaquesquales, 146
Tlaxcala, 103
Tomatlán, barrio of, 57
Tools, 109. *See also* Artisans
Torquemada, Nicolas de, 106–7
Torrez, José de, 30
Torrez, Josefa de, 97
Torrez, Lorenzo de, 59
Tovar, José de, 119
Tovar, Juan de, 119
Traza, 10, 16, 20, 42, 164. *See also* Indians; Segregation
Tribute, 18, 21, 66, 92

Vagabonds, 21, 37, 104
Valle, José de, 120
Vásquez de Espinosa, Antonio, 15
Vecinos, 15, 114, 161
Vega, Matías de, 102
Vega Y Vique, Gerónima de, 119–20
Velasco, Juan de (wheelwright), 145
Velasco, Juan de (witness of riot of 1692), 140–41
Velasco, Luis de, I, 17
Velasco, Luis de, II, 12
Velásquez, Diego, 154
Velásquez, Domingo, 68
Verdugo, Juan Alejo, 91
Viceroys: in conflict with archbishops, 46–

47; as patrons, 47–48. *See also* Galve, Gaspar de Sandoval Silva y Mendoza, conde de; Government officials; Judicial system
Villagrán, María de, 150–51
Villalta Enríquez, José de, 97

Wage rates: of repartimiento Indians, 45; of militiamen, 150; in panaderías, 189–90n66; of journeymen, 191n13
Wheat: supply for Mexico City, 13; failure of 1691 harvest, 129; production in eighteenth century, 129. *See also* Maize
Wills: as source on transmission of surnames, 59–60; limitations of, 107–8, 117–18; and casta elite, 110; racial identifications in, 121
Women: and popular celebrations, 36; in urban economy, 37, 42, 191n6; and capital punishment, 39, 158; and use of surnames, 59–66 *passim;* outnumbering men in Mexico City, 68; as domestic servants, 91, 104–5; social mobility of, 107; problems in determining source of wealth of, 118; evacuated from Royal Palace during riot of 1692, 145; and alhóndiga, 157, 158; participation of, in riot of 1692, 157–58; urban *vs.* rural, 158

Zumárraga, Juan de, 15
Zavala y Velasco, Isabel de, 98

"*A superb book, of obvious interest not only to Latin Americanists but also to those who study race relations in a hemispheric context.*"
—Frederick P. Bowser, Stanford University

In this distinguished contribution to Latin American colonial history, R. Douglas Cope draws upon a wide variety of sources—including Inquisition and court cases, notarial records, and parish registers—to challenge the traditional view of *castas* (members of the caste system created by Spanish overlords) as rootless, alienated, and dominated by a desire to improve their racial status. On the contrary, the *castas*, Cope shows, were neither passive nor ruled by feelings of racial inferiority; indeed, they often modified or even rejected elite racial ideology. *Castas* also sought ways to manipulate their social "superiors" through astute use of the legal system. Cope shows that social control by the Spaniards rested less on institutions than on patron-client networks linking individual patricians and plebeians, which enabled the elite class to co-opt the more successful *castas*.

The book concludes with the most thorough account yet published of the Mexico City riot of 1692. This account illuminates both the shortcomings and strengths of the patron-client system. Spurred by a corn shortage and subsequent famine, a plebeian mob laid waste much of the central city. Cope demonstrates that the political situation was not substantially altered, however; the patronage system continued to control employment and plebeians were largely left to bargain and adapt, as before.

A revealing look at the economic lives of the urban poor in the colonial era, *The Limits of Racial Domination* examines a period in which critical social changes were occurring. The book should interest historians and ethnohistorians alike.

R. DOUGLAS COPE is assistant professor of history at Brown University.

The University of Wi...
Madison, Wisconsin

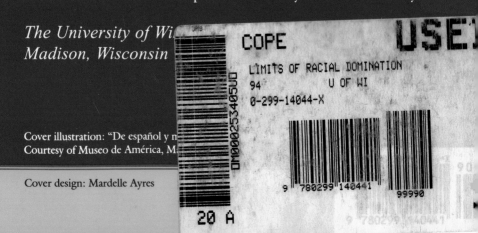

Cover illustration: "De español y m...
Courtesy of Museo de América, M...

Cover design: Mardelle Ayres